POLITICS FROM A TO Z

For general information on our other products and services or to obtain technical support, please contact our Customer Care Department within the U.S. at (866) 744-2665, or outside the U.S. at (510) 253-0500.

Zephyros Press publishes its books in a variety of electronic and print formats. Some content that appears in print may not be available in electronic books, and vice versa.

ISBNs: Print 978-1-62315-637-4 | eBook 978-1-62315-638-1

POLITICS FROM A TO Z

GREAT WARS
INSPIRING LEADERS
MAJOR REVOLUTIONS
CURRENT POLICIES
BIG IDEAS

RICHARD GANIS | INTERVIEW WITH NOAM CHOMSKY

CONTENTS

***Bolded** entries indicate major discussions*

E

F

G

H

I

J

K

L

S

T

U

V

W

Z

POLITICS FROM A–Z

PERESTROIKA

OLIGARCHY

LIBERTY

IMPERIALISM

TYRANNY

IMMIGRATION

COMMUNISM

AUTHORS OF OUR OWN DESTINY

WORLD & AMERICAN POLITICS IN THE 21ST CENTURY

AN INTERVIEW WITH NOAM CHOMSKY

Q: Professor Chomsky, let's start with a basic question. Are people in control of their own destiny? More specifically, are American people fully aware that they themselves are the creators of their own laws, and how does that dispose them towards their institutions?

NC: First of all, the majority of American people today don't accept the assumption that it is they who create their institutions and who run their country. The last time I looked at the polls, about 80% of the population felt that the government is made up of a few big interests looking out for themselves and not for the people. You could see this at the elections. Although I don't have the exact figures at hand, there's a very striking fact: opinions of Congress are extremely low—in the teens. Nevertheless, probably 98% of incumbents get reelected. What this tells you is that, essentially, people are aware that they don't have a choice and that they're not taking part in running the country. In fact, you can see this in many other ways: take April 15, the day when taxes are paid. In a democratic society, where people would feel that they are shaping their own lives, this would be a day of celebration. The spirit would be "We're getting together as a community to put our resources into implementing policies that we have chosen. What could be better than that?" Well, that's not the way it is here. Instead, it's a day of mourning when some alien force that has nothing to do with us comes to steal our hard-earned money.

Q: Would you say that we have become so apathetic and conformist that we even lack the desire to resist?

NC: I don't think "apathetic" is the right word, I'm also not sure "conformist" is the right word. People feel hopeless. Take the Obama campaign in 2008. Campaigns in the US are run by the public relations industry and elections are, basically, bought. The Obama campaign was a case in point. In fact, as you may know, the advertising industry gives an award each year for the best marketing effort of the year. In 2008 they gave it to Obama, whose campaign beat Apple in "Best Marketing of the Year."

There was really very little talk about issues. Real political issues were off in the side somewhere and, to start with, most people didn't even know what they were. The words that were being repeated over and over again, in typical advertising campaign style, were "hope" and "change." Well, that's meaningless. But it does work: advertisers understand popular moods. The people wanted "hope" and "change" which means that they didn't have hope and they didn't like what existed. Now, that's not apathy, it's a mark of a kind of disintegration of society. I'm old enough to have lived through a real depression, the Great Depression. My family were mostly working people, not well-off by any means. But, in a way, it was a less psychologically depressed time. There was a sense of hopefulness; the sense that there is a way out of this, that there are possibilities, things that can be done, like organize the CIO (Committee for Industrial Organization), get involved in programs of reform—there were opportunities to be grasped. There is no such general feeling in the country now—but it's not apathy. I think what it is is the success of an incredible propaganda campaign, the scale of which is very little understood, although there's good scholarship on it: after the Second World War, there was an enormous campaign by the business classes to drive out of people's heads any conception of democracy, concern for one another, feeling able to do anything, and so on. And it had its successes.

Q: Nowadays it looks like things are driven by invisible and unaccountable entities: the markets, capitalism. What's your view on that?

NC: That's a concocted image; its basis in reality is extremely slight. First of all, do we have capitalism? Do we live in a market society? People who write these things, write them on computers and send them by the Internet. Where did computers and the Internet come from? They came mostly from the kind of place where I am sitting right now: research institutions that in these days were largely funded by the Pentagon. These products (computers, email) are, for the most part, the result of a very dynamic and creative state sector of the economy. Is this capitalism?

Computers and the Internet were in the state sector for decades before they were handed over to private enterprises for profit. That's not unusual; in fact, that's how most of the economy works. It's an economy in which one of the leading principles is that the public pays the costs and takes the risks whereas the profit is privatized. We're seeing this in such a striking way today that it cannot even be concealed. It's the so-called "too big to fail" principle, by which the government is bailing out the financial markets that crashed when they tried to live up to market principles, leading to disaster. Their bailout means that they're basically public utilities, except with private profit. To begin with, then, it's only a partial market system, a limited form of state capitalism. And can it not change? Of course it can.

Q: In our societies we affirm, in theory at least, the equal rights of all cultures while knowing that there are cases of regimes that constantly, systematically, and massively violate those principles. Should we consider these digressions as interesting exceptions, or do we have a duty to take a stance, including the use of force?

NC: It's quite often useful to adopt a principle that is frequently voiced but rarely applied: look in the mirror. American society was founded as what George Washington called "an infant empire" that was willing to create its territory by what the founding fathers themselves recognized to be extermination (their words). That's one of the original sins of this society and the effects continue to linger. The other is slavery. Lets take a look at slavery. We know what slavery was and what its horrors were. After the Civil War it was technically supposed to have ended. However, if you look at the facts, after about twenty years it began to be reinstituted directly in the South—and with the complicity of the North. What was instituted was, literally, a criminalization of black life through laws such as "vagrancy" or "talking too loud." This was devised as a means to throw much of the black male population into prison, where they would stay permanently through various other machinations and from which they created the basis of a good part of the modern industrial society: mines, steel mills, cotton, and so on. In fact, if you look at the details, it was worse than slavery. Under slavery, the slave-owners owned the slaves as capital and so they took care of them. But in this system there was no sense of responsibility. This continued until the Second World War. During World War II, when industrial labor was needed, there was a kind of opening for black males that lasted through the following several decades, during which there was a very rapid and highly egalitarian growth, the so-called Golden Age of Capitalism. In the 1970s, the financialization of the economy began and this window of opportunity was closed. Since about 1980, the incarceration rate has shot way up, reaching higher levels than in any other industrialized society. I think England is second, far behind the US, and others are even farther behind. This phenomenon has no relation to crime, and it concerns, to a substantial extent, black males. That's reinstituting slavery; prison slavery, in fact, since these inmates work as prison labor. So, if you look at the whole history, from the beginning of the slave trade until today, slavery has barely ended. Sure enough, it's taken somewhat different forms, it's not as rigorous today as it was after Reconstruction—but it's there and it has tremendous effect on the society. Well, is that a property that meets the condition that you described? Should we invade ourselves by force to overcome it?

Q: What are your views on China and Russia? It seems they may be able to live in a peaceful coexistence with the US, but they will never accept American guardianship, and the assumption that they can be conscripted into a campaign to convert the world to American-style democracy seems unfounded.

NC: There's a presupposition in the question that I cannot accept. Do we want to convert the world to a world in which 80 percent of the population think that their government is run by a few big interests looking after themselves? A world in which citizens regard themselves as helpless to influence governmental policies?

Do we want a world, to take a case in point, where 85 percent of the population believe that their government should adopt the policies of every other government and negotiate drug prices to cut them down from their exorbitant level and their government doesn't even put it on the agenda? Is that the kind of world we want to convert people to? People talk about the model of American democracy and the American way of life, but they do it in abstraction from reality. It actually reminds me of what was written by a leading figure and one of the founders of the realist school of international affairs, Hans Morgenthau. He once wrote an interesting book which had a lot of truth in it. The book was called *The Purpose of American Politics*. In this book, he claims that the United States is unique in the world and has a transcendent purpose, unlike any other country. This transcendent purpose is to bring about freedom. But Morgenthau, being a good scholar and going through history, observed that we have not lived up to this transcendent purpose. Case after case, this purpose has, in fact, been radically violated. So, he said, we should think of what actually happened as just the "abusive" history. The "real" history is how what happened is reflected in our minds. He then went on to point out, correctly, that to deny historical reality on the basis of the abusive history is like the error of atheism that questions the magnificence of God. Unfortunately, he was not trying to write a satire. He was describing actual intellectual life, except describing it honestly.

Q: **What about 9/11 and its symbolism? There have been authors like Don DeLillo who said that the 9/11 attacks were not targeted against the West but specifically against the US. On the other hand, there are countries, like France, who insisted they were attacked together with the United States.**

NC: Any serious specialist, whether its Michael Scheuer, the chief CIA analyst who was following Saddam Hussein, or academic specialists, they all know perfectly well that the 9/11 attacks were directed against United States policy. Of course it was an attack on the West, since the West supports US policy—US policy in the Middle East, that is. You may say that it was a monstrous terrorist attack and claim that they were mistaken about American policy, but there is very little doubt that people who follow Al-Qaeda seriously say "They mean what they say." And what they're saying is: "You're attacking Islam and we are going to defend ourselves." Incidentally, that's another good example of propaganda. What I'm going to say is almost unintelligible in the West, but let me say it anyway. 9/11 was a horrible atrocity. But it could have been worse; let me give you an example. Suppose that Al-Qaeda had bombed the White House, killed the President, established a military dictatorship, tortured several hundred thousand people, set up a major international terrorist center that was overthrowing governments and killing people all over the world, brought in a bunch of crazed economists who drove economy into its worst recession in decades. Suppose that had happened. Wouldn't that be a lot worse than September 11, 2001? Well, it did happen: on September 11, 1973—the only thing I did was change the numbers to per capita equivalents, which is a proper measure. This is what happened on what is sometimes called "the first 9/11" in South America: the overthrow of the government of Chile, backed by the United States. Why wasn't that an atrocity? Why didn't that change the world? In terms of the societal effects, it's much greater than what we call 9/11. But that was our terror, our violence, so it doesn't count. And that's only one of innumerable examples. We have to learn to look at ourselves if we want to talk seriously about the world.

Q: One thing that is fundamentally different between the US and Europe is the role religion plays. In fact, judged by almost any standard, the US is a less secular country than Turkey. In no other highly industrialized country is there widespread belief in Satan or an official movement contesting Darwinian theory. Where should we look for the origins of this and what tools does it provide for the understanding of American society?

NC: It's a very important question—and definitely too complex for me to answer it briefly. To begin with, we should look back to the early colonists who came from England. They came from a providentialist culture, namely, a culture immersed in the conception that providence has laid out a plan for history and we are carrying out God's will. For example, when the first colonists came to New England in the 1620s and King Charles I gave the charter to the Massachusetts Bay Colony, this charter said something along the lines of "the purpose for this plantation is to save the natives from their Pagan misery." When John Winthrop gave his famous sermon in which he said that "We are the city on the hill," he was using the framework of what is now called "the responsibility to protect" or "humanitarian intervention," the notion that we are coming to save you. In fact, the great seal of the colony of Massachusetts has on it a picture of an Indian with a scroll coming out of his mouth saying "Come over and help us." So, this is a perfect example of humanitarian intervention in the name of the Lord. And that runs through a good part of American history. It's a long stream of providentialism that has never ended and which has repeated revivals, like in the 1950s. So, in a word, yes, it's a deep feature of the culture and it goes way back to the origins. What influences us on policy, however, is debatable, since we're also a very secular society. Freedom is, actually, guaranteed to an extent that is probably unique in the world.

This never-before-published conversation with Noam Chomsky, illuminating the importance of politics in public life, happened in 2009. It has been edited for content.

purpose aforesaid,
D SHALL BE
NIZE AND MAINTA

ABSOLUTISM

A government is said to be *absolutist* when its powers are unlimited and concentrated in the hands of a single centralized authority. Absolutist regimes lack institutional processes—such as judicial review and **elections** (page 92)—that would enable citizens to contest the laws and decrees of the ruling power. Absolutism is thus closely associated with forms of government such as **despotism** (page 83), **dictatorship** (page 84), and **totalitarianism** (page 240); in these cases, the powers of the sovereign are likewise unrestrained and all-encompassing. Another well-known example of absolutism is absolute monarchy. In the medieval era, absolute monarchs were backed by the **Divine Right** (page 87) doctrine. Later, in the early modern period, their leadership was sanctioned by **social contract** (page 221) theorists such as Thomas Hobbes. From the sixteenth century through the eighteenth century, many of the countries of Western Europe were ruled by kings who placed all of their subjects under their absolute power. Monarchs such as King Henry VIII of England were even able to corral the church—whose authority was pitted against that of the state at the time—under their influence.

AGRARIANISM

There are two common usages associated with the term *agrarianism*. On the one hand, it may refer to a philosophical stance that exalts the values of agrarian communities over those of urban ones: the simple, self-sufficient, and wholesome lifestyle of the independent farmer is deemed superior to the complex, commercial, and potentially corrupt ways of the urban dweller. Such sentiments were maintained by **United States** (page 248) president Thomas Jefferson, who declared small yeoman farmers "the most valuable citizens."

On the other hand, "agrarianism" may refer to a political standpoint that supports reclaiming **land** (page 146) from the wealthy and redistributing it to the poor or landless. The origins of this idea can be traced back to the agrarian laws of ancient Rome. Known as *Lex Sempronia Agraria*, the laws were implemented by Roman politician Tiberius Sempronius Gracchus, who seized public lands held by Rome's rich patricians and transferred them to the poor. Today such policies are referred to as land reform. The modern land reform movement took hold in eighteenth and nineteenth-century England and Ireland, and spread throughout the world during the demise of European **colonialism** (page 61). Agrarian land reform efforts were central to the **decolonization** (page 77) campaigns in the Arab world and Africa.

AL-QAEDA

The name *al-Qaeda* gained instant notoriety in the aftermath of the attacks on the World Trade Center and the Pentagon on September 11, 2001; for many, it became virtually synonymous with global **terrorism** (page 238). Al-Qaeda—the "base" or "the foundation" in Arabic—was formed between 1988 and 1989 under the leadership of Osama bin Laden, an adherent of militant Islamism who had previously been involved in the Mujahideen guerilla war against Soviet forces in Afghanistan. The organization is unlike traditional militant groups such as the Irish Republican Army, which are backed by the authority of a state attempting to obtain political power; it is a non-state entity that operates via a global,

A

decentralized network of "cells," each acting independently and without knowledge of the others' identity. Al-Qaeda also differs from customary forms of militancy in that it is not driven by one specific political conflict. Instead, the group has a wide-ranging set of objectives, including the establishment of a new worldwide Islamic caliphate, a form of government based on its own strict interpretation of sharia law (sharia is a religious legal system rooted in the sacred texts of Islam, the Quran and the Hadith). To achieve its aims, al-Qaeda advocates armed warfare against certain religious, national, and political groups—notably Americans, socialists, Hindus, Christians, Jews, the State of Israel, and various Islamic sects—which it views as sworn enemies of its own "true" version of Islam and hence of all "righteous Muslims."

The call for militant conflict against its alleged enemies, often referred to as jihadism, has been the force behind the wave of terrorist activities that al-Qaeda has either directly sponsored or approved since its formation in the late 1980s. The most spectacular and deadliest of these actions to date—the al-Qaeda-backed 9/11 attacks—gave rise to a global "War on Terror" (a term coined by US President George W. Bush). As the main sponsors of this campaign, the United States and Great Britain have judged the continued existence of al-Qaeda to be a clear and present danger to global and national security. This has been the US's official justification for the execution of Osama bin Laden in Pakistan in 2011; the invasion and occupation of Afghanistan from 2001 to the present; and the subjection of detained al-Qaeda operatives to "enhanced interrogation techniques" (or torture, in the view of critics) at sites such as the Guantanamo Bay Naval Base.

Al-Qaeda leader Osama bin Laden claimed responsibility for the September 11, 2001, terrorist attacks. He was killed by US military forces in 2011.

A

AMERICAN REVOLUTION

The *American Revolution* was staged by the rebel forces of the thirteen American Colonies between 1765 and 1783. Known as the Patriots, these forces wanted to overthrow the colonial rule of the British monarchy and replace it with a new, independent **republic** (page 205). The Revolution gained momentum in 1765, sparked by a particular thorn in the side of the colonists—namely, Great Britain's resolve to collect duties on goods such as molasses and sugar. The Patriots denounced these taxes as unfair, as they had no representation in the government that had imposed them, and for many years refused to pay.

Their protests came to a head in 1773 when, disguised as American Indians, several members of a group of Patriots called the Sons of Liberty boarded vessels docked in the Boston Harbor and proceeded to destroy their cargoes of taxed British tea. The action, known as the Boston Tea Party, has become one of the most celebrated events of the Revolution. In retaliation, the British imposed the punitive Coercive Acts on Massachusetts, which served only to further antagonize the rebels. As their cause gained momentum, the Patriots established their own government in opposition to the rule of the British Crown. (Not all American colonists supported the rebel campaign, however: some, known as the Loyalists, were content to remain British subjects.)

The first military salvos of the American Revolutionary War erupted in the towns of Lexington and Concord, Massachusetts, in April 1775, where the Patriot militia clashed with the forces of the British Army and emerged victorious. They went on to initiate the Patriot Suffolk Resolves, a declaration announcing their break with the Royal government of Massachusetts. From this point onward, the conflict escalated into a full-scale civil war between the Patriots (later assisted by French, Spanish, and Dutch forces) and the British/Loyalist coalition.

As the campaign progressed, the Patriots succeeded in suppressing the Loyalists and replacing some of the governments of the thirteen colonies with extralegal legislative bodies known as Provincial Congresses. The rule of King George III was declared **tyrannical** (page 244) and an affront to the colonists' "rights as Englishmen." In July 1776, a countrywide body called the Continental Congress convened in Philadelphia to declare the colonies free states. In issuing its famous *Declaration of Independence*, the Congress affirmed the Enlightenment ideals of **liberalism** (page 152) and **republicanism** (page 206). It further repudiated monarchy and **aristocracy** (page 30) as forms of government inconsistent with the principles of **freedom** (page 107) and equality.

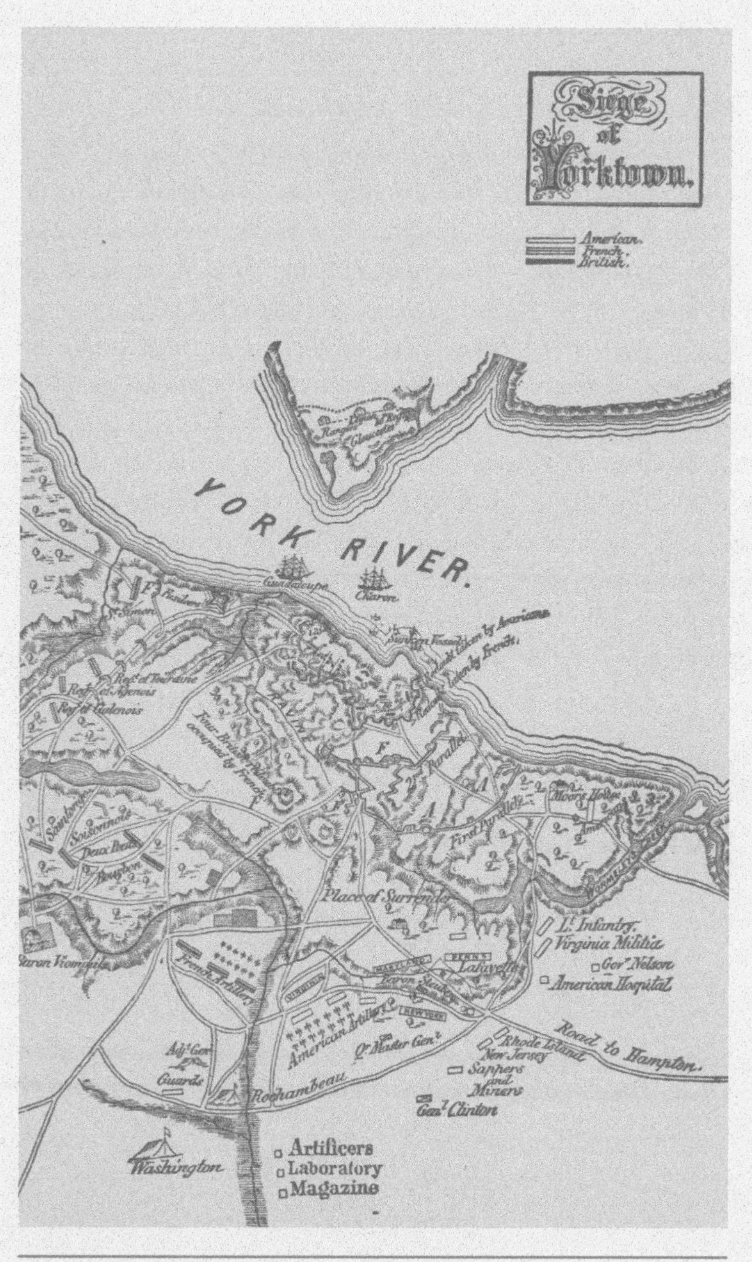

George Washington received help from over 5,000 French troops who fought alongside Patriot soldiers, forcing the British to surrender and laying the way for US independence.

1765 *Great Britain's unfair duties on goods; no colonist representation in the government*

1773 *Boston Tea Party; imposition of Coercive Acts*

1775 *Lexington and Concord, Mass.: Patriot militia clash with British Army*

1776 *Continental Congress, Philadelphia: Declaration of Independence*

1776 *General Washington expels the British from Boston*

1778 *Patriots defeat British forces at the Battle of Saratoga*

1781 *Siege of Yorktown (left): with French assistance, the Americans crush the British*

1783 *Fighting ends with signing of peace treaty between the United States and the British Empire*

In 1776, under the leadership of General **George Washington** (page 257), the Patriot Army expelled the British from Boston (the Crown, however, retained control of New York City until the end of the war). Washington faced formidable resistance from the British, who obstructed access to ports and held a number of other cities for short periods. After the Patriots defeated the British forces at the Battle of Saratoga in 1778, the conflict moved into the American South. While the British had some success in South Carolina, they and their Loyalist allies ultimately proved no match for the Patriot Army. Assisted by the French, the Americans crushed the British at the Siege of Yorktown in 1781, a victory that ultimately brought the war to an end.

The conflict was officially terminated in 1783, when the two parties signed a peace treaty that declared the United States an independent nation wholly separate from the British Empire. Most of the land south of the Great Lakes and east of the Mississippi River was brought under US control. Spain took possession of Florida, while the British retained Canada. Although the Americans promised the British that they would respect the rights of the Loyalists, the latter were ruthlessly suppressed; they became the targets of various acts of violence, including lynching. Under the

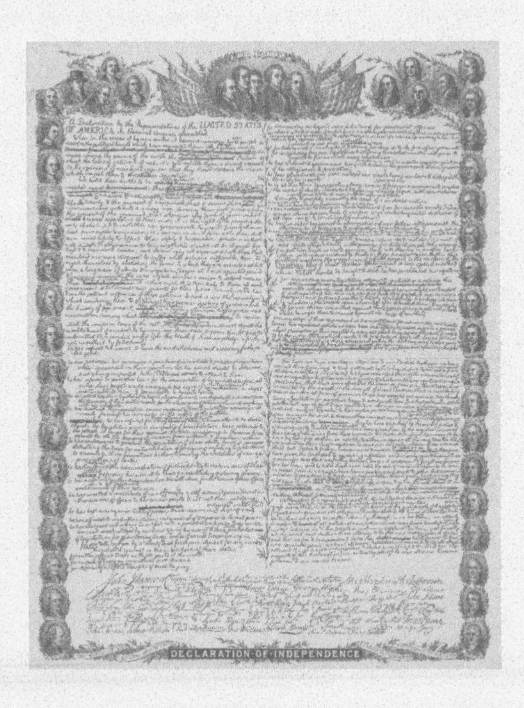
DECLARATION·OF·INDEPENDENCE

weight of the onslaught, many of them fled to Canada as refugees.

In the aftermath of the Revolution, a representative system backed by democratic **elections** (page 92) was established under the US **Constitution** (page 72). In principle, the new government was accountable to all the citizens of the republic. However, owing to an agreement known as the "Three-Fifths Compromise," the Southern slaveholding states gained higher proportions of electoral votes and seats in **Congress** (page 69) than they would have otherwise held. This arrangement enabled them to amass power and preserve the institution of slavery for an additional eighty years. The new political system was based on the principles of **federalism** (page 105) and the **separation of powers** (page 216), which divided the government into three branches: the executive, the judicial, and the legislative. The **civil rights** (page 54) guaranteed by the Constitution's **Bill of Rights** (page 37) are often cited as principles in whose defense the American Revolution was fought.

(Opposite, left) The Declaration of Independence was issued on July 4, 1776, though a peace treaty was not signed until 1783. (Left) Soldiers clash at Lexington, one of the first military battles of the Revolution.

ANARCHISM

The ancient Greek root of the term *anarchism* can be translated as "without a leader or ruler." In its modern usage, "anarchism" generally refers to the absence of an external authority whose **laws** (page 147) people are obliged to follow. Anarchists maintain that institutional arrangements such as the **state** (page 229), the economy, and religion are impediments to the maximization of human **freedom** (page 107), which they take to be a principal moral objective. They reject the idea that the consent of the people legitimates the authority of the sovereign; the subordination of human beings to the law, they argue, cannot be justified by a supposed contractual arrangement between them and their government, as **social contract** theorists (page 221) would have it. Two of the most influential anarchist thinkers of the nineteenth century, Pierre-Joseph Proudhon and Peter Kropotkin, claimed that the propertied and privileged had always utilized the laws and institutions of the state to consolidate power and exercise control over the public, private, and economic lives of ordinary citizens.

In line with the **socialists** (page 224), anarchists are generally opposed to **capitalism** (page 44), which they see as being dominated by exploitative **elites** (page 94); they believe the emancipation of the working class depends on capitalism's demise. They disagree, however, on what system ought to replace it. Both the collectivist and mutualist varieties of anarchism argue that individuals should be allowed to privately own and control the product of their labor. This view is rejected, however, by anarchist-**communists** (page 64), who think the maximization of individual freedom depends on the collective ownership of material resources and goods. For their part, individualist anarchists endorse a "labor for labor" system of exchange and the retention of **free-market** (page 108) forces. Finally, anarcho-**syndicalists** (page 235) maintain that the economy should be democratized and

A

placed under the control of multiple, decentralized worker cooperatives unconstrained by state authority.

Anarchist thinking is strongly anticlerical: while some anarchists are not ideologically opposed to the practice of private spiritual reflection, most denounce organized religion as an institution seeking to entrench its own authority. Moreover, they say, contemporary religious organizations have allied themselves with secular governments, thus becoming part of the general system of repression that binds ordinary citizens to the disciplinary authority of the state.

(Opposite) Anarchist thinker Peter Kropotkin, author of *Memoirs of a Revolutionist*, maintained that all state institutions serve the interests of the elite.

ANTI-SEMITISM

For millennia, the Jewish people have suffered discrimination, prejudice, hatred, violence, and genocide at the hands of various individuals, groups, and nations. The term *anti-Semitism* was coined in Germany in the nineteenth century, to replace the more vulgar-sounding *Judenhass* (or "Jew hatred"). Although *Semite* is an umbrella term encompassing all of the Semitic-speaking peoples of the Near East, the term anti-Semitism is now used to refer to derogatory attitudes and practices against Jews in particular. Over the ages, the mistreatment of Jews has been defended on the basis of their supposedly inferior religious beliefs, race, culture, and social and economic practices. Jews have been stereotyped as Christ-killers, money-grubbing bankers and usurers, unclean social outcasts, racial misfits, and conspirators secretly plotting to achieve world domination.

The most notorious twentieth-century manifestation of anti-Semitism was the Holocaust, perpetrated by **Adolf Hitler**'s (page 124) Third Reich during the 1930s and 1940s; it resulted in the extermination of nearly six million Jews. Hitler's crimes, however, are only the tip of an iceberg of state-sponsored violence against Jews dating back thousands of years. Today, in many nations, Jews continue to be the target of both subtle and blatant forms of anti-Semitism.

APARTHEID

In the twentieth century, few political systems were more notorious and reviled than the racial segregation regime imposed on South Africa from 1948 to 1994, and on South-West Africa from 1948 to 1990. South African *apartheid* ("the condition of being apart," in Afrikaans) restricted the **civil rights** (page 54), **freedoms** (page 107), and movement of blacks and other nonwhite ethnic groups, who comprised the majority of the population. It was instigated by the National Party (NP) in coalition with the *Broederbond* organization.

The NP built on the ideological principles of racial segregation brought to South Africa by the colonial Dutch Empire, which had ruled the nation from 1642 to 1795. Upon winning the general elections of 1948, it enacted the basic legal framework of apartheid. The population was officially divided into four main racial categories: "whites," "blacks," "coloreds," and "Indians." The latter two groups were further divided into various sub-classifications. Residential areas were segregated along racial lines, as were education, healthcare, and other public institutions and facilities. The policy of residential ghettoization was brutally enforced from 1960 to 1983, during which time the state uprooted some 3.5 million nonwhite South Africans and relocated them to specially designated areas. In 1970, blacks were stripped of political representation and of their status as citizens of South Africa. Legally, they were now recognized as citizens of ten tribal homelands known as *bantustans*. Although the *bantustans* were given some formal powers of self-government, in reality they remained under the autocratic rule of the apartheid state.

From the outset, the imposition of apartheid was staunchly resisted by nonwhite South Africans; numerous popular uprisings and public demonstrations were staged to contest its legitimacy and demand its removal. Eager to squelch the dissension, the regime resorted to brute force and intimidation: it murdered anti-apartheid protesters (during the Sharpeville Massacre of 1960, for example) and imprisoned many of the movement's key leaders, including Steve Biko and **Nelson Mandela** (page 161). The government's tactic of political repression served only to radicalize opposition groups such as the African National Congress (ANC), which came to believe that violence and militancy were warranted after the failure of **nonviolent resistance** (page 179).

Mounting internal resistance, coupled with foreign nations' economic sanctions against the regime, began to take their toll in the late 1980s. Having been reduced to pariah status by the international community, the

(Opposite) South Africa's apartheid regime lasted from 1948 to 1994, codifying racial segregation throughout the country. Black leaders like Nelson Mandela fought tirelessly to bring it down.

A

apartheid government sensed its own imminent collapse. South African President F.W. de Klerk took the first steps toward dissolving apartheid. In 1989, he released several activists from prison; among them was Mandela's political mentor, Walter Sisulu. In 1990, he released Mandela himself. Soon thereafter, De Klerk agreed to hold talks with the ANC and an assortment of other anti-apartheid organizations. These negotiations led to the annulment of remaining apartheid laws in 1991, and to multiracial elections in 1994. When the final votes were tallied, ANC President Mandela emerged as the nation's first democratically elected black leader.

For many, South Africa still bears the social and psychological scars left by a system of racial discrimination and violence that lasted over forty years. The term *apartheid* has become so infamous that it is now widely used to refer to any political system subjecting certain groups of citizens to systematic segregation, discrimination, and/or the denial of civil rights on the basis of race, ethnicity, or religion.

A

APPARATCHIK

The term *apparatchik* has become part of everyday English; it is often used to mock or ridicule someone who is seen as a "soulless bureaucrat." The word is a holdover from the former **Soviet Union** (page 226), where it was used to describe lower-level officials who worked in the *apparat* (or apparatus) of the government or the Communist Party. In contrast to other workers in Soviet society, some *apparatchiks* did not retain their positions for life, and many had to wait until midlife before receiving their appointments. They were derided for being incompetent, lazy, and focused on bureaucratic details rather than on the overall quality of their work. Upper-level officials (the *Nomenklatura*) would often shuffle *apparatchiks* between different positions, with little regard as to whether or not they had the necessary skills and training. This further solidified the *apparatchiks'* reputation as an interchangeable, and basically useless, part of the Soviet Union's vast governmental bureaucracy. During the Cold War, the term *apparatchik* was used liberally in Western propaganda, as a way of underscoring the Soviet economic system's inferiority to **free-market** (page 108) **capitalism** (page 44).

APPEASEMENT

In **foreign policy** (page 107), *appeasement* is a **diplomatic** (page 86) strategy aimed at avoiding direct military conflict by making concessions. The policy of appeasement is most often associated with British Prime Minister Neville Chamberlain's attempt to pacify German leader **Adolf Hitler** (page 124) during the late 1930s, thereby hoping to stave off a war with his **Nazi** (page 175) regime. The fact that Chamberlain's efforts were ultimately unsuccessful is often regarded as the chief reason why appeasement later fell into disrepute. Indeed, politicians in the **United States** (page 248) and other nations now often use the term as an epithet against adversaries whom they accuse of being "dovish" out of fear or weakness. Some, however, are less critical of appeasement, insisting that it is often a necessary and effective approach to conflict resolution.

During the Cold War, the US and Britain refused to adopt a posture of appeasement toward the **Soviet Union** (page 226), their bitter ideological rival. British Prime Minister Anthony Eden was likewise eager to avoid the tactic during the Suez Crisis of 1956. (He had, in fact, resigned as Foreign Secretary in the 1930s to protest Chamberlain's policy of

(Opposite) Neville Chamberlain (far left), Adolf Hitler (center), and other European leaders at the 1938 signing of the Munich Agreement, allowing Germany to annex the Sudetenland.

appeasement toward Benito Mussolini's Italy.) He made his anti-appeasement sentiments known to Egypt when he brought Britain, alongside France and Israel, into an armed conflict with President Gamal Abdel Nasser's government. US President Lyndon Johnson's reluctance to end American involvement in the Vietnam War stemmed, at least in part, from his refusal to appease North Vietnamese leader Ho Chi Minh. Distaste for appeasement was also a principal factor behind the First Iraq War, which began in 1990. Vice President Richard Cheney and Secretary of State Madeline Albright were especially vocal opponents of the idea, insisting that the US should not negotiate with Iraqi President Saddam Hussein from a position of "weakness."

Some have argued, however, that equating appeasement with weakness is simpleminded and misguided. British historian Paul Kennedy, among others, has claimed that appeasement can be an important tool of modern **statecraft** (page 230). He cites the British approach to the US in the latter half of the nineteenth century as an example: during this time, Britain allowed the emerging superpower to assume control of the Western Hemisphere, thus using appeasement to manage and stabilize the international system.

A

ARAB SPRING

The *Arab Spring* refers to a series of revolutionary movements that began to sweep through the Arab world in 2010. The "Spring" portion of the term is an allusion to two predecessor movements: the 1848 Springtime of Nations—a wave of political upheavals against feudal rule in Europe—and the 1968 Prague Spring—a revolt against the domination of the **Soviet Union** (page 226) in Czechoslovakia.

The first major rebellion of the Arab Spring was the Tunisian Revolution of December 2010, which managed to oust Tunisia's longstanding President Zine El Abidine Ben Ali in January 2011. The regimes of the Arab World soon began to teeter and fall like dominoes: Egypt, Libya, and Yemen all deposed their rulers just over a year after Ben Ali's removal. Civil uprisings broke out in Bahrain,

A

and demonstrators filled the streets of Syria, Algeria, Iraq, Jordan, Kuwait, Morocco, and Sudan, among other countries.

The revolutionary campaigns of the Arab Spring made use of many time-honored resistance strategies, including **strikes** (page 231), demonstrations, and marches. These protests, which were sometimes violent and sometimes peaceful, were accompanied by chants of a popular slogan: "The people want to bring down the regime!" One especially notable feature of the Arab Spring was its widespread use of social media—largely on the part of younger protesters—to organize, communicate, and mobilize popular support. In fact, the Arab Spring was one of the first political movements of its kind to utilize social media as a means of outmaneuvering the state. The backlash was at times brutal, involving the use of pro-government militias and armed assaults on demonstrators. In some cases, state violence was greeted with civil violence.

Behind the Arab Spring lay widespread dissatisfaction with the regimes that governed the region, some of which were constituted as **dictatorships** (page 84) or **absolute** (page 15) monarchies. The deep discontent with these governments has been attributed to a number of factors, including sharp disparities between the incomes of everyday citizens and those of the elites, chronic human rights abuses, political corruption, high levels of unemployment, skyrocketing food prices, and a high incidence of famine. These and other long-standing problems fueled the desire for alternative political structures—particularly among Arab youth, who constituted a significant and highly vocal segment of the various resistance movements. For many, the Turkish model of democratic **elections** (page 93), economic growth, and an Islamist government coupled with a secular constitution seemed like an appealing and tenable alternative.

By 2013, the enthusiasm of the Arab Spring and its hopes of change had been largely dashed; its initial victories were followed by a region-wide wave of violence and repression. The effects of this reversal of political climate, which has been referred to as the Arab Winter, were clearly demonstrated in Egypt. In 2013 Mohamed Morsi, who had become Egypt's first democratically elected president just a year earlier, was removed from office in a military coup d'état. His government was replaced by an authoritarian regime that proceeded to suppress the **civil liberties** (page 54) of Egyptian citizens. The Arab Winter also gave rise to civil wars in a number of Arab countries, including Syria and Yemen. Other Arab

(Opposite) Beginning in Tunisia in December 2010, and later in Egypt in January 2011, the Arab Spring uprisings spread like wildfire throughout the Middle East, resulting in the overthrow of various regimes. Social media gave voice to youth disillusioned with high unemployment rates and autocratic rule.

nations have had to contend with escalating political instability and, in some cases, internal insurgencies. The political fallout from the Arab Winter has up to now contributed to an estimated 250,000 deaths and created millions of political refugees. Because of its effects, approximately sixteen million people were in need of humanitarian relief in Syria, Egypt, Iraq, Jordan, Lebanon, and Turkey in 2014.

A

ARISTOCRACY

An *aristocracy* is a government run by an **elite** (page 94) class or a small group of individuals who are believed to be the most qualified to rule. The ancient Greek philosophers Plato and Aristotle described it as the rule of a few individuals who, by virtue of their superior moral and intellectual capacities, are best suited to uphold the interests of society at large. Which rulers are in fact "the best" is, of course, an entirely subjective question: one person's aristocracy may be another person's plutocracy (a government in which a few privileged individuals rule with the aim of further entrenching their own wealth and power). The line between aristocracies and other types of government may thus, at times, be difficult to draw. Moreover, some regimes are not technically aristocracies, but nevertheless harbor aspects of these types of government. For example, although monarchies are officially the province of a single ruler, they are often dominated by an aristocratic class. Likewise, because representative democracies aim to elect the best rulers, they, too, entail an aristocratic element.

Historical examples of aristocratic classes include the nobility of medieval Europe, which ruled the continent's feudal societies prior to the advent of **liberal** (page 152)

(Opposite) Late-eighteenth-century Europe was ruled by an aristocracy that passed down power through family lines.

republicanism (page 206) in the late eighteenth century; the Brahmans, who wielded enormous political influence over the ruling warrior caste of India; the Spartiates, an elite class of men who held power in Sparta during the Classical period of Greek civilization; the ancient Greek *Eupatridae*, the ruling nobility of the Attica region; and the Optimates, the "best men" who dominated the Senate during the late Roman Republic.

Throughout history, most aristocracies have been organized according to the **hereditary principle** (page 123). Some, however, have been nonhereditary, drawing their members from various sectors of society's upper strata—leading figures within the church or the business community, for instance. Even in nonhereditary aristocracies, political power may be passed down in a hereditary fashion, since members of the upper social stratum frequent the same privileged circles and tend to intermarry. In his 1956 book, *The Power Elite*, the sociologist C. Wright Mills set forth an argument along these lines in relation to the political, economic, and military elites of advanced industrial societies.

A

ART AND POLITICS

As one of the most significant elements of a **culture** (page 74), *art* has long played an important role in shaping societal attitudes regarding *politics*. At the same time, it has served as an avenue of resistance to prevailing political opinions. Throughout history, kings, popes, and the wealthy have patronized the arts, often with the objective of utilizing these works to advance their own agendas. In fact, politically motivated artistic patronage was responsible for many of Europe's great cathedrals, churches, paintings, and sculptures.

In the modern era, works of art were brought under the orbit of the **capitalist** (page 44) market and made available for sale alongside other commodities; this dramatically impacted the nature of their production. The commodification of art was a subject of particular interest to the Frankfurt School, a philosophical tradition that arose in Germany in the 1920s. Its proponents argued that the "culture industry" of modern societies had subjected art to processes of standardization and "massification." Denuded of all potential revolutionary impulses, they added, a commodified work of art embodied the rationalized logic of the capitalist economy, thereby impoverishing the political imagination of the masses and producing a docile, compliant body politic.

The Catholic Church regularly patronized Renaissance artists to produce work extolling its doctrines, as when Pope Julius II commissioned Michelangelo's masterpiece in the Vatican's Sistine Chapel.

AUTONOMY

The word *autonomy* is derived from the Greek *autonomia*, or "freedom to live according to one's own law." Aspects of this idea can be found in the theories of ancient Greek thinkers such as Plato and Aristotle. Our contemporary understanding of autonomy, however, grows out of the tradition of Enlightenment **liberalism** (page 152). Perhaps the most succinct summation of the meaning of autonomy was provided by Immanuel Kant in 1784: "Have the courage to use your own understanding!"[1] The autonomous individual thinks and acts without the guidance of another, without reliance on the authority of time-honored traditions and inflexible systems of belief. Thus, for Kant, autonomy is the hallmark of a rationally, morally and politically "mature" individual. In contrast, "immature" individuals remain content to blindly follow the pre-established rules, customs, and formulas of an external authority, thereby relinquishing control over the direction and content of their own lives. This state of irrational immaturity is a comfortable place to be, says Kant, as it relieves the "cowardly" and "lazy" person of the risks associated with questioning settled beliefs and cherished assumptions—risks that must be taken if moral and intellectual progress is to be made. Politically, Kant's view of autonomy is a direct challenge to the **Divine Right** (page 87) doctrine of the old feudal orders of Western Europe, which linked the rule of the king to the infallible, unquestionable authority of God.

Kant's view of autonomy was upheld a century and a half later in the **utilitarian** (page 252) and **libertarian** (page 154) doctrines of John Stuart Mill, despite some important philosophical differences between the two thinkers. For Mill, that aspect of the individual's conduct "which merely concerns himself, his independence, is, of right, absolute. Over himself, over his body and mind, the individual is sovereign."[2]

While autonomy appears to free the individual from knee-jerk obedience to majority opinion, rigid doctrines, and **tyrannical** (page 244) state authority, it also raises a basic question: does autonomy give one the license to do whatever one pleases? For thinkers such as Mill, preventing harm to others is the only legitimate basis for constraining the individual from freely pursuing his or her own opinions, tastes, and objectives; indeed, this is the sole purpose of the state's civil **law** (page 147). Where there is no prospect of any such harm, the law must remain silent, leaving the individual autonomous and free to form and revise his or her own ends.

B

BERLIN WALL

Of all the events leading to the demise of the **Soviet Union** (page 226), none is more emblematic than the collapse of the *Berlin Wall* in 1989. The story of its rise and fall is as fascinating as it is complex. For almost thirty years, the Wall served as an unshakeable barrier between the two halves of a formerly unified German nation: the German Democratic Republic (GDR) to the east, and the Federal Republic of Germany (FDR) to the west. Erected in August 1961 by the GDR, the structure featured large concrete walls topped by barbed wire and punctuated by imposing guard towers. A special area along its East German side was carved out; known as the "death strip," it was fortified with various defense structures, including anti-vehicle trenches.

For the GDR, the Wall served a vital strategic purpose: it buffered the Eastern Bloc nations against potential infiltration by counterrevolutionary elements from the West. Indeed, the official name given to the Wall by the GDR was the "Anti-Fascist Protection Rampart." On the other side of the border, the structure was generally perceived as a means of corralling the population of the GDR and preventing it from defecting to the West. This impression was reinforced by the renowned vigilance of the East German border guards, who killed roughly two hundred of the approximately five thousand people who attempted to escape over the Wall between 1961 and 1989. Clearly, it was more than just a physical barrier: it was a potent symbol of the great ideological "Iron Curtain" that separated East and West during the Cold War.

The order to begin construction of the Berlin Wall was issued on August 12, 1961, by GDR State Council Chairman Walter Ulbricht. Police and military units were summarily dispatched to close the border, while East German soldiers and workers proceeded to demolish the streets and erect barbed wire edifices—the first stages of the commanding ninety-six-mile-long fortification that would separate East and West Germany for almost three decades. The construction of the Wall was overseen by forces from the National People's Army and the Combat Groups of the Working Class. At this point, the somber aims of the GDR's project were readily

The 96-mile-long Berlin Wall separated communist East Germany from the capitalist West for nearly three decades.

apparent to the citizens of East Germany: to flee across the border would mean having to contend with obstacles like chain fences and minefields, as well as patrols that had been given shoot-on-sight orders.

The Berlin Wall effectively ended travel between the two German states, splitting family members on opposite sides of the divide and depriving many East Berliners of the jobs they had once held in the West. It also had the effect of isolating the city of West Berlin, leaving it surrounded by the hostile territory of the GDR. The reaction on the part of West Berliners was fierce: mayor Willy Brandt led public demonstrations against the barrier—he even dubbed it the "Wall of Shame"—and strongly rebuked the United States for failing to intervene.

Over the ensuing decades, the Wall continued to be widely unpopular on both sides of the divided German nation, even as the East German regime remained committed to maintaining it. By 1989, however, the political climate in the Eastern bloc had begun to change: a program of liberalization, associated chiefly with Soviet leader Mikhail Gorbachev's policies of *glasnost* and ***perestroika*** (page 190), was eroding the political authority of the pro-Soviet governments of Eastern Europe. In the West, Cold War ideologues were quick to seize upon the mounting tide of dissension in the hope of hastening the demise of the Soviet system. In a 1987 speech at the Brandenburg Gate, US President Ronald Reagan delivered his famous demand: "Mr. Gorbachev, tear down this wall!"

East Germany was by no means immune to the shifting political winds: in November of 1989, a wave of protests against the East German government swept the nation. In the face of mounting civil unrest, the GDR allowed its citizens to cross the border into West Berlin and West Germany. Scores of East Germans did so, to the welcoming cheers of West Berliners on the other side. The Berlin Wall was now officially defunct. It was relieved of its armed watchmen and turned over to the masses, who hacked away at its concrete flanks in pursuit of souvenirs. Its fall laid the groundwork for the formal reunification of Germany in October 1990. Under the authority of the new German state, the wall was demolished between 1990 and 1992.

BILL OF RIGHTS

Collectively, the first ten amendments to the United States **Constitution** (page 72) are known as the *Bill of Rights*. Under the bill, American citizens are guaranteed various personal freedoms, judicial proceedings are safeguarded against undue governmental interference, and the federal government's authority over the affairs of US states and the general public is limited. Initially, the Bill of Rights was meant to apply to the federal government alone; however, it was eventually extended to each of the fifty states under the Fourteenth Amendment.

The Bill of Rights was crafted from a raft of thirty-nine constitutional amendments presented to the **House of Representatives** (page 126) by James Madison in 1789. Madison wrote the amendments in a bid to appease his Anti-Federalist opponents, who felt that the Constitution gave the federal government too much authority and were thus against its ratification. From the original thirty-nine proposals Madison had hoped to incorporate into the main text of the Constitution, the US **Congress** (page 69) composed twelve amendments. In 1791, ten of these—Articles Three through Twelve—were approved by the necessary number of states as amendments to the Constitution.

The Bill of Rights, the first amendments to the US Constitution, was approved in 1791.

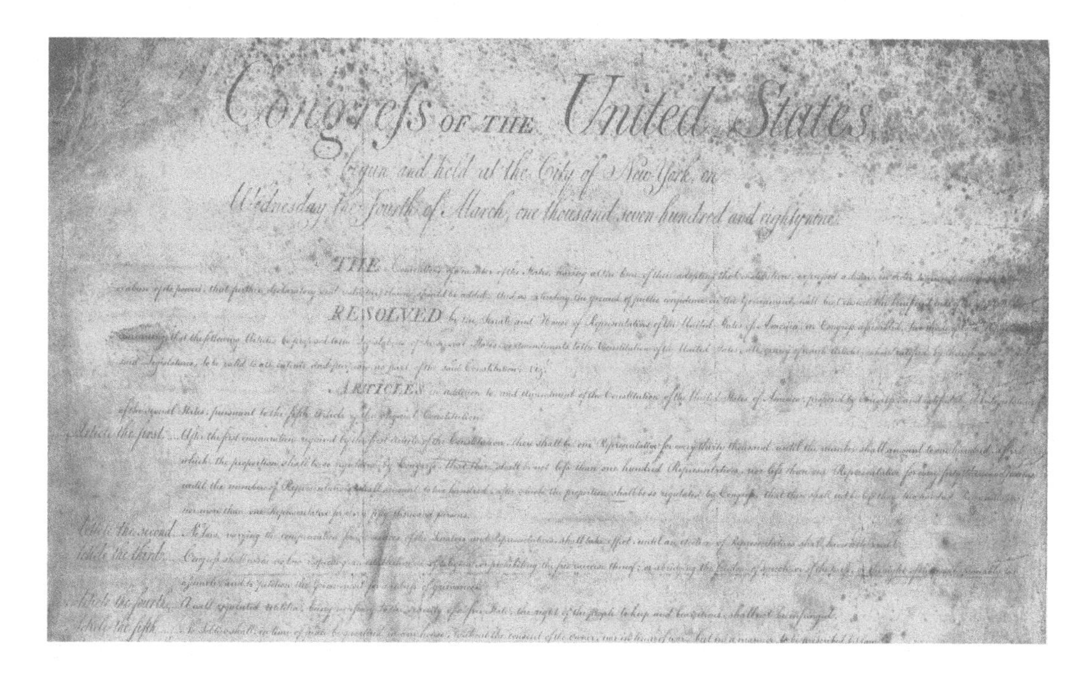

Congress of the United States,
begun and held at the City of New-York, on
Wednesday the fourth of March, one thousand seven hundred and eighty nine.

THE

RESOLVED

ARTICLES

Consistent with the ideals upheld in modern **liberalism** (page 152) and in legal documents such as the **Magna Carta** (page 160), the Bill of Rights grants a number of **rights** (page 208) and **freedoms** (page 107) to American citizens. These include the freedoms of religion, speech, the press, and public assembly. Americans are also guaranteed the right to "keep and bear arms," and are protected against "unreasonable search and seizure." Crime suspects cannot have their personal effects confiscated by governmental authorities without "probable cause." A grand jury indictment is required before bringing those charged with serious crimes to court, and all defendants are entitled to a speedy, public trial overseen by an impartial jury of their peers. Rights that are not explicitly noted in the Constitution devolve to the citizens, and powers not reserved for the federal government devolve to the states. Neither the federal government nor state governments can arbitrarily abridge the rights upheld in the Constitution.

Since its ratification in 1791, the Bill of Rights has become a pivotal resource for advocates of **civil rights** (page 54) and those seeking to guard against the abuse of state power. Its initial impact on judicial rulings in the United States was limited. However, in the twentieth and twenty-first centuries, it has figured prominently in many Supreme Court decisions.

B

BLACK PANTHER PARTY

The *Black Panther Party* (BPP) arose amidst the social, cultural, and political turmoil of 1960s America. Established in 1966 in Oakland, California, by Huey P. Newton and Bobby Seale, the group espoused a more radical set of objectives and political tactics than those of the **civil rights** (page 54) movement led by **Martin Luther King, Jr.** (page 141). While both King and the BPP sought to end institutional racism, poverty, police brutality, and the war in Vietnam, the BPP pushed beyond these goals. It championed both **socialism** (page 224) and—in its early phase—black nationalism: the view that black people should be governed by the principle of self-determination and remain independent from white, European society. It also rejected the civil rights movement's strategy of **nonviolent resistance** (page 179). While Newton once insisted that the group "never advocated violence," the BPP openly promoted militant self-defense of black and minority communities. It established armed citizens' patrols to monitor the actions of the police, and some of its members were involved in armed confrontations.

Despite its stance on armed resistance and its reputation for violence (reinforced

(Opposite) A Black Panther Party member at a 1970 Washington, DC, convention. The BPP advocated armed revolution and self-sufficiency within the black community.

by media images of its gun-toting, leather-jacketed leaders), the Panthers placed various community social programs at the core of their agenda. One of the most well-known of these initiatives was the Free Breakfast for Children Program, which provided food for poor youth in inner-city neighborhoods throughout the US.

Early leaders such as Stokely Carmichael, who assumed the role of BPP Prime Minister in 1968, focused on the need to reclaim black masculinity, leaving little room for women in the party leadership. Carmichael was also staunchly opposed to bringing whites into the movement, claiming that this would be inconsistent with the nationalist principles of Black Power. However, the party would later adopt a more inclusive stance, seeking to unite women, nonblack minorities, and whites in its revolutionary campaign. At this point, the party's initial emphasis on black nationalism began to recede. Its focus shifted to a **Marxist**-Leninist (page 166) critique of the class structure of **capitalist** (page 44) society, and to a **Maoist**-inspired (page 163) effort to build a revolutionary internationalist movement. The Panthers positioned themselves at the fore of this movement, whose aim was to overthrow the capitalist economic system.

The BPP's radical objectives did not escape the attention of the power structure that it sought to dismantle. As he had done with King and the civil rights movement, Federal Bureau of Investigation (FBI) Director J. Edgar Hoover mobilized his counterintelligence program (COINTELPRO) to discredit and undermine the Panthers, which he deemed "the greatest threat to the internal security of the country." At the FBI's direction, a number of prominent figures in the Panther hierarchy were jailed. Others were killed in police

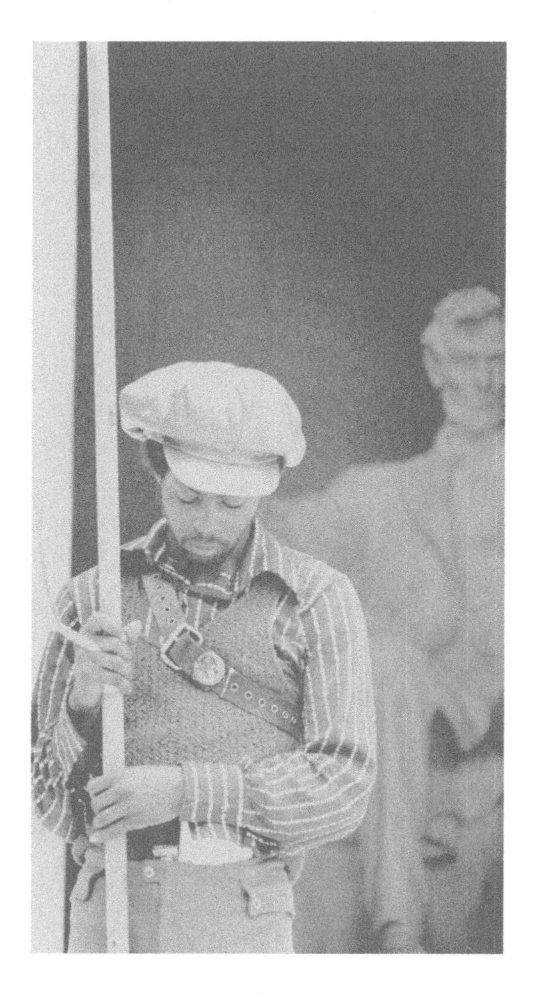

raids, including the leader of the BPP's Chicago chapter, Fred Hampton: in 1969, tipped off by an FBI informant, the Chicago police stormed into Hampton's apartment and shot him as he slept.

While Hoover had hoped to destabilize the party leadership, stripping it of critical resources and personnel, his initial efforts backfired. The negative publicity surrounding the political repression of the Panthers heightened sympathy for the party within the black community and among radical and progressive whites. One BPP supporter was the white actress Jean Seberg, who herself became the target of a COINTELPRO campaign that included surveillance, intimidation, and the planting of stories in the press designed to tarnish her reputation in Hollywood. A further endorsement came from actress Jane Fonda, who rallied behind the campaign to free Huey Newton from an Oakland prison where he was being held for allegedly killing a police officer.

In 1970, the power of the Black Panther Party was at its height: its membership had swelled to the thousands and it had established branches in sixty-eight American cities. However, thanks largely to the FBI-orchestrated anti-Panther campaign in mainstream media, public support for the party would soon decline. The group became increasingly isolated and its leadership began to fragment. Some of its leaders were expelled, while others defected. Among those who remained, persistent infighting undermined efforts to contain the damage and reinvigorate the movement. Party membership continued to dwindle during the 1970s, dropping to just twenty-seven members by 1980.

The legacy of the Black Panther Party, like that of other revolutionary movements and organizations of the 1960s and 1970s, remains controversial. Critics maintain that much of the group's revolutionary rhetoric and posturing was but a cover for the violent, criminal activities in which its leadership was covertly engaged. Supporters, however, hail the Panthers for establishing vitally needed social programs for poor and minority communities, and for risking life and limb in the struggle against international capitalism and imperialism.

BOLSHEVISM

Bolshevism refers to the political doctrines and practices of the Bolsheviks. Founded in 1905 by Vladimir Lenin and Alexander Bogdanov, the Bolsheviks were a faction of the Marxist Russian Social Democratic Labor Party (RSDLP). Breaking with a rival RSDLP faction known as the Mensheviks, the Bolsheviks came to power during the **October Revolution** (page 184) of 1917. They were so named because their side tended to prevail on a majority of issues ("Bolshevik" means "majority" in Russian).

Operating under a principle known as "democratic centralism," Bolsheviks were expected to carry out decisions that had been finalized by majority vote; however, they remained free to publicly debate political issues. Once in power, believing that Europe was going to enter a period of generalized civil war, the leading Bolsheviks urged their fellow parties in the Communist International (Comintern) to adopt a quasi-military model of organization that came to be known as the "vanguard" or "Leninist" type of party. In the aftermath of the October Revolution, the Bolsheviks led the wider Russian Revolution, which ultimately resulted in the establishment of the **Soviet Union** (page 226) in 1922. After the Revolution, they became the Communist Party of the Soviet Union.

BOURGEOISIE

Many historians have portrayed the *bourgeoisie* as a "middle class" that entered the European scene during the late Middle Ages. They locate this new social stratum somewhere between the upper-class nobility and the mass of peasants and city workers. Indeed, many urban figures of the time—merchants, guild masters, financiers, and government officials, to name a few—could count themselves among neither the ruling **aristocracy** (page 30) nor the throngs of "the lowly and the insulted" (to borrow a phrase from the philosopher Ernst Bloch).

At the dawn of the modern era, during the seventeenth and eighteenth centuries, many of the bourgeoisie began to adopt **capitalism**'s (page 44) novel economic principles. Some abandoned the medieval doctrine of divine predestination in favor of Protestantism, which sociologist Max Weber would later describe as the "spirit of capitalism" due to its emphasis on hard work, self-denial, and the production of "good works." The **French Revolution** (page 109) of 1789 was Europe's first great "bourgeois revolution": by the time it was over, the bourgeoisie had managed to wrest control of the **state** (page 229) from the nobility of the *ancien régime*, while stripping old feudal landlords of power over the means of production. In his writings, Karl Marx used the term "bourgeoisie" to refer to the class of property owners who came to control this new socioeconomic order.

B

Marx also spoke of a lower class of shopkeepers and small businessmen, which he referred to as the "petite bourgeoisie." Along with the peasantry and the aristocracy, the petite bourgeoisie was for him an "anachronistic" class—a holdover from the old feudal order. Unlike the working class and the bourgeoisie proper (capitalism's two main strata), the petite bourgeoisie still espoused traditional social and religious values, while capitalism profaned "all that is holy."

In his book on *The Mass Psychology of Fascism*, Wilhelm Reich argued that the petite bourgeoisie's reactionary values predisposed it to embrace **fascism**'s (page 101) ideological assault on reason, individual **freedom** (page 107), and the basic ideals of the Enlightenment. The beliefs of the bourgeoisie proper, on the other hand, posed an ideological challenge for the fascist movement—a challenge which its leaders addressed by dismissing the bourgeoisie as a morally degenerate class. Benito Mussolini, who led fascist Italy from 1922 to 1945, portrayed the members of the bourgeoisie as social parasites, hedonists, and crass materialists who served only to undermine the greatness of the Italian state and its people. (He was nevertheless careful to spare the capitalist economic order over which the bourgeoisie presided from such assaults.)

Marx was likewise a critic of the bourgeoisie proper, albeit on decidedly different terms. In the *Manifesto of the Communist Party*, he and his associate Friedrich Engels praised this class for revolutionizing the means of production and spearheading advances in science, industry, and technology—these, they argued, could one day free humanity from the drudgery of menial labor. The bourgeoisie was also to be lauded for tearing down feudalism's ossified, parochial traditions and proclaiming the universal values of **liberty** (page 155), equality, and fraternity in the context of a new **republican** (page 206) order. The capitalist system, however, kept the bourgeoisie's emancipatory ideals at the level of mere ideology; their realization would only come with the arrival of a new **communist** (page 64) society.

BUREAUCRACY

In simplest terms, *bureaucracy* refers to **government** (page 118) by agencies or offices with specified functions. The sociologist Max Weber, the first great theorist of the modern bureaucracy, argued that modern societies exhibit a cultural tendency toward rationalization or "disenchantment": they replace the authority of established traditions and prerational systems of belief with "instrumental reason," a perspective that enjoins one to adopt suitable means to achieve prescribed ends. The modern bureaucracy, said Weber, appeals to this instrumental reason in order to legitimate its organizational structure.

Weber portrayed the bureaucracy's operations as circumscribed by well-codified and exhaustive rules, aimed at assuring the fulfillment of organizational goals. The rule-bound nature of the bureaucracy encourages the establishment of a **hierarchical** (page 123) structure. Inside it, one finds individuals who are trained to carry out specific functions. These are typically of an "abstract" nature—involving the processing of files or documents, for example. Accordingly, bureaucracies are inclined to mete out rewards such as job security in exchange for services rendered.

For Weber, another remarkable feature of bureaucracy is its capacity to routinize and rationalize "charisma"—the personal attributes of a particular individual that inspire devotion in others. Bureaucracy, Weber claimed, does not extinguish charisma but rather "demystifies" it so that it can be made consistent with the notion of instrumental reason. Weber's analysis was highly prescient in this regard: it anticipated, for example, the phenomenon of German **Nazism** (page 175). Nazi leader **Adolf Hitler** (page 124) was certainly a charismatic figure, but his was a decidedly "domesticated" type of charisma, well-suited to the depersonalized bureaucratic apparatus of death and destruction over which he presided.

From Weber's standpoint, bureaucracy's tendency to "disenchant the world" comes at a terrible cost: it leaves little room for individual creativity and **freedom** (page 107). Building on Weber's work, Theodor Adorno, Max Horkheimer, Herbert Marcuse, and others associated with the so-called Frankfurt School, highlighted the tendency of advanced industrial societies to subordinate more and more spheres of life to the logic of bureaucratic control and administration.

C

CAPITALISM

Capitalism is an economic system in which **property** (page 199) is privately owned. The owners of private property, known as capitalists, acquire the output of the work performed for them by laborers and sell it on the **free market** (page 108). In so doing, they accumulate value as profit, rent, or interest, depending on the type of property owned. In general, workers have few or no assets with which to generate income, other than their own capacity to labor. They are thus obliged to enter into a contractual relationship with the capitalists, agreeing to sell them their labor for a specific period of time and at a set wage or salary. However, because the intensity at which this labor is to be performed is generally not specified, they are often pressed into increasing their productive output during the prescribed period of employment.

Although markets have existed throughout human history, private market relations constitute the economic foundation of a capitalist society. Capitalism thus represents a fundamental departure from all previously existing orders. In his influential 1944 study, *The Great Transformation*, Karl Polanyi observed that in pre-capitalist societies, markets were subordinated to a broader cultural framework wherein social and economic relationships were determined on the basis of status and rank. Under capitalism, however, market relations themselves become the framework for determining how social status, space, time, and virtually every other aspect of the culture are to be constituted. Indeed, as the first economic order in history to institutionalize self-sustaining economic growth, capitalism increasingly brings more and more aspects of human existence under its own economic orbit, creating a world system beyond the self-conceptions and designs of any particular culture.

These sweeping changes could not have been realized without an associated shift in the terms in which the **state** (page 229) and its legal order are structured. The most critical development in this regard has been the secularization of the state's foundations, a change that removed blood **rights** (page 208), rank, and social status (among others) as criteria for who is allowed to rule. In developed capitalist societies, the state's political **sovereignty** (page 226) does not ride on the ambiguities and restrictions of sedimented traditions, and its political authority is clearly distinguished from an independent sphere of activity predicated on the defense of **property** (page 199). As the Enlightenment thinkers John Locke and Adam Smith observed, such limits on the scope of **government** (page 118) are required in order to sustain an economic system based on the imperative to expand value incessantly.

The state's valorization of private property rights means that under capitalism, universal access to **land** (page 146) and other natural resources is neither legally nor institutionally recognized. Rather, a relatively small number of property owners remain in control of the production process, while the remainder of the population is left without significant amounts of property and without any legal rights to appropriate privately held resources and assets. Involvement in market relations thus becomes inevitable.

In his seminal nineteenth-century text, *Capital*, German thinker Karl Marx described how the capitalist market compels workers to compete with one another for the opportunity to sell their labor to the capitalists. Because labor supply always outstrips its demand, a "reserve army of labor" is created. The existence of this enduring replacement pool makes workers dependent on employment terms offered by the capitalists, who are then able to negotiate wages down to minimum subsistence levels. Marx further argued that, rather than compensate workers fully for the value they generate, capitalists are obliged to extract some "surplus value" in order to revolutionize the means of production and, ultimately, generate more surplus. Because the production process is not under their control, workers remain alienated from their own activity, the products of their labor, and their relations with themselves and the natural world. Thus, in Marx's view, exploitation is built into the capitalist system of production on a structural level.

In addition to his analysis of the nature and logic of capital accumulation, Marx is renowned for his account of how ideology is deployed to reproduce capitalist relations of production. Modern states, he noted, are founded with the ideals of **liberty** (page 155) and equality in mind. By virtue of their control over the means of production, however, capitalists are able to wield these *universal* ideals to legitimate and further their own *particular* class interests. Marx praised capitalism for laying the material and conceptual foundations for a truly liberated social order, but maintained that such an order can only be achieved by overturning capitalism and establishing a classless, **communist** (page 64) society.

C

CHRISTIANITY

Christianity is the largest religion in the world today. In 2012, 31.5 percent of those affiliated with a religion (some 2.2 billion people) were Christians. Since its rise over two millennia ago, Christianity has been tightly interwoven with the history of Western civilization. It has had a major influence on the development of Western art, literature, philosophy, and culture. In politics, its impact has been similarly profound.

The Christian Church coalesced into a dominant political force during the Middle Ages, when it seized the reins of power from the Roman Empire and established a collection of Christian church-states across Europe. With the **papacy** (page 187) of Gregory VII in the late eleventh century, its power, wealth, and influence grew exponentially. It established its own system of courts, whose authority dominated virtually all aspects of everyday life from education to marriage. Even the secular laws of medieval society were stamped with the Church's ideological imprint. During the late Middle Ages, many European kings were granted **absolute** (page 15) authority over their subjects under the doctrine of **Divine Right** (page 87).

(Opposite) The belief that Jesus Christ is the son of God is at the center of Christianity's teachings, which have reached all corners of the world, often through violent conquest.

C

The patronage of the medieval Catholic Church accounts for some of mankind's greatest architectural achievements, while its educational institutions became the basis of the modern university system. During the Renaissance era, Christian artists such as Michelangelo, Leonardo da Vinci, Bach, Mozart, and Beethoven produced some of the world's most renowned artistic masterpieces. The Church also collected taxes and earmarked them for the construction of orphanages, hospices, and hospitals for the elderly, as well as for the provision of food for victims of famine and poverty. Some have credited such activities with laying the foundations of the modern **Welfare State** (page 259).

The Church was rather less progressive with regard to slavery. In ancient times and during the reign of the Roman Empire, it maintained that slaves should be treated humanely, but nevertheless recognized the institution of slavery as legitimate. The Church's position softened somewhat in the early medieval period, when it objected to the enslavement of Christians. While several popes attempted to defend slaves against ill-treatment, it was not until 1839 that Pope Gregory XVI condemned slavery outright for Christians and non-Christians alike.

The period spanning the fourteenth through the eighteenth centuries brought significant upheaval and transformation to the Christian world. Beginning in 1492, Christianity began to expand beyond the confines of Europe, eventually leaving its mark on every corner of the globe. During

the first half of the sixteenth century, however, the unity of the Church was broken by the Protestant Reformation, which ended the dominance of Catholicism in Europe. Toward the end of this period, Christianity would face a formidable challenge from the Age of Enlightenment, which confronted its foundational doctrines and belief in divine revelation with new perspectives—notably those of science, rationality, secularism, and individual **freedom** (page 107). As the Enlightenment ushered in the demise of the old feudal order, adherents of Christianity were forced to adapt the tenets of their religion to the **liberal** (page 155) conditions of the modern world.

In so doing, many Christians have found a striking continuity between the teachings of **Jesus** (page 138)—the main figure of their faith—and the modern ideals of social **justice** (page 140) and **human rights** (page 128). During the twentieth century, **Martin Luther King, Jr.** (page 141) and other **civil rights** (page 54) campaigners appealed to Christian teachings to justify their nonviolent **civil disobedience** (page 53) movements. Similarly, taking its name from a passage in the Book of Isaiah in which the people are counseled to "beat their swords into ploughshares," the Plowshares Movement in the US draws heavily on Roman Catholic doctrine to protest the continued existence of **nuclear weapons** (page 180). Meanwhile, liberation theology—which arose in Latin America in the 1950s and is sometimes described as a kind of Christianized **Marxism** (page 166)—has interpreted Jesus's moral principles as a call against the unjust social and political treatment of the poor and oppressed.

While these social movements emphasize Christianity's adaptation to the values of modernity, many Christians adopt a decidedly **conservative** (page 71) vantage point. Conservative evangelicals and others affiliated with the contemporary Christian right espouse highly traditional views on sexuality, marriage, gender roles, contraception, abortion, pornography, evolution, sexual education in public schools, and other matters. They often think of those who have found a progressive or **socialist** (page 224) message in the teachings of Jesus as deeply misguided. In their view, Jesus is not so much counseling Christians to help the poor and promote social justice, as he is adjuring them to affirm and preserve established Christian mores. With so many internal battles over its true meaning, contemporary Christianity is perhaps best described as a collection of highly divergent Christianities.

(Opposite) Leonardo da Vinci's fifteenth-century masterpiece, *The Last Supper*, depicts Jesus and his disciples prior to his Crucifixion—the event that turned him into a martyr.

C

WINSTON CHURCHILL

1874	*Born in England*
1940–1945	*First term as Prime Minister*
1951–1955	*Second term as Prime Minister*
1953	*Awarded the Nobel Prize in Literature*
1953	*Suffers a major stroke*
1965	*Dies at the age of 90*

Winston Churchill is often hailed as one of the greatest political leaders of the twentieth century, but his long career in politics was not without controversy. Churchill served two terms as Prime Minister of the United Kingdom: one from 1940 to 1945, and another from 1951 to 1955. He was also a military officer, an artist, a historian, and the author of numerous books for which he was awarded the 1953 Nobel Prize in Literature.

Churchill was born in 1874 to an aristocratic family that was part of the Duke of Marlborough's line. Before entering politics, he was a war correspondent and an army officer, serving tours of duty in British-ruled India, the Sudan, and the Second Boer War. His various campaigns were fodder for the books that he would later write.

As a Conservative, Churchill assumed several positions in the Liberal government of Henry Herbert Asquith prior to **World War I** (page 262)—namely, those of President of the Board of Trade, Home Secretary, and First Lord of the Admiralty. He retained his Admiralty post during the war, but left the government in the aftermath of a botched military maneuver in the Gallipoli peninsula that resulted in a temporary victory for the Ottoman Empire. After a short stint as a battalion commander on the Western Front, Churchill was back in politics. Under the Liberal government of David Lloyd George, he took up several defense-related Cabinet positions that he would later incorporate into the Ministry of Defence. He became Chancellor of the Exchequer—a post that had once been his father's—under the Conservative Premiership of Stanley Baldwin.

In these roles, Churchill took a number of controversial stands. Notably, he opposed the demands for greater home rule that were being raised in pre-Independence India. He also had a checkered record regarding labor issues: he is rumored to have ordered an attack on coal miners in the Rhondda Valley during his early years in Parliament—a move that damaged his reputation in Wales and among Labour Party stalwarts.

During the early 1930s, Churchill raised alarms about **Nazi** (page 175) Germany's mounting threat to Europe, and pushed for the rearmament of the British military. The onset of **World War II** (page 266) found him at his former post as First Lord of the Admiralty, this time under Conservative Prime Minister Neville Chamberlain. When Chamberlain resigned in May 1940, Churchill took over the Premiership. Prior to the start of the war in 1939, the British stood alone in their vigorous opposition to **Adolf Hitler**'s (page 124) regime. As the nation's new leader, Churchill showed his resolve to resist the German onslaught. He defended the Allied campaign in his numerous speeches and radio broadcasts, despite the domestic privation it caused and the deaths of almost half a million citizens. He persevered in his war efforts until victory over Nazi Germany was declared.

In the elections of 1945, the ruling Conservatives were defeated by the Labour Party. However, Churchill remained in the government as Leader of the Opposition. It was in this capacity that he delivered the famous address that helped popularize the term "Iron Curtain"—a metaphor for the ideological battle and physical boundary that separated the **communist** (page 64) East and the **capitalist** (page 44) West during the Cold War.

Churchill's departure from the Prime Minister's chair lasted just six years; he was reelected to the post in 1951. Although the war was well behind him, his political palate was far from satisfied. On the foreign affairs front, he oversaw Great Britain's involvement in a number of conflicts, including the Malayan Emergency, the Mau Mau Uprising, the Korean War, and a coup d'état in Iran. At home, his government enforced tighter workplace and housing regulations, and a number of house-building initiatives were undertaken.

In 1953, Churchill suffered a major stroke, which led to his retirement from the Premiership in 1955. He nevertheless continued to serve in the government as a Member of Parliament until 1964. He died the following year, at the age of ninety. Despite his many controversial political moves, opinion polls continue to rank him as one of the most highly esteemed and influential Prime Ministers in British history.

(Opposite) Winston Churchill served multiple political and military roles before rising to power as British Prime Minister and leading the Allied forces during World War II.

CITY-STATE

A *city-state* is an independent city that has **sovereignty** (page 226) over its own political, economic, and cultural affairs, as well as those of its adjacent territories. The earliest city-states are believed to have arisen between 1000 and 800 BC; the term "city-state," however, did not enter popular usage until the late nineteenth century. Since then, historians have used it to describe the municipalities of ancient and medieval Italy, as well as the model for political life that took hold during the classical period of Greek civilization.

For Aristotle, the highest level of human existence was to be achieved within the context of the city-state, or *polis*. Aristotle characterized the citizens of the city-state as "political animals" who deliberate over questions of the "good life." A *polis*, he believed, was corrupt if it did not adopt the good life as its ultimate end, but instead remained focused on the concerns of the "mere life"—the acquisition of material wealth as an end in itself, for example.

The city-states of ancient Greece were limited in size, and were distinguished from other political systems by their high level of patriotism and independence. Many were established in the ancient world and assumed a wide range of political incarnations. They were the birthplaces of numerous advancements in the fields of art, literature, and philosophy, laying the cultural foundations for Greco-Roman civilization.

Ironically, the fierce independence that helped nurture their achievements also contributed to their downfall: due to their disinterest in forming a defensive union or federation, they were easy prey for the conquering Macedonians, Carthaginians, and Romans. (While Rome itself was initially constituted as a city-state, it would later adopt a centralized government with expansionist objectives, ultimately morphing into an empire that swept the city-state from the political landscape of the ancient world.)

City-states underwent a revival in some of the more prosperous regions of eleventh-century Italy. In the modern era, Enlightenment thinker Jean-Jacques Rousseau weighed in on their side. Offering Geneva and Corsica as examples, he argued that of all possible political arrangements, the city-state was best suited for implementing **democracy** (page 78) and the "general will" of the citizenry.

CIVIL DISOBEDIENCE

Civil disobedience is the act of refusing to abide by certain edicts or **laws** (page 147) imposed by a domestic government or foreign occupying power. It is carried out by individuals, civic groups, or political movements with the aim of exposing and ultimately changing policies, practices, and institutions that they deem unjust or illegitimate. Civil disobedience commonly avoids the use of violence. In such cases, it qualifies as a form of **nonviolent resistance** (page 179).

Civil disobedients generally do not reject the legal system as such. Rather, having found that their grievances cannot be redressed through established legal avenues, they attempt to break specific laws. Their aim in so doing is to raise awareness of higher extralegal principles that the existing order has either ignored or actively precluded. Civil disobedients are aware that their lawbreaking activity is considered criminal by **state** (page 229) authorities; in submitting to the attendant punishments, they hope to illustrate the injustice of prevailing norms and practices, while provoking government officials and the public at large to support their demands for change.

Proponents of revolutionary political action maintain that civil disobedience is an

Mahatma Gandhi's "noncooperation movement" was a form of peaceful civil resistance against British colonial rule in India.

insufficient tactic, since it accepts the legitimacy and permanence of present institutional arrangements and fails to call for the fundamental restructuring of society as a whole. Most **conservatives** (page 71) also reject the strategy of civil disobedience, but for different reasons. They argue that, in flouting the authority of established laws as they see fit, civil disobedients have lurched toward **anarchy** (page 22). For conservatives, obedience to prevailing laws and institutions is necessary in order to promote self-discipline and prevent individual **liberties** (page 155) from being exercised irresponsibly.

In political philosophy, arguments on behalf of civil disobedience have been advanced by writers as diverse as Thomas Aquinas and Henry David Thoreau. Its modern conception is significantly indebted to the ideas of Indian anti-**colonialist** (page 61) **Mahatma Gandhi** (page 114) and those of American civil rights leader **Martin Luther King, Jr.** (page 141). The principle of civil disobedience received qualified support from the international tribunal that presided over the trials of Nazi war criminals in Nuremberg, Germany, after **World War II** (page 266). The judges maintained that, under circumstances where crimes against humanity are legally sanctioned, individuals may be held accountable for failing to break the state's prevailing laws.

C

CIVIL RIGHTS/LIBERTIES

Civil rights and *civil liberties* are related, but not identical, concepts. Usually backed by the force of **law** (page 147), **governments** (page 118) extend civil rights to their citizens, protecting them equally and granting them equal opportunities to participate in the social and economic life of the nation. Civil liberties, however, are **freedoms** (page 107) that individuals obtain when governments *refrain* from exercising authority over their personal affairs.

In contrast to natural rights and **human rights** (page 128)—which are presumed to be bestowed upon people by nature or God—civil rights are not inherent rights; rather, they issue from the authority of the **state** (page 229), which guarantees and upholds them under law. Because the state is a changeable institution, the content and scope of civil rights laws will vary greatly over time, often reflecting prevailing societal attitudes regarding which individuals and groups are entitled to their protections. The first ten amendments to the **Constitution** (page 72) of the **United States** (page 248), collectively known as the **Bill of Rights** (page 37), enumerate a number of basic civil rights, including the right to a fair trial before a jury of one's peers.

(Opposite) The 1963 March on Washington led by Martin Luther King, Jr. was a pinnacle of the US civil rights movement.

Over the course of the past two and a half centuries, modern representative **democracies** (page 78) have gradually extended the compass of their civil rights laws, applying them to groups that have been historically denied full and equal citizenship on the basis of religion, race, ethnicity, gender, or other personal attributes. This has often been a response to action from disadvantaged groups themselves. For instance, the campaign for women's **suffrage** (page 233) in America—which began in the mid-nineteenth century under the leadership of Elizabeth Cady Stanton, Susan B. Anthony, and other activists—led to the passage of the Nineteenth Amendment to the US Constitution in 1920. Similarly, during the 1950s and 1960s, pressure from the African-American civil rights movement led by **Martin Luther King, Jr.** (page 141) resulted in **Congress** (page 69) passing the Civil Rights Act of 1964 and the Voting Rights Act of 1965—two landmark pieces of legislation for the African American community. Many other civil rights struggles across the

C

globe, including the Northern Ireland resistance movement and the campaign against South African **apartheid** (page 24) led by **Nelson Mandela** (page 161), were inspired by King's movement in America.

As noted, civil liberties differ from civil rights in that they are dependent not on government action, but rather on government inaction: they arise when the government abstains from encroaching on citizens' private affairs. A variety of civil liberties are upheld in the Bill of Rights, including the freedom to express one's thoughts and opinions, the freedom to assemble publicly, and the freedom to engage in the religious practices of one's choice.

In its role as a mediator of disputes between Americans and their government, the Supreme Court has declared various constitutionally guaranteed civil freedoms and rights universal, extending them to US citizens to whom they were previously denied. Thus, the federal judiciary has restricted local and state governments' authority to abridge civil rights and liberties as they see fit. This process, which has become known as the incorporation or nationalization of the Bill of Rights, has been carried out under a broadened interpretation of the Equal Protection Clause of the Fourteenth Amendment of the Constitution. One recent example is the Supreme Court's 2015 ruling in *Obergefell v. Hodges*, which extended the right to marry to same-sex couples.

Many observers have noted that contemporary representative democracies will at times abrogate constitutionally protected civil freedoms and civil rights, particularly when threats to national security are perceived to be great. Some have alleged, for example, that in carrying out its campaign to defend **homeland security** (page 125) and combat global **terrorism** (page 238) in the aftermath of the 9/11 attacks on New York City and Washington, DC, the US government has infringed upon the constitutionally guaranteed privacy rights of many Americans. Preventing governments from undermining the civil rights and liberties of their citizens has been a principal objective of nonprofit organizations such as Human Rights Watch, Amnesty International, and the American Civil Liberties Union.

While civil rights and liberties are typically guaranteed in the constitutions of modern nation-states, they are also protected by international agreements such as the 1950 European Convention on Human Rights, the **United Nations** (UN) (page 245) International Convention on the Elimination of All Forms of Racial Discrimination of 1965, the UN International Covenant on Civil and Political Rights of 1966, and the UN International Covenant on Economic, Social, and Cultural Rights of 1966.

C

CIVIL SERVICE

The term *civil service* refers to the entire body of employees within a **government**'s (page 118) civil administration: postal workers, county clerks, and highway patrol officers, among others. The civil service is thus distinct from the government's **military** (page 168) sector and its body of elected officials. In most contemporary representative **democracies** (page 78), civil service personnel are selected according to their performance on specialized examinations, and promoted on the basis of merit ratings.

Examinations were first used to select civil officials during the Chinese Han dynasty of 206 BC to AD 220. In the West, however, this practice was not institutionalized until the modern era: in the mid-seventeenth century, King of Prussia Frederick Wilhelm established a competitive selection process for civil officials. The royal administration of France was eventually transformed into a civil administration, courtesy of reforms initiated by **Napoleon Bonaparte** (page 172) in the early nineteenth century. The term "civil service" itself did not take hold until the mid-nineteenth century, when it was applied to civil employees within the English government, as well as to the British administration of **colonial** (page 61) India. The British civil service remains extremely powerful and well-regarded, although it has at times been accused of **bureaucratic** (page 43) inflexibility and elitism.

For many years, the standing of the American civil service trailed far behind that of Great Britain's, in large part due to the "spoils system" that prevailed in the Jacksonian era of 1820 to 1845. Under this system, political parties would hand out government jobs to their supporters after winning an **election** (page 92). In 1871, due to pressure from reformers, **Congress** (page 69) granted the president the power to establish admission standards for public service jobs and gave President Ulysses S. Grant the authority to appoint the first Civil Service Commission. The short-lived body was brought back to life by President James A. Garfield with the passage of the Pendleton Civil Service Reform Act in 1883. The law, which made specialized tests compulsory for civil service job candidates, aimed to eliminate the system of political patronage that had allowed elected officials to hire and fire civil servants on the basis of partisan ties. Over the years, US presidents have expanded the authority of the Civil Service Commission and increased the number of federal departments falling under its jurisdiction. Since 1978, the commission's powers have been divided between the Merit Systems Protection Board and the Office of Personnel Management.

C

CIVIL WAR

The American Civil War was a pivotal event in the history of the **United States** (page 248), where it is often referred to simply as the *Civil War*. The 1861–1865 campaign pitted the Confederate forces of the South against the Union forces of the North. In January 1861, seven Southern slaveholding states reconstituted themselves as the Confederate States of America and declared their independence from the United States. The South's secession from the Union was motivated by two principal issues that had not been resolved by the **American Revolution** (page 18) one century earlier: first, whether political **sovereignty** (page 226) should reside mainly with the federal government or with the individual states; second, whether the rights of the states (notably the right to maintain the institution of slavery) superseded the guarantees of individual **liberty** (page 155) and equality before the law, set forth in the US **Constitution** (page 72). The South's position on these questions was clear: it refused to be bound by the central authority of the Union and sought to establish a Confederation that allowed each state to retain control over its own internal affairs.

The South's declaration of secession was deemed illegal by both outgoing Democratic President James Buchanan and incoming Republican President **Abraham Lincoln** (page 156). A peace conference aimed at bringing about a diplomatic end to the dispute was not successful. The Confederate forces attacked the Union-held Fort Sumter in South Carolina on April 12, 1861, signaling the official start of the war. The initial seven member states grew to eleven when four additional Southern states joined in. However, several slaveholding border states were soon under the control of the Union, preventing their defection to the Confederacy. In a bid to further undermine the Confederate cause, Lincoln implemented a naval blockade designed to cripple the Southern economy. He also limited **civil liberties** (page 54) and suspended the writ of **habeas corpus** (page 120) in Maryland—a directive that was at one point imposed upon the entire nation. Lincoln's *Emancipation Proclamation* of 1863 declared the abolition of slavery an official objective of the war. The four-year conflict, which resulted in the deaths of an estimated seven hundred and fifty thousand military personnel and an unknown number of civilians, ended with Confederate General Robert E. Lee's surrender to Union General Ulysses S. Grant on April 9, 1865. Efforts to rebuild and reintegrate the battered nation were undertaken over the next twelve years, during the period known as Reconstruction.

(Opposite) The battles of Fort Sumter (top left), Gettysburg (top right), and Antietam (bottom), after which Lincoln issued the Emancipation Proclamation, were among the deadliest of the US Civil War.

purpose aforesaid, I do order and declare that ALL PERSONS HELD AS SLAVES
SHALL BE FREE! and that the Executive Government of the United
AND MAINTAIN THE FREEDOM of said persons.
A. Lincoln

C

CLASS

Any overview of the modern idea of *class* must begin with the pioneering analysis of the nineteenth-century German author Karl Marx. Marx argued that classes do not arise in societies where the process of production is controlled by each individual member, and where resources and material goods are distributed equitably; they only exist in societies where one group of people privately controls the means of production. This group can extract "surplus value" from members of the productive working class, who invest more time producing than is necessary to assure their own subsistence. The owners of the means of production are then able to appropriate whatever is left over to reproduce themselves as a class. In Marx's view, whether the relationship is one of master and bondsman, **aristocratic** (page 30) landlord and peasant, or **capitalist** (page 44) and wage laborer, class divisions are present in all societies where the means of production are not owned by the direct producers, and where surplus value is thus forcibly extracted from them.

Although he did not deny that exploitative class relations are a feature of modern societies, the German sociologist Max Weber was critical of Marx's account of class. Weber focused on other forms of domination, which he envisioned as having a more central place in the modern landscape. In his seminal 1922 essay "Class, Status, Party," he depicted a class as a collection of individuals who are basically disconnected from one another, but who nevertheless share the same "life chances." Life chances might include one's ownership of the means of production, but they can also include professional skills or educational background, for instance. Similar life chances are sufficient to classify people as members of the same class, but they offer no guarantee that such individuals will act together, as Marx maintained. Weber went on to discuss other forms of non-economic domination that forestalled the capacity for class action altogether. The French sociologist Émile Durkheim contributed to the discussion by arguing that the coherence of modern classes is based on the "organic solidarity" of their members, who take up complementary roles within a highly specialized division of labor.

COLLECTIVISM

From the standpoint of *collectivism*, humans require a form of social organization suited to their status as interdependent beings. Collectivism is thus often contrasted with individualism, which places the interests and **rights** (page 208) of the individual above those of the collective. This basic assumption aside, collectivism is associated with a wide range of competing political perspectives.

Various collectivist ideas emerged within the tradition of the modern European Enlightenment. The eighteenth-century philosopher Jean-Jacques Rousseau, for example, advocated for a social order in which individuals submit to the "general will" of the collective. In so doing, they lose none of their **liberty** (page 155) or **autonomy** (page 33): the universal laws they obey are precisely those they have prescribed for themselves. Despite important differences, nineteenth-century thinker Georg Wilhelm Friedrich Hegel and **communist** (page 64) theorist Karl Marx likewise prioritized the collective as a framework for their respective projects of human emancipation. Normatively, the **fascist** (page 101) movements of the twentieth century were at odds with **Marxism** (page 166) and other forms of collectivism; fascism, however, is also associated with the collectivist tradition, given its rhetorical investment in the idea of an authentic "people's community" to which the concerns of particular individuals are subordinated.

COLONIALISM

The process whereby one political power acquires, maintains, and expands control over other territories is known as *colonialism*. Under colonialism, an unequal set of relationships between the colonial regime and the colonized territory is established. Convinced of its superiority and prerogative to rule, the colonizing power redefines the lives, cultures, and institutions of the colonized people to suit its own interests and objectives. It rejects the idea of conciliation or diplomacy and dominates the colonized territory, often subjecting its indigenous population to exploitative **labor** (page 143) practices and discriminatory or **racist** (page 200) attitudes and policies.

The modern era of colonialism began in the early fifteenth century with the dawn of the so-called Age of Discovery. During this period, Spain and Portugal sent naval fleets across the oceans and conquered large swaths of newly discovered territory. The trading posts that were established on these lands soon evolved into full-fledged colonies; their control was parceled out between the Spanish and Portuguese Empires under the Treaty of Tordesillas in 1494 and the Treaty of Zaragoza in 1529, with further support from the **papacy** (page 187). The age of global colonialism kicked into high gear as the British, French, Dutch, and Danish Empires entered the scene and proceeded to colonize much of Asia, Africa, and the Americas. In an effort to strengthen their national treasuries, the

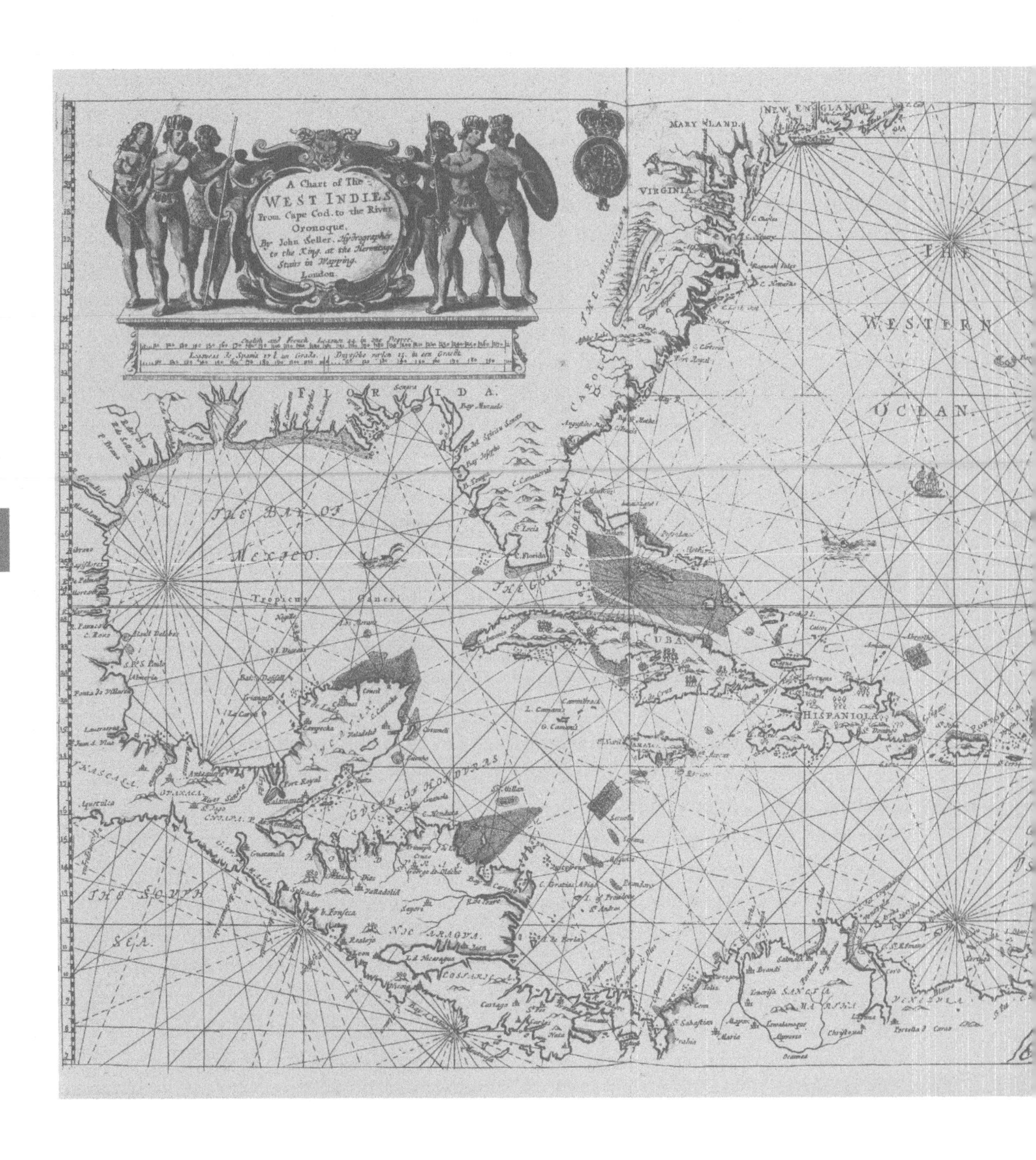
A Chart of The
WEST INDIES
From Cape Cod. to the River
Oronoque.
By John Seller. Hydrographer
to the King. at the Hermitage
Stairs in Wapping.
London.
NEW ENGLAND
MARY LAND.
VIRGINIA
FLORIDA.
THE BAY OF
MEXICO.
Tropicus
Cancri
THE
WESTERN
OCEAN.
CUBA
HISPANIOLA
THE SOUTH
SEA.
C. Florida

conquering powers instituted mercantilist policies that barred their colonies from trading with rival empires.

Following the revolutionary wars in the **United States** (page 248) and Latin America, a fresh wave of colonial expansion took hold between 1820 and 1939. This period saw the rise of the German and Belgian Empires, which were soon joined by Italy, Britain, Portugal, France, and Spain in the struggle over control of African territories. Meanwhile the Russian, Ottoman, and Austrian Empires showed little interest in overseas expansion, confining themselves to the conquest of neighboring lands. After **World War I** (page 262), the German and Ottoman Empires were dissolved and divided up among the victorious Allied forces under mandates from the **League of Nations** (page 148). Japan then joined the ranks of the world's major colonial powers, setting its sights on territories that were already under the control of the British, French, Dutch, and Americans. Its colonial ambitions were a principal factor behind the outbreak of **World War II** (page 266).

For some critics, colonialism was not simply a game of global conquest pitting powerful empire-building nations against one another; it was also indicative of a worldview whereby Western empires were superior to non-Western societies, and were therefore entitled to dominate them. These so-called **postcolonial** (page 191) critics add that the prevailing beliefs of Western culture are replete with colonialism's ethnocentric biases: the self-understanding and lived experience of colonized people are largely excluded from the "grand narratives" of Western art, literature, and philosophy; what emerges instead is a portrait of colonized subjects who are less than human and unable to shape their own destinies. Such misguided assumptions have led to the **paternalistic** (page 190) claim that the colonial project is—in Rudyard Kipling's words—"the white man's burden."

The colonialist project has encountered resistance since its inception. In the mid-twentieth century, movements for **decolonization** (page 77) gained significant momentum. Backed by the **United Nations** (page 245) Special Committee on Decolonization, they ultimately led to the demise of European colonialism and to independence for the former colonies.

(Opposite) A seventeenth-century nautical map depicting colonial territories at the height of European imperial expansion.

COMMUNISM

According to the political doctrine of *communism*, an ideal society would be one where social and economic classes cease to exist and where property and all means of production are collectively owned and controlled. Communism would thus serve as a replacement for the class-divided, market economy of **capitalism** (page 44), in which property is privately held. This general proposal aside, the idea of communism has been interpreted in many different ways by both theorists and political activists. For some, communism should resemble the arrangements instituted by the former **Soviet Union** (page 226), under which property was controlled by a single-party **state** (page 229). In this model, decision-making about the production and distribution of material goods is highly centralized, and accompanied by the use of authoritarian practices to quash those perceived to be at odds with the regime's ideological objectives. Others repudiate the Soviet example as a betrayal of the communist ideal. **Anarchist**-communists (page 22), for example, advocate for the collective ownership of property, but see the state as a hindrance to the maximization of human **freedom** (page 107).

The term communism—which derives from *communis*, the Latin word for "shared" or "common"—first entered the political lexicon in the 1840s. However, visions of a society modeled along communist lines date back to antiquity. In *The Republic*, for instance, Plato imagined a social order governed by an **elite** (page 94) group of "guardians," who would be responsible for upholding the interests of the community at large. Believing that they would be corrupted by the private ownership of property, Plato maintained that they should share material goods and live together in large families where spouses and children would be likewise held in common.

Other notions of communism emerged from what Karl Marx would later call the "misty realms of religion." A simple type of communism was practiced by the first Christians, whose disdain for private property was inspired by a passage from the New Testament, "The Believers Share Their Possessions" (Acts 4:32–37). Stirred by similar impulses within **Christianity** (page 46), later monastic orders espoused that their brethren should take vows of poverty and share their material possessions with one another and with the poor. Monastic communism would in turn influence the author Thomas More who, in his 1516 *Utopia*, imagined a world where money had been eradicated and all material goods were held in common. Other fictional models of communism would follow, including Italian

(Opposite) In the 1848 *Communist Manifesto*, Karl Marx declared that workers must seize the means of production through revolution.

C

Manifest
der
Kommunistischen Partei.
Veröffentlicht im Februar 1848.
Proletarier aller Länder vereinigt euch
London.

Bolshevik leader Vladimir Lenin led the 1917 October Revolution in Russia, overthrowing the monarchy and founding what would become the Soviet Union.

380 BC *Plato's Republic mentions communal living as political ideal*

1534 *Anabaptists attempt a communist government in Münster, Germany*

1642 *English "Diggers" form short-lived collectivist government*

1848 *Marx and Engels publish* Communist Manifesto

1917 *Lenin writes* State and Revolution, *spearheads October Revolution*

1945–1991 *Cold War rages between capitalist West and communist Eastern Bloc*

1989 *Fall of the Berlin Wall*

C

Dominican philosopher Tommaso Campanella's *City of the Sun*, published in 1623. Around this time, there were also a number of efforts to put the ideal of communism into practice. In the Münster Rebellion of 1534 to 1535, for example, radical Anabaptists established a short-lived communist government in the Westphalian city of Münster. Later, during the English Civil Wars of 1642 to 1651, a group of Protestant radicals known as the Diggers attempted to create an agrarian form of communism under which the earth would be shared by all as "a common treasury."

The German thinker Karl Marx is undoubtedly the most renowned modern theorist of communism. Although he sometimes used the terms "communism" and **"socialism"** (page 224) interchangeably, he ultimately believed the former to be a higher and more advanced form of the latter. In his 1875 "Critique of the Gotha Programme," Marx spoke of an initial "lower" phase of communism, to be established in the immediate aftermath of the working class's victory over the capitalist order. In this transitional stage, the workers would assume control of the **state** (page 229) and the economy, while continuing to pay people according to the length and intensity of their work. In the *Manifesto of the Communist Party*, Marx and his associate Friedrich Engels referred to this first phase of the communist revolution as the "dictatorship of the proletariat," during which workers utilize the state as an instrument for defending and sustaining the revolution. However, communism will be fully realized only upon the transition to the next and final phase, in which all class divisions are abolished, the state (in Engels's phrase) "withers away," and production is organized in such a way that humanity regains control over its own laboring activity.

In his 1917 book *State and Revolution*, **Bolshevik** (page 41) leader Vladimir Lenin emphasized the distinction between a lower socialist stage of communist society and a later phase that would establish true communism. Lenin's Bolsheviks gained control of the Russian state in the **October Revolution** (page 184) of 1917, adopting the name All-Russian Communist Party a year later. Much to the chagrin of defenders of the original Marxian ideal, the word "communism" has since been widely associated with single-party, authoritarian models of governance that were later instituted in the Soviet Union, the People's Republic of China, and other nations.

COMMUNITARIANISM

As a political philosophy, *communitarianism* places itself at odds with the **liberal** (page 152) tradition: it prioritizes the interests of the community over those of the individual. Communitarians maintain that a community's stability should be protected, and a collective sense of civic duty promoted. The community should be a locus of political and moral action, for it is within the context of its traditions and institutions that individuals develop attachments, identities, relationships, and an expression of their social needs—it is within this context, in short, that they find meaning.

Communitarians see liberalism, with its emphasis on individual **liberty** (page 155) and **autonomy** (page 33), as a threat to this objective. Liberal individualism, they argue, has hobbled the ability of communities to address problems such as **racism** (page 200) and **poverty** (page 193), because their political agents remain isolated from one another and operate solely under the power of their own sovereign wills. In a liberal society, communitarians add, ideals such as value neutrality, natural **rights** (page 208), and rugged individualism reign at the expense of public policies and values; individuals are set adrift in a sea of meanings from which they must pick and choose on their own.

Communitarians thus reject the contention, advanced by the Enlightenment philosopher Immanuel Kant, that moral maturity is predicated on one's capacity to think and act autonomously, i.e., without the guidance of another. For the well-known communitarian author Michael Sandel, for example, there are some cultural, religious, and institutional traditions that have a hold on people "beyond their consent." Such traditions, Sandel argues, should not be relinquished in the face of a "better argument," as liberalism imagines; insofar as they transcend the cause of truth, they should not be subjected to processes of verification and falsification. They are worth preserving because they allow the community to achieve moral and civic objectives that are essential to its way of life. For their part, liberals maintain that communitarianism carries the danger of ensnaring people within cultures, religions, and other institutional frameworks without allowing them the option of rejecting their normative prescriptions.

C

CONGRESS

The *Congress* is the national lawmaking body of the United States. Established under Article One of the US **Constitution** (page 72), it is divided into two chambers: the **House of Representatives** (page 126) and the **Senate** (page 212). The building in which it meets is called the Capitol; its north wing hosts the Senate, and its south wing the House. The Congress is sometimes nicknamed Capitol Hill after the neighborhood in Washington, DC, in which it is situated.

Members of the Senate (Senators) and members of the House (Representatives or Congresspersons) are chosen in state and district elections, respectively; state governors, however, have the authority to fill unexpected vacancies in the Senate by appointment. Since the mid-nineteenth century, members of the two chambers have generally been affiliated with either the **Republican Party** (page 206) or the **Democratic Party** (page 82)—independents and members of third parties are rarities in contemporary US politics. There are 100 Senators and 435 Representatives in Congress, for a total of 535 voting members.

Congresspersons are elected for two-year terms. They represent the residents of a specific geographical constituency or district, whose boundaries are determined by each state on the basis of population size. Each state, however, is allotted just two Senators, regardless of its geographic size or number of residents. Senators are elected to six-year terms, and their elections follow a staggered cycle: every two years, one-third of the one-hundred-member Senate is up for election.

The basic mandate of Congress is to make federal law. Under the **separation of powers** (page 216) doctrine—a key principle of the **federalist** (page 105) system—Congress is the only branch of the national government with such authority. While each chamber deliberates separately, the consent of both the House and the Senate is required in order for a bill to be passed into law. However, the specific powers of each chamber differ. The **Constitution** (page 72) gives the House the authority to initiate impeachment cases and introduce revenue-raising bills. For its part, the Senate has the power to ratify treaties, approve presidential appointments, and decide impeachment cases opened in the House. As an example, the House brought impeachment charges against President Andrew Johnson in 1868 and against President Bill Clinton in 1998; in both cases, the accused officials were acquitted by the Senate.

Some critics have noted that, since the end of **World War II** (page 266), Congress has increasingly focused on making laws that cater to narrow economic interests (tax subsidies for wheat and soybean producers, for instance). They argue that, by and large, Congress has delegated its authority to make general legislation to the **President** (page 194), one of whose main objectives is to promote the interests of

C

the **capitalist** (page 44) class as a whole while leaving the interests of its various sectors in the hands of Congress.

A number of factors are said to lie behind this shift. First, a Congress member's continued tenure in office often depends on ongoing support from businesses, organizations, and lobby groups based in his or her home state (in the case of Senators) or congressional district (in the case of Representatives). Such groups are generally well-financed, well-organized, and well-positioned to pressure legislators into passing bills favorable to their interests—notably, through the contribution or withdrawal of campaign funds.

Second, the constitutional organization of Congress leaves it ill-equipped to formulate coherent national policies. Passing a bill is a long, tortuous process, since it requires the approval of both congressional chambers. Legislation benefitting particular industries, wealthy individuals, and other narrow interests often wends its way through Congress with relative ease—of relevance only to specific legislators and facing little opposition from members of Congress with no special stake in it. This is not the case, however, with national legislation. Here, opposing interests often result in either a stalemate or some hybrid policy with little connection to the original. Moreover, Congress has become increasingly insulated from public sentiment. This is especially true of the Senate, set up by the framers of the Constitution as a check on the more democratic, "leveling" tendencies of the "People's House."

Thus, the structural features of Congress have turned it into what Edward S. Greenberg has called "a halting, conservative, and indecisive" organization when it comes to formulating general legislation. Corporate and civic groups in need of decisive action at the level of national policy "have generally turned to the other, more energetic institution—the presidency."[3] This is not to say that Congress lacks the power to undermine the president's legislative agenda; it has such authority, and has often exercised it. However, it has increasingly played the role of a naysayer to the president's policy proposals, rather than that of an active initiator of comprehensive national legislation.

CONSERVATISM

Conservatism is a political doctrine that advocates for the maintenance of a society's traditional social practices and institutions. It distinguishes itself from competing perspectives such as **Marxism** (page 166) and classical **liberalism** (page 152), which seek to better society and redress abuses of state power through modernization and change. Conservatives contend that rather than transform prevailing norms and political arrangements, the proper objective of **government** (page 118) is to preserve the time-honored traditions, policies, and lifestyles behind society's organic unity and stability. They are thus highly suspicious of governmental activism, and of liberal and radical movements that adopt anti-traditionalist stands.

While he did not use the term himself, late eighteenth-century thinker Edmund Burke helped galvanize the conservative cause. He rejected the anti-traditionalism and violence that accompanied the **French Revolution** (page 109), and advocated for the restoration of pre-Revolutionary forms of social organization. Contemporary conservatives do not subscribe to Burke's reactionary desire to revert to a previous political order. They do, however, share his interest in maintaining the patriarchal family, the church, and other traditional institutions; these are necessary, they believe, in order to instill the value of self-discipline and curb the irresponsible exercise of individual **liberty** (page 155).

CONSOCIATION

Consociation refers to a type of **democracy** (page 78) sometimes found in nations that are sharply divided along racial, ethnic, religious, linguistic, or regional lines. In a consociational democracy, issues of concern to the society at large are resolved by a coalition of officials representing its major segments, while each segment retains decisional **autonomy** (page 33) over its own immediate concerns. Consociation thus differs markedly from majoritarian democracy, in which decisions are made by popular vote. Consociational democracies have been implemented throughout the world, but have been particularly prevalent in Europe. Some contemporary examples of consociation include the governments of Switzerland, Belgium, and South Africa.

Supporters of consociation argue that it offers important advantages: it promotes governmental stability, averts possible political violence, assures democracy's long-term survival, and allows political power to be shared by groups that are otherwise deeply divided. Some critics counter that consociation does little more than entrench existing ideological, religious, and ethnic antagonisms, placing it at odds with a more cosmopolitan ideal of democratic participation seeking to break down artificial barriers among human subjects. Dutch political scientist Arend Lijphart is recognized as one of the leading authorities on the theory and practice of consociation.

CONSTITUTION

Since coming into force in 1789, the *Constitution* has served as the chief legal document of the **United States** (page 248) and the blueprint for its main governing institutions. Consistent with the doctrines of **federalism** (page 105) and the **separation of powers** (page 216), the first three articles of the Constitution split the national government into three branches, each with its own limited sphere of authority. The articles provide for a law-enforcing executive branch with the **President** (page 194) as its chief; a law-interpreting judiciary with a system of **federal courts** (page 103); and a lawmaking **Congress** (page 69) which is itself divided into two chambers: the **House of Representatives** (page 126) and the **Senate** (page 212).

Procedures for amending the Constitution are also specified. To date, twenty-seven amendments have been added to the document's main body. Known collectively as the **Bill of Rights** (page 37), the first ten amendments are aimed at limiting the powers of **government** (page 118), protecting individual **liberties** (page 155), and upholding principles of **justice** (page 140).

In 1787, prior to the Constitution's ratification, a Constitutional Convention gathered in Philadelphia. Its aim was to revise the Articles of Confederation, under which the government had been operating since gaining independence from Great Britain in the **American Revolution** (page 18). Delegates such as James Madison and Alexander

George Washington is depicted presiding over the 1787 Constitutional Convention, where the political foundations of the newly independent government were laid.

Hamilton, however, were more interested in establishing new governmental arrangements than in repairing existing ones.

Among the more pressing problems for the drafters of the Constitution was the issue of **slavery** (page 217): how could its continued existence be squared with the **liberal** (page 152) ideals of **freedom** (page 107) and equality that the new republic sought to defend? In a bid to sustain the slave system, delegates from Southern states attempted to increase their power within the government by demanding that all the inhabitants of each state be represented in the House and in the Electoral College. While opponents of slavery advocated for limiting representation to free men (slaves, after all, could not vote), it was eventually agreed that slaves would be represented at a rate of three-fifths of their actual numbers. This "Three-Fifths Compromise" enabled slave-holding states to consolidate power within the government and preserve the institution of slavery until the passage of the Thirteenth Amendment some eighty years later. In 1920, full suffrage rights were finally granted to **women** (page 106) under the Nineteenth Amendment. Throughout US history, numerous social movements have sought to defend the **civil rights** (page 54) of marginalized groups by appealing to ideals upheld in the Constitution.

CORRUPTION

When something is *corrupt*, it is generally understood to have deteriorated physically or declined qualitatively from an original or pristine state. Political theorists and philosophers have likewise appealed to the idea of an initial, presumably unblemished set of standards as a basis for judging the corruption of a society's institutions and political actors.

Some of the most significant contributions to the theorization of corruption were made during the Italian Renaissance of the fourteenth to sixteenth centuries. Influenced by the work of ancient thinkers like Aristotle and Cicero, Renaissance authors such as Leonardo Bruni promoted the ideal of **republicanism** (page 206), which stressed the importance of civic **virtue** (page 255) and the active participation of citizens in political life. Working together, the citizens of the republican **city-state** (page 52) were enjoined to make decisions about the common good and contribute to its realization. Pursuits at odds with this goal (the quest for wealth, luxury, power, or glory, for instance) were seen as distractions, and thus as agents of corruption; practices that fostered civic virtue, a sense of mutual self-regard, and the achievement of the common good were viewed as safeguards against it. Later, during the Enlightenment era, the **social contract** (page 221) theorist Jean-Jacques Rousseau drew upon both ancient and Renaissance philosophy to develop one of the most significant and influential theories of republican virtue.

Some have argued that the problem of corruption was not just a concern for the civic republican tradition of continental Europe; it was also an important element of American political thought. The theorist J.G.A. Pocock, for example, has argued that in addition to being influenced by **liberalism** (page 152), the founders of the **United States** (page 248) **republic** (page 205) upheld the ideal of civic virtue, positioning it as a bulwark against the onset of corruption.

Today, the rhetoric of corruption is taken up by those on both sides of the political spectrum, sometimes with highly moralistic overtones. **Conservatives** (page 71) condemn present societies as corrupt on account of their alleged fall from an earlier "golden age" whose traditions and past glories are in need of resuscitation. For their part, liberals and progressives decry corruption as the hallmark of a society where socially privileged **elites** (page 94) have the power to flout domestic and international legal arrangements in the service of their own narrow economic and political interests.

CRONYISM

See *nepotism.*

CULTURE

Culture is an especially difficult term to define, as its meanings are manifold and highly contested. One of the first significant efforts to flesh out a modern concept of culture was undertaken by the German philosopher Johann Gottfried von Herder in the late eighteenth century. In surveying the existing literature, Herder observed that the terms "culture" and "civilization" had frequently been used interchangeably. Dissatisfied with this slippery usage—which suggested a single, unified framework of human development—Herder separated these two concepts and set forth a theory of "cultures." Later anthropologists would take up his idea of "culture-in-the-plural." No longer seen as a monolithic, "one-size-fits-all" concept, culture was now said to be varied and multiple, existing in different places and times. From this vantage point, even the same nation could be host to an array of different cultures.

An early champion of the culture-in-the-plural thesis was the anthropologist Franz Boas. Boas argued that each culture's value systems, norms, and beliefs must be understood on their own terms, rather than in relation to a preexisting, universal template. From this relativist vantage point, Boas rejected the idea of innate racial inferiority; he argued that it was not nature, but rather variations in culture, that accounted for differences among people across the world.

His and other anthropologists' attempts to move beyond earlier exclusionary definitions of culture were not without opponents, however. The English poet and cultural critic Matthew Arnold, for example, distinguished between low (or popular) culture and high (or "sublime") culture, defending the latter as an ideal to be carried forth in the "pursuit of perfection." Some of the most trenchant criticisms of this view have come from writers associated with the late twentieth-century **postcolonialist** (page 191) tradition, whose sympathies lie with the culture-in-the-plural argument. The literary theorist Edward Said, for example, linked the ideal of high culture to the European project of **imperialism** (page 132). In his seminal 1979 text *Orientalism*, Said portrayed high culture as a fabrication of the Occident, one that is aimed at erasing the multiple cultures of the Orient and absorbing their internal frames of reference into the dominant narratives of European **colonialism** (page 61).

Although the high culture/low culture distinction is generally associated with **conservative** (page 71) thinkers, it has also been upheld by writers on the left side of the political spectrum. In their 1947 book *Dialectic of Enlightenment*, the Frankfurt School theorists Max Horkheimer and Theodor Adorno provided a rigorous analysis of how the modern "culture industry" destroys the division between high culture, which elevates the individual to the level of an **autonomous** (page 33) subject, and popular culture, which reduces people to commodified, non-thinking objects. In opposition to a popular culture that does little more than produce a compliant body politic, Adorno and Horkheimer sought to defend high culture as a reservoir of meaning and potential revolutionary agency. For his part, the German philosopher Walter Benjamin was more optimistic. He acknowledged that the distinction between high and low culture is being eroded in the modern age, especially given the rise of the mechanical mass reproduction of art. However, he claimed, this is not necessarily a bad thing: modern popular culture has the potential to neutralize earlier ideals of artistic genius and mastery, thus creating an opening for the masses to participate in the production of a new form of culture.

D

DAOISM

Founded in the late fourth century BC by Laozi, *Daoism* is a philosophical, ethical, and religious tradition of Chinese origin. In the third century BC, Laozi's teachings were interpreted and elaborated in Master Zhuang's work, *The Zhuangzi*, which has been described by some commentators as being essentially **anarchist** (page 22) in nature. Daoism encourages its adherents to live in harmony with the Dao, or the "way." Finding the "way" requires constant meditation and the achievement of a state of mental stillness. As a religious system, Daoism espouses ethical values such as compassion, moderation, and humility.

There are significant differences between its beliefs and practices and those of the Judeo-**Christian** (page 46) tradition. In particular, Daoism is sometimes viewed as less punitive: it is not dominated by a divine figurehead who doles out sanctions to a fearful flock. This perception helped increase its popularity (and that of other Eastern religions) among Westerners in the 1960s and the 1970s. Along with Confucianism, Daoism is currently one of the two main religious traditions in China. It is also widely practiced in other Asian and Southeast Asian countries.

DECOLONIZATION

Decolonization refers to the process of dismantling **colonialism** (page 61), the rule of colonial empires over colonized territories. The goal is for these territories to acquire political and economic independence. Decolonization has generally involved either nonviolent or militant struggles for national liberation, waged by indigenous pro-independence movements with the occasional assistance of foreign powers.

Over the last two hundred years, the political landscape of the world has been altered by several waves of decolonization. The Spanish Empire dissolved in the nineteenth century, while the Russian, Austro-Hungarian, German, and Ottoman Empires collapsed after the conclusion of **World War I** (page 262) in 1918. Following the end of **World War II** (page 266) in 1945, the colonial powers of Europe were weakened politically and financially. They also had to reckon with two newly emerged superpowers, the **United States** (page 248) and the **Soviet Union** (page 226), which had both expressed opposition to European colonial rule. Poorly positioned to contest the national independence movements that were sweeping through the colonized world, the empires of Great Britain, the Netherlands, Italy, Japan, France, Belgium, and Portugal ultimately met their demise. The satellite republics of the Soviet Empire also gained their independence upon the dissolution of the Soviet Union in 1991.

Mahatma Gandhi (center) with Louis and Edwina Mountbatten, the last British rulers of India, who oversaw the postcolonial partition of India and Pakistan.

DEMOCRACY

Democracy is a concept upon which many—if not most—contemporary governments have staked their political legitimacy. However, the precise meaning of democracy, and the question of whether it makes sense to apply it to any existing political system, are the subject of ongoing controversy. The term *democracy* is derived from the Greek *dēmokratía*, or "rule of the people." The ideal itself is believed to have originated in Ancient Greece; it found its most famous champion in Cleisthenes, who led a democratic city-state in Athens from 508 until 507 BC. However, Athens was also home to some of democracy's fiercest critics. Aristotle decried democracy as the corrupt flipside of an ideal form of government known as polity, while Plato rejected it in favor of his famous concept of a **republic** (page 206) ruled by "philosopher kings."

While a few experiments in limited democracy arose during the late Middle Ages—the Polish-Lithuanian Commonwealth of 1569 to 1795 being one of them—arguments for extending it to the population at large did not take hold until the early modern period. Here the term reemerged in the philosophy of Enlightenment **liberalism** (page 152). It attracted defenders such as Jean-Jacques Rousseau, who argued for implementing it in small city-states like Corsica. It also drew a fair number of detractors, including Thomas Hobbes—an advocate of **absolutism** (page 15)—and Immanuel Kant, who likened democracy to a kind of **despotism** (page 83) aimed at promoting the interests of the majority at the expense of individual liberty and the "general will." James Madison's case for **federalism** (page 105) was rooted in a similar anxiety about the prospect of "pure" democracy, a system in which citizens take part directly in governmental affairs. In "Federalist No. 10," he insisted that direct democracy would promote factionalism, and position the propertyless majority—who have a "rage for paper money" and similar "wicked projects"—to infringe upon the property rights of the wealthy minority. Madison is generally understood to be an advocate of indirect or representative democracy, in which citizens entrust representatives to rule on their behalf. However, he does not employ the term "representative democracy" to characterize his own point of view in "Federalist No. 10," nor is there a single instance of the word "democracy" in the American Constitution—a document of which Madison was a principal architect. The word is also absent from the US Declaration of Independence.

Debates over the relevance of democracy for modern political life continue to rage,

(Opposite) James Madison, the fourth president of the United States, believed that an indirect form of democracy was necessary to protect the interests of wealthy landowners.

as do arguments about its precise meaning. Despite these disagreements, democracy is usually said to involve a situation in which the government is charged with carrying forth the will of the citizenry, and the citizenry, for its part, has the capacity to oversee the actions of the government and guard against abuses of political power. In the modern era, various institutional arrangements have been proposed to foster democratic rule and increase the accountability of governments to their citizenries—for example, free and fair **elections** (page 92), a system of just and equitable **laws** (page 147), and bargaining among competing interest groups as a means of striking compromises and shaping public policies.

Debates over the relevance of democracy for modern political life continue to rage, as do arguments about its precise meaning.

D

Some commentators have recently argued that a robust interest-group process accounts for the fundamentally democratic nature of most contemporary Western political systems, which are best characterized as pluralist democracies. Interest-group bargaining and lobbying, according to this view, is evidence of the direct involvement of a variety of citizens in the political process, making it a more powerful gauge of a nation's democratic capacities than elections, which are after all little more than intermittent expressions of an individual's political opinions.

Efforts to portray contemporary Western political orders as pluralist democracies have been challenged from various quarters. Marxist critics, for example, have insisted that the characterization is deeply misguided, based as it is on the erroneous assumption that interest groups with competing agendas bargain and extract concessions from one another on a more or less level "playing field." Edward S. Greenberg notes that when applied to the American political system, the perspective of pluralist democracy overlooks something fundamental: it fails "to take into account the highly unequal influence of social classes or to recognize the disproportionate political power exercised by the giant corporations and their ancillary organizations."[4] Indeed, for critics like Greenberg, the argument for democratic pluralism can be exposed as **ideological** (page 131): it wraps contemporary Western societies in a false ideal that serves only to disguise and legitimize their underlying conditions of power and domination.

Many argue that despite regular elections, modern Western pluralist democracies are not truly democratic due to the influence of corporate interests in the political process.

D

DEMOCRATIC PARTY

The contemporary American political system is dominated by two political parties: the **Republican Party** (page 206) and the *Democratic Party*. Founded in 1828, the Democratic Party has the distinction of being the oldest currently existing political party in the world. Its roots can be traced to the Democratic-Republican Party, established in 1792 by Thomas Jefferson, James Madison, and other opponents of the Federalist Party of John Adams and Alexander Hamilton. Some three decades later, Andrew Jackson removed the "Republican" portion of the party's name and founded the modern Democratic Party. Jackson went on to become the first Democratic President of the United States in 1829.

Since 1912, the Democratic Party has tended to adopt more progressive stances on social and economic issues than the Republican Party. The policy differences between the two became especially pronounced during the 1930s, when Democratic President **Franklin D. Roosevelt** (page 209) inaugurated his New Deal reforms. Roosevelt's **Welfare State** (page 259) became the basis of a revised version of American **liberalism** (page 152), developed and supported by his party in the ensuing decades. According to this perspective, the federal government should administer various social and healthcare programs; protect the environment and the rights of consumers and labor unions; regulate at

least some of the activities of private enterprise; and assure social **justice** (page 140), and **civil rights** (page 54) protections for minorities, immigrants, and economically disadvantaged communities.

In recent years, many Democrats have retreated from the basic principles of Roosevelt's welfare state, thus blurring the ideological differences between the Democratic and Republican parties. This shift in perspective became particularly apparent during Bill Clinton's presidency (1993-2001). A member of the New Democrats coalition, Clinton proved more open to deregulating the economy and reducing the role of the federal government in social welfare—both Republican ideals. Famously declaring that "the era of big government is over," he introduced a series of "welfare reforms," presided over the large-scale deregulation of big business, and championed the elimination of barriers to international investment and trade. He also ordered cruise missile strikes against the Iraqi Intelligence Service's headquarters in Baghdad, among other overseas military interventions. Many of Clinton's domestic and foreign policy positions were upheld by his successors, Republican George W. Bush and Democrat Barack Obama.

(Opposite, left to right) Democratic US presidents have included Andrew Jackson, the founder of the Democratic Party, and Bill Clinton, a "New Democrat."

DESPOTISM

The term *despotism* derives from the Greek *despótēs*, loosely translated as "master," "lord," or "holder of power." In antiquity, it was used to characterize the governments of the Egyptian Pharaohs and the Byzantine Emperors. Throughout the ages, despotism came to be associated with any political system (from small chiefdom to imperial superpower) whose essential functions remain under the exclusive control of a single individual or group. Despotic regimes are sometimes viewed as more or less equivalent to **dictatorships** (page 84), governments headed by unaccountable rulers who are concerned solely with maintaining and advancing their own power and authority. Historically, however, various writers have judged the idea of despotism far less harshly. Enlightenment figures such as Thomas Hobbes portrayed a type of despotism known as **absolutism** (page 15) as the only political arrangement capable of assuring social stability and peace—the distinctly moral ends of Hobbes's **social contract** (page 221). For his part, John Stuart Mill argued that despotism is a necessary means of bringing "backward" peoples into the fold of modern, "civilized" nation-states. Arguments for such "benign" forms of despotism have receded, however. Today, despotism tends to be associated with more negative concepts such as **oligarchy** (page 182) and **totalitarianism** (page 240).

D

DICTATORSHIP

In a *dictatorship*, a single individual or small group of persons has absolute control of the **government** (page 118), unchecked by any of its branches or the principles of its constitution. In the ancient Roman Republic, temporary magistrates would sometimes be appointed and endowed with extraordinary powers during periods of crisis. The political philosophers of the era were careful to distinguish such dictators from **tyrants** (page 244), however. Tyrants, they claimed, often use brute force or other illegal methods to obtain their positions, and proceed to rule **despotically** (page 83) by terrorizing the populace and suppressing its **civil liberties** (page 54). Like ancient tyrants, but unlike ancient dictators, modern dictators have little intention of relinquishing their exceptional powers after a prescribed period of time; rather, their objective is to maintain and expand their authority, often employing mass propaganda techniques to assure popular support.

With the collapse of the old **hereditary** (page 123) monarchies and **colonial** (page 61) European empires in the nineteenth and twentieth centuries, dictators became a major presence on the world stage. In nineteenth-century Latin America, dictators known as *caudillos* seized power from weak national governments with the aid of their own private armies, and anointed themselves the leaders of territories that had recently gained independence from Spanish colonial rule. Among their ranks were Argentinian dictator Juan Manuel de Rosas and Mexican dictator Antonio López de Santa Anna.

In the twentieth century, Latin America's provincial dictators were replaced by national rulers who emerged from **nationalist** (page 170) elements within the **military** (page 168). Such dictators straddled both sides of the political spectrum: some of them defended the interests of privileged economic **elites** (page 94), while others implemented left-wing social reforms on behalf of the poor. In the aftermath of **World War II** (page 266), constitutional governments were set up in Asia and Africa by the departing Western colonial powers. They soon proved susceptible to dictatorial rule: in some cases, dictators seized power through military coups; in others, elected prime ministers or presidents used their positions to consolidate power, squelch the opposition, and institute long-term, one-party dictatorships.

While **Adolf Hitler**'s (page 124) Nazi Germany and Joseph Stalin's **Soviet Union** (page 226) espoused sharply divergent ideological doctrines and political objectives, both have been described as **totalitarian** (page 240) dictatorships. Taking hold in the 1920s, **Nazism** (page 175) and Stalinism each gave absolute authority over the affairs of the state to a single mass party headed by a charismatic figure. The leader's rule was buttressed by a "cult of personality" that obliged

D

government officials and the society at large to defer to his authority without question. Both Hitler and Stalin employed brute force, ideological manipulation, and modern technology to quash dissenting opinions and legitimize the power structures over which they presided. Dictatorial rule was also instituted in the satellite Socialist republics established in Central and Eastern Europe after World War II. These regimes would ultimately dissolve, along with the Soviet Union, in the early 1990s. The People's Republic of China, created in 1949 under the leadership of **Mao Zedong** (page 163), has also been described by many as a dictatorship.

Throughout the nineteenth and twentieth centuries, various representative **democracies** (page 78) have exercised dictatorial powers during national emergencies, suspending constitutional **rights** (page 208) and limiting civil freedoms. During the American **Civil War** (page 58), for example, US President **Abraham Lincoln** (page 156) disallowed the writ of **habeas corpus** (page 120) and limited the freedom of the press; President **Franklin D. Roosevelt** (page 209) sent Japanese-American citizens to internment camps during World War II. Similar to the dictatorial magistrates of ancient Rome, the executives of these regimes were relieved of their extraordinary authority at the end of these wartime crises.

D

(Left to right) Antonio López de Santa Anna of Mexico; Joseph Stalin of the Soviet Union.

DIPLOMACY

Diplomacy is an avenue through which nations can settle disputes with one another without resorting to **war** (page 256). It is typically carried out by professional diplomats, who represent their **states** (page 229) in international negotiations. Unlike **military** (page 168) strategy, whose goal is to subdue the enemy through brute force, diplomacy attempts to engage disputing parties in a tactful, non-confrontational manner in order to reach an unforced solution to a given conflict. Some critics reject this portrayal of diplomacy. They argue that it is often a game in which negotiators use their rhetorical skills to produce agreements favorable to the nations they represent, introducing an element of concealed coercion into the process. As the Italian diplomat Daniele Varè once observed, "Diplomacy is the art of letting someone else have your way."

Today, diplomacy is often attempted under the auspices of the **United Nations** (page 245), either to prevent the outbreak of war or to resolve disagreements regarding economic, cultural, environmental, or **human rights** (page 128) policies.

DIRECT ACTION

Employed by individuals, civic groups, and social movements, *direct action* is a political tactic aimed at calling attention to an existing set of problems, usually with the hope of compelling some sort of change. It is often contrasted with institutionalized political processes such as **elections** (page 92) and **lobbying** (page 158). It may involve lawful, nonviolent activities like demonstrations and boycotts, as well as illegal, violent acts such as sabotage and **property** (page 199) destruction.

The concept was first introduced in connection with the **labor** (page 143) struggles of the early twentieth century, and was analyzed by William Mellor in his 1920 book *Direct Action*. Curiously, Mellor viewed direct action as a strategy available to both workers and employers: both **striking** (page 231) laborers and factory owners staging employment lockouts, for example, are engaging in forms of direct action. Today, direct action is usually seen as a tool of the non-powerful and the marginalized.

The strategy of nonviolent direct action was a prominent feature of **Mahatma Gandhi**'s (page 114) movement for Indian independence, as well as the American **civil rights** (page 54) campaign led by **Martin Luther King, Jr.** (page 141).

D

DIVINE RIGHT

During the Middle Ages, the doctrine of *divine right* gave political legitimacy to the absolute authority of the king. It was the basis for the rule of many of the royal monarchs of feudal Europe, including James I of England (1603–1625) and Louis XIV of France (1643–1715). Jacques-Bénigne Bossuet, a preacher in Louis XIV's court, was a renowned champion and popularizer of the theory. The divine right doctrine held that the king, as God's mortal representative on earth, was beholden solely to the divine will. No person (whether commoner or noble) was entitled to question his decisions. The king enjoyed exclusive, sweeping political powers, and could rule over his subjects in any manner that he deemed consistent with God's infallible commandments. All other governmental officials and institutions (including the church) were regarded as mere delegates; they remained entirely under his control and were obliged to submit passively to his rulings. Efforts to curtail the king's powers or remove him from the throne—even in cases in which he appeared to be acting **tyrannically** (page 244)—were seen not only as legal and moral crimes, but also as sacrilegious affronts to his divinely derived authority. Not surprisingly, **regicide** (page 204), or the killing of a king, was considered to be an especially flagrant and detestable form of blasphemy, punishable by both torture and execution.

As the feudal era drew to a close, the doctrine of divine right began to be challenged in the newly emerging philosophies of modern **liberalism** (page 152). Thomas Hobbes, generally regarded as the founder of this tradition, disputed the idea that the monarch's political power is rooted solely in God's will. According to his **social contract** theory (page 221), the king's authority stems not from God but from the citizens of the commonwealth themselves, who, upon leaving their uncivilized "state of nature," surrender to their sovereign some of their natural rights and freedoms. In return, the king must act not on behalf of God but on behalf of citizens, carrying forth their will to be governed by **laws** (page 147) that will ensure peace and social stability. Thus, although the king's powers remain absolute, the foundation of his rule remains distinctly *secular*. Later social contract theorists like John Locke upheld Hobbes's critique of divine right, even as they challenged his defense of monarchical **absolutism** (page 15).

E

ECOLOGY

Interest in *ecology*—the study of the relationship between living organisms and the natural environment—has grown steadily in recent decades. The famous 1972 photograph taken by the Apollo 17 spaceship, which depicted Earth as a small "blue marble" adrift in the vast blackness of space, is often credited with raising awareness about the interconnectedness of all life on our planet. This awareness was accompanied by growing concerns about human-caused degradation of natural environments and the life they support. By the early 1970s, various organizations and social movements were created to advocate for new policies aimed at protecting the Earth's ecology and forestalling what became known as the "ecology crisis." Their ongoing campaign pins much of the blame on the prevailing model of industrial production, pointing to its role in depleting the Earth's natural resources and destroying its natural habitats. In order to restore, rebalance, and improve the relationship between humans and ecosystems, sustainable patterns of production and consumption are

(Opposite, left to right) The 1971 "blue marble" image of Earth changed how humans view the environment; wind power gaining ground as an alternative to fossil fuels.

called for. These include the use of renewable sources of **energy** (page 95)—such as solar, wind, and geothermal energy—which have lighter "ecological footprints" than conventional, petroleum-based energy sources like coal and natural gas.

Some campaigners adopt an "Earth Stewardship" approach, in which humans play a leading role in protecting and preserving Earth's natural environments. A more radical view is taken up by proponents of "deep ecology." Rather than regard the environment as something that should be preserved because it serves human needs and interests—a stance associated with **environmentalism** (page 96)— deep ecologists emphasize the intrinsic worth of ecological systems and the life they sustain. From this more holistic perspective, the destruction of the complex web of relationships between living organisms and their environments is a threat not just to human survival but to the natural order of the planet.

Critics of the ecology cause insist that the environment is not as fragile as activists have alleged, and that ecologists' concerns (including the alarms raised about climate change) are overblown. While such criticism often comes from the business community, industry has not shied away from using the "green" symbolism of the ecological movement to market its products. Some claim that this practice, known as "greenwashing," promotes the economic interests of corporations while doing little to benefit the Earth's ecology.

E

ECONOMY AND POLITICS

Economic life, centered on the production of goods and services, and political life, focused on the governance of people, have been intricately linked throughout history. Indeed, it would be surprising if something as fundamental to the existence of a human community as its system of production did not at least pique the curiosity of those in charge of its political affairs.

The connection between *politics and economics* has been a prominent theme in philosophy since antiquity. The association was formalized in the late eighteenth century with the emergence of a new discipline known as political economy, associated with the French physiocrats, and with British authors such as Adam Smith and David Ricardo. The timing of political economy's arrival was perhaps not surprising, for this was precisely the point at which **capitalism** (page 44) was taking hold as a world system *in lieu* of Europe's old feudal economy; in the continent's new constitutional **republics** (page 205), the **state** (page 229) was denied significant involvement in economic life. The attempt to theorize the relationship between the new **free-market** (page 108) economy and the state became one of the principal tasks of the early political economists.

Adam Smith wrote of the "invisible hand" of the free market, calling for little government regulation, in his seminal eighteenth-century work, *The Wealth of Nations*.

E

EDUCATION

Since the formation of the earliest communities, human beings have recognized the importance of passing down knowledge, traditions, values, and technical skills to succeeding generations. Various systems of *education* have been devised to accomplish this objective. In preliterate societies, oral histories, narratives, and stories were the primary mode of knowledge transmission. As human societies began to develop and expand on their erudition, more formal types of education became necessary.

Circa 387 BC, the ancient Greek philosopher Plato founded the first European institution of higher learning in Athens. The Egyptian city of Alexandria, renowned for the extraordinary collection of texts housed in its Royal Library, soon replaced Plato's Academy as the ancient world's intellectual hub. Upon the collapse of the Roman Empire, literate scholarship in Western Europe became the preserve of the Catholic Church. The cathedral schools founded by the church in the early Middle Ages evolved into medieval universities, many of which in turn developed into the universities of modern Europe.

During the Middle Ages, Islamic science and mathematics flourished throughout the Middle East. Later, the European Renaissance ushered in a remarkable period of philosophical and scientific innovation. Assisted by Johannes Gutenberg's mid-fifteenth-century invention of the printing press, education in the arts, sciences, religion, and philosophy blossomed. The Renaissance laid the foundations for the modern era's more secularized and rationalized system of education.

Some have characterized modern education as being ensnared within a "dialectic of enlightenment" (as the German philosophers Theodor Adorno and Max Horkheimer termed it). On the one hand, the modern academy has freed itself from the parochialisms, supernatural cosmologies, and theological orthodoxies of its medieval forerunner. Students today have access to a storehouse of information that the librarians of ancient Alexandria could have scarcely dreamt of. Moreover, the opportunity to acquire knowledge for its own sake is available, at least in principle, to most modern learners. On the other hand, the current trend toward the "rationalization of education" has increasingly focused learning on matters of importance to large business interests. In fact, private corporations have themselves become involved in the running of the academy, providing funding for schools, textbooks, research grants, and so forth. Additionally, for some, an educational system where standardized multiple-choice tests take priority over critical discourse represents no advance at all.

ELECTIONS

Elections are a mechanism for deciding which individuals should hold public office. Throughout history, human societies have employed different types of electoral systems. In ancient Athenian **democracy** (page 78), for example, candidates were chosen by lot; Athenian democrats believed this would assure the overall fairness of the process. In modern **parliamentary democracies** (page 189), officeholders are chosen by popular vote: citizens cast their ballots for those candidates whose platforms most closely align with their own views. Depending on the conventions of the particular political system, elections may be used to fill offices in some or all levels of the government (national, regional, local) and in some or all of its branches (legislative, executive, judicial). Once in office, political representatives are charged with formulating laws and policies consistent with the preferences of those who have elected them. If citizens find that government officials have failed to adequately represent them, they have the opportunity to reject those officials in subsequent election cycles; this makes elections an important mechanism of democratic accountability.

In North America and Europe, full **suffrage** (page 233) rights—which include the right to vote and the right to stand for public office—were initially granted to predominantly white, male owners of **land** (page 146) and **property** (page 199). Over the past two centuries, numerous campaigns have successfully pressured governments into making suffrage universal, that is, no longer based on eligibility criteria such as property ownership, race, and gender.

Many modern parliamentary democracies utilize an electoral system known as proportional representation, in which candidates gain seats in the parliament based on the proportion of votes cast for their party. Some observers argue that proportional representation offers important advantages over first-past-the-post elections, held in countries such as the United Kingdom and the **United States** (page 248). Here, those candidates who win a simple plurality of votes are elected to office, while the remaining candidates gain nothing. As many citizens feel that their votes will be "wasted" on minority-party candidates who stand little chance of being "first past the post," the political scene tends to be dominated by a few major parties. Advocates of proportional representation claim that it broadens the political complexion of the government by opening it up to minority parties and independent candidates. Others, however, reject the system on the basis that it allows extremist parties to gain a foothold in the government.

ELECTIONS (US)

In the **federalist** (page 105) system of the **United States** (page 248), elections are held at the national, state, and local levels. Most elected government officials are elected by popular vote; the one exception is the **president** (page 194), who is elected by delegates under a system known as the Electoral College. The president has the power to appoint Supreme Court justices and other federal officials, meaning that some positions within the national government are unelected. While many modern **parliamentary democracies** (page 189) utilize proportional representation, the US has a "winner-take-all" electoral system, in which the candidate who receives a simple plurality of votes wins. For example, in an election where candidates A, B, and C receive 45 percent, 35 percent, and 20 percent of the votes, respectively, candidate A is the victor despite having failed to earn an absolute majority.

Throughout US history, numerous struggles have been waged over the right to participate in elections and hold political office. Led by activists such as Elizabeth Cady Stanton and Susan B. Anthony, a movement for women's **suffrage** (page 233) arose in the nineteenth century. The hard-fought campaign took some seventy years, but eventually resulted in the removal of gender-based voting

Abraham Lincoln's 1860 presidential campaign banner. At the time, African Americans, and women of any race, were not yet allowed to cast ballots.

restrictions with the passage of the Nineteenth Amendment to the **Constitution** (page 72) in 1920. Despite legally mandated universal suffrage, political barriers were erected in many US states to prevent African Americans from participating equally in the electoral process. The American **civil rights** (page 54) movement's demand for the removal of such barriers helped assure the passage of the Voting Rights Act of 1965.

Some critics question the utility of American elections as mechanisms of **democratic** (page 78) accountability, pointing to the fact that political campaigns in the US often depend on contributions from large corporate interests. Although **Congress** (page 69) has passed the 1971 Federal Election Campaign Act and various other campaign finance reform laws, cash from large private donors and corporate political action committees continues to flow into the coffers of candidates for high political office—leaving labor unions, civic organizations, poor people, and other less powerful groups with far less leverage over the electoral process. Some argue that, before the first ballot has been cast, US presidential elections are skewed in favor of those who are able to raise the requisite level of funds (Barack Obama's 2012 presidential campaign alone cost close to $1.12 billion), and those who are willing to adopt political agendas hospitable to the economic interests of their well-heeled financial backers.

ELITES

Small groups of people who possess a disproportionate amount of a nation's **wealth** (page 259), social privileges, or political power are known as *elites*. Elite rule can take different forms: it may be based on social status or rank, as in **aristocracies** (page 30); high levels of wealth, as in some **oligarchies** (page 182); or real or perceived qualifications, as in **meritocracies** (page 168).

The rule of elites is often contrasted with **democratic** (page 78) rule, in which the operations of the government are subject to citizen oversight and control. Many critics have questioned whether this is the case in contemporary representative democracies; they argue, for example, that large corporations exert inordinate leverage over the political process by virtue of their superior economic resources. This idea is developed in C. Wright Mills's highly influential 1956 book, *The Power Elite*. Influenced by the ideas of Max Weber, Mills notes that in modern industrial societies, members of political, economic, and military elites travel in the same privileged social circles: they attend the same exclusive clubs and educational institutions, and often intermarry. In so doing, he claims, they arrive at mutually reinforced assumptions about their high social standing and their associated prerogative to dominate the national political decision-making process.

ENERGY

Energy is a natural resource used to produce goods that serve human needs. The machinery of the modern industrial economy operates chiefly on petroleum-based energy sources such as natural gas and oil. Under the prevailing system of global **capitalism** (page 44), control over energy reserves is primarily entrusted to large corporations. However, not all **governments** (page 118) have been content to consign the fate of these resources to the mechanisms of the **free market** (page 108) alone: some have championed energy conservation, the development of alternative energy technologies, and other policies aimed at assuring environmentally sustainable energy usage.

Many observers contend that such efforts have done little to reduce the ecological impact of the modern petroleum-based economy. In addition to being responsible for significant amounts of environmental pollution, the widespread use of coal, gas, and oil has been implicated in global climate change, a development that has the potential to trigger perhaps irreversible environmental collapse. Many have argued that the **United Nations** (page 245) 1992 Kyoto Protocol on climate change is likewise insufficient, and that more comprehensive steps must be taken on an international level to avert such an outcome.

ENTREPRENEURIALISM

An *entrepreneur* is an individual responsible for at least some of the strategic decision-making functions of an organization, typically a private business. Prior to taking on this meaning, the word "entrepreneur" had long been part of the French language. In the early sixteenth century, it was applied to leaders of **military** (page 168) expeditions. Soon, members of other types of occupations—including architects and those contracted to build bridges, roads, and harbors—were also being called entrepreneurs. In the mid-eighteenth century, Richard Cantillon employed the term in a technical sense, claiming that the basic function of the entrepreneur was to bear the risks of buying and selling at uncertain prices.

It was in the **United States** (page 248) that it first began to be thought of as a function separate from either ownership of the means of production or control over the supply of capital. In particular, the distinction between capitalists and entrepreneurs was emphasized by Francis A. Walker in the late 1870s. Walker portrayed entrepreneurs as the principal drivers of industrial development because they, unlike capitalists, were prepared to face the potentially unwelcome consequences of their risk-taking activities. In 1882, Frederick B. Hawley endorsed Walker's view that risk-taking was the distinctive characteristic of the entrepreneur. He even went so far as to place entrepreneurial risk-taking

E

alongside land, labor, and capital as one of the principal factors of production.

Although economists seemed to lose interest in entrepreneurialism for some time, the Great Depression of the 1920s and 1930s refocused their attention on the critical role it played in generating profits. Joseph Schumpeter credited entrepreneurial innovation with spearheading progressive changes that ultimately led to the creation of interest and profit. He argued that the changes for which entrepreneurs are responsible often have the effect of stimulating other entrepreneurs to engage in risk-taking ventures. Entrepreneurial innovation thus tends to occur in clusters, which yield additional profits and upswings in economic activity. In this context, Schumpeter drew a key distinction between the functions of entrepreneurs (who make strategically important decisions) and the functions of managers (who are primarily responsible for maintaining and overseeing everyday business operations). His work on entrepreneurialism significantly impacted the development of economic theory throughout the twentieth century, and remains an important influence on economic scholarship today.

ENVIRONMENTALISM

Environmentalism refers to the perspectives and practices of organizations and movements seeking to protect and improve Earth's natural environments. Although it is sometimes understood as equivalent to the broader **ecology** (page 88) movement, environmentalism more specifically refers to established, lawful efforts to safeguard the environment from human-caused destruction. From the standpoint of environmentalism, the natural world matters insofar as its wellbeing (or lack thereof) is linked to human needs and interests. This outlook is exemplified by the work of organizations such as the Sierra Club, the World Wildlife Fund, and Citizens for a Better Environment. These well-recognized groups are principally concerned with pressuring governments into adopting more environmentally sustainable policies and placing tighter controls on polluting and natural habitat–destroying industries. Environmentalism thus differs from the more radical outlooks and political tactics adopted by some activists within the wider ecology movement. Among the latter, for example, the organization Earth First! has maintained that the Earth's complex, biodiverse ecosystems should be conserved simply for their own sake, independently of their utility for human beings. To get its points across, the group has at times engaged in minor acts of vandalism.

ESPIONAGE

The purpose of *espionage*, or spying, is to obtain confidential information from a **state** (page 229), individual, private corporation, or other entity. It is usually carried out covertly by a **government** (page 118) or private agency against targets that wish to keep the desired information undisclosed. Espionage operations are thus, of necessity, clandestine (in many cases, they are also illegal). This sets espionage apart from the more general practice of "intelligence gathering," in which information is collected legally from public sources.

The most common espionage scenario is that of a state seeking to discover another state's **military** (page 168) secrets with the purpose of gaining a strategic advantage in an existing or potential armed conflict. Posing as members of a military or civilian organization, spies may attempt to appropriate the targeted group's technology or engage in acts of sabotage. Spies known as *agents provocateurs* may incite group members into committing crimes in order to discredit them, entice them to defect, or sew dissension within their ranks—by planting intentionally provocative rumors, for example. From the late 1950s through the early 1970s, this tactic was employed by the US Federal Bureau of Investigation's COINTELPRO initiative, which covertly monitored, infiltrated, and gathered information about various domestic political organizations.

EUROPEAN UNION

The *European Union* (EU) is an international federation of mainly European nation-states. Founded in 1993 under the Maastricht Treaty, it is an outgrowth of organizations established in the 1950s: the European Coal and Steel Community (ECSC) and the European Economic Community (EEC). The idea behind these international bodies was similar to that driving the formation of the **United Nations** (page 245) in 1945. In the aftermath of **World War II** (page 266), the victorious Allies were eager to prevent a recurrence of extreme nationalistic belligerence such as that which led the Axis Powers to wreak havoc across Europe and other parts of the world. For many, this required a united Europe. The cause was taken up by members of the newly formed European Movement International and by students of the College of Europe, some of whom went on to become leading European politicians.

Their efforts led to the establishment of the ECSC in 1952. Offering its member states access to a common market for coal and steel, its aim was to promote regional economic integration. This objective was furthered by the creation of the EEC in 1958 under the Treaty of Rome. The European Atomic Energy Community was also established at this time; its purpose was to secure a dedicated nuclear power market in Europe. Additional steps toward European integration were taken in the ensuing decades. The adoption of the 1985 Schengen

E

Agreement, for example, broke down the political borders of Europe by permitting the citizens of member states—as well as those of some nonmember states—to travel across the continent without passport controls.

With the dissolution of the **Soviet Union** (page 226) in 1991, the opportunity arose to incorporate some newly independent nations to a growing European union. On November 1, 1993, German Chancellor Helmut Kohl and French President François Mitterrand signed the Maastricht Treaty, bringing the EU officially into effect. The organization's objectives include the integration of the European economy and the advancement of peace, **human rights** (page 128), and social **justice** (page 140). To further these causes, a number of supranational institutions have been established within the EU. They include the Council of the European Union, the European Commission, the EU Court of Justice, the European Council, the European Court of Auditors, and the European Central Bank. The organization itself is governed by the European Parliament, whose members are elected every five years by EU citizens.

The EU has fundamentally transformed Europe's political landscape. There are

currently twenty-eight member states, nineteen of which are also members of the Eurozone (this means they adopt the euro as their official currency). The economy of the EU—the world's largest—is organized into a single market whose common legal system is binding on all member states. Its countries are home to more than five hundred million people—approximately 7.3 percent of the world's inhabitants.

Numerous objections have been leveled against the EU's project of European integration, both from within the continent and from without. This diverse body of criticism is collectively known as Euroscepticism. Right-wing critics argue that the existence of the EU poses a threat to the **sovereignty** (page 226) of European nation-states: it hinders their capacity to determine their own laws and monetary policies, and erodes their unique cultural traditions. Such sentiments are especially strong in the United Kingdom, which has long insisted on retaining its own currency and remaining outside the Eurozone. Britain is also home to the right-wing, anti-**immigration** (page 129) UK Independence Party, a Eurosceptic organization that has enjoyed significant successes in both local and European Parliament elections in recent years.

For left-wing critics, some of the EU's main deficits include its lack of **democracy** (page 78) and its overinvestment in trade and economic development issues. This position has been upheld by philosopher Jürgen Habermas, who, lamenting the fact that "the EU has become a financial market-oriented technocracy," has called for the "democratization of the European Union and democratic management of the European Council."[5]

While Habermas worries that the EU has prioritized the economic objectives of Europe's business elites at the expense of Immanuel Kant's ideal of a cosmopolitan federation of nation-states, the Nobel Committee appears to be more optimistic about the organization's progressive capacities: in 2012, it awarded the EU the Nobel Peace Prize for its contributions "to the advancement of peace and reconciliation, democracy, and human rights in Europe."[6]

(Opposite) The European Union launched in 1993 as a way of bringing Europe under a single political and economic umbrella during the fall of the Soviet Union.

EXCEPTIONALISM

The term *exceptionalism*, or exceptionality, is used in reference to nations, political movements, or historical epochs that view themselves as so extraordinary or unusual that they need not be bound by prevailing norms or institutional arrangements. In the late eighteenth century, the theme of exceptionalism emerged in the writings of Johann Gottlieb Fichte and Johann Gottfried Herder. The two German thinkers spoke of an organic community of people, the *Volk*, characterized by its own unique historical, linguistic, and cultural traditions. The *Volk*, they argued, resides at the core of society, expressing its "national spirit" or *Volksgeist*. Inspired by this idea, various exceptionalist political movements took hold in nineteenth-century Europe, culminating in the extreme militant **nationalism** (page 170) of the **fascist** (page 101) campaigns of the mid-twentieth century.

Throughout history, exceptionalism has figured prominently in the political ideologies of many nations. It was evident, for example, in the nineteenth-century doctrine of "Manifest Destiny," which celebrated the unique virtues and traditions of the American people and helped legitimate the conquest of the Western Frontier of the **United States** (page 248). In the century that followed, exceptionalism reemerged in the doctrines of America's Cold War ideologues, who positioned the nation at the forefront of a march toward a global **free-market** (page 108) economy. In its campaign against the "**communist** (page 64) menace," they argued, the US was entitled to flout both domestic and international conventions regarding **human rights** (page 128), codes of **warfare** (page 256), and so on.

Some observers maintain that, despite the end of the Cold War in 1991, the US has continued to espouse exceptionalism. They suggest that since then, and particularly since the 9/11 attacks on its soil, it has been reluctant to participate in international treaties that would hinder its operations against hostile nations and **terrorist** (page 238) organizations like **al-Qaeda** (page 16).

In the early 1990s, political scientist Samuel Huntington used the now popular phrase "clash of civilizations" to describe the shift away from Cold War disputes over ideological and economic doctrines toward conflicts over religious and cultural worldviews. While many have cast doubt on Huntington's thesis, it seems clear that exceptionalism, in whatever guise, remains the backdrop for many political conflicts in the world today.

F

FASCISM

Between 1919 and 1945, several mass political movements emerged throughout Central, Southern, and Eastern Europe—movements whose legacy of death and destruction the world still grapples with. These movements and their associated ideologies are encompassed under the term *fascism*. Not only was the fascist cause wildly popular in countries where its leaders managed to attain state power; it also attracted large followings in Western Europe and in many nations outside the continent, including the **United States** (page 248) and South Africa.

The first fascist head of state in Europe was Benito Mussolini, who became Prime Minister of Italy in 1922—some eleven years prior to **Adolf Hitler**'s (page 124) ascendancy to the German Chancellorship. Mussolini's National Fascist Party derived its name from *fasces*, a Latin term referring to a bundle of elm or birch rods (often with an axe inside it), which the ancient Romans used to symbolize the formidable powers of their penal system.

Fascist ideologies and movements differ in important ways, but there are several broad points of agreement: they roundly reject **parliamentary democracy** (page 189), **Marxism** (page 166), and **liberalism** (page 152); they aim for a hierarchal society in which elites rule; they support extreme militaristic **nationalism** (page 170); and they subordinate the interests of particular individuals to those of an authentic "people's community," in whose name the fascist state is organized.

Beyond this, there remains much scholarly debate about the true nature of fascism. Some regard it as a genuinely radical movement in the **Jacobin** (page 137) tradition of the **French Revolution** (page 109), promising a sweeping cultural "renewal" and the birth of a "new man"; for others, it is little more than a fearful, reactionary assault on the liberal ideals of the European Enlightenment and the emancipatory objectives of international **communism** (page 64). Some are struck by the incomprehensibility and irrationality of the fascist worldview; others view it as the pinnacle of **capitalist** (page 44) rationality and **bureaucratic** (page 43) efficiency, as evidenced by the systematic mass exterminations

carried out in the **Nazi** (page 175) concentration camps.

Although the fascist parties of Germany, Italy, and Japan were dissolved upon the conclusion of **World War II** (page 266), fascism was not so easily swept under the rug. By the late 1940s, fascist-oriented parties and movements were already on the rebound in Europe, Latin America, and South Africa. Today, various neofascist organizations continue to attract significant followings throughout the world.

(Opposite) Benito Mussolini (left) and Adolf Hitler (right) pushed fascist nationalist ideologies that inspired fear and adulation, making them among the most reviled political figures of the twentieth century.

FEDERAL COURTS

In the **United States** (page 248), *federal courts* comprise the judicial branch of the national government. The basic mandate of the federal judiciary is to interpret the law, making its powers distinct from those of the executive (law-enforcing) and legislative (lawmaking) branches of the government. The federal judiciary is divided into three levels. From highest to lowest, they are the Supreme Court, the courts of appeal (or circuit courts), and the district courts. The establishment of the Supreme Court was mandated under Article Three of the US **Constitution** (page 72), which also gave **Congress** (page 69) the power to create the other courts and determine aspects of their jurisdiction. Federal court judges are appointed by the **president** (page 194) with the approval of the **Senate** (page 212). They effectively hold lifetime appointments, leaving their positions only upon resignation, death, or impeachment by the **House of Representatives** (page 126) and subsequent conviction by the Senate.

As the court of final appeal, the Supreme Court hears cases that come to it from the lower federal appellate courts. It decides which cases to entertain, operating under a power granted to it by Congress and known as discretionary review. It has the final say in all issues involving federal law, and it is the final interpreter of federal constitutional law.

Some observers maintain that, far from being a neutral adjudicator of constitutional law, the Supreme Court has been a highly politicized institution from its inception: it has focused on protecting the economic interests of the elites rather than those of the less powerful or the disadvantaged. This bias became readily apparent in the second half of the nineteenth century, when the Court issued a raft of decisions granting industrial corporations personhood **rights** (page 208) and **freedom** (page 107) from undue governmental interference in their operations.

To be sure, the Court has issued many important rulings over the years—rulings upholding equality of opportunity and the **civil rights** (page 54) of everyday Americans. Its landmark 1954 decision in *Brown v. Board of Education*, for instance, ended racial segregation in public schools. However, some maintain that such rulings have done little to alter the underlying conditions of class inequality in the US. Edward S. Greenberg has argued that, rather than serving as "the foundation of a genuinely democratic political life," the principal objective of the Court and the federal court system at large has been to assure that "those who own the main economic assets of society are secure in their control, use, and enjoyment of such assets."[7]

The US Supreme Court is often called upon to decide the constitutionality of government actions, such as school segregation and the prohibition of gay marriage.

FEDERALISM

The political doctrine of *federalism* underlies many **democracies** (page 78) in the world today, including that of the **United States** (page 248). Consistent with the principles of **social contract** (page 221) theory, federalism sees the citizens of the nation as bound by covenant with their representatives, who must govern on their behalf and remain accountable to them through various democratic rules and institutions.

In a federalist system, the national government is typically divided into various branches—each with its own specific obligations and authority—according to the **separation of powers** (page 216) doctrine. State control is further divided between the central government, which is given certain exclusive powers applicable to the entire nation, and smaller governmental units such as states or provinces, which are granted localized authority and rights. Some powers are shared between local governments and the central government and its various political subdivisions.

The framers of the US **Constitution** (page 72) presented various arguments for the implementation of a federalist system. Chief among them was the desire to prevent **tyranny** (page 244), a form of government in which political power is used to service the interests of the ruling elite rather than those of the citizenry at large. The power of the central government, it was argued, could be checked by splitting it up into separate branches (legislative, judicial, and executive); these branches would oversee one another and guard against abuses of power. Tyranny could also be avoided if some of the federal government's authority was parceled out to the individual states, which would further serve as "laboratories" for fresh ideas and programs. Meanwhile, the election of both state and national officials would give citizens greater oversight over the doings of their government. The basic idea was to balance a strong central government—capable of guaranteeing social order —with individual **liberty** (page 155) and states' **rights** (page 208).

Be that as it may, James Madison and other authors of the Constitution were keenly aware of the risks of granting the general public an excessive amount of control. Madison in particular argued that "pure" **democracy** (page 78) would imperil the **property** (page 199) rights of the wealthy "minority." He therefore incorporated institutions such as the US **Senate** (page 212) into the American model of federalism. These institutions were meant both to protect elite rights and to check the "leveling" impulses of the masses.

F

FEMINISM

Feminism is a broad term that seeks to encompass a range of philosophical, political, moral, and cultural movements focused on women's concerns. Given the extremely wide scope of issues and groups it has been identified with, some have argued that it is more appropriate to speak of feminisms, in the plural. Most overviews divide feminism into three main chronological phases or "waves." The first wave is associated with the **liberal** (page 152) feminist campaigns of the 1800s and early 1900s; the second wave arose in the 1960s and 1970s, focusing on issues such as reproductive **rights** (page 208) and workplace equality; and the third and most recent wave began in the 1990s and has further expanded the domain of feminist concerns, turning attention to matters such as **racism** (page 200) and class discrimination.

F

Held in Seneca Falls, New York, in 1848, the first major women's rights convention in the **United States** (page 248) demanded, among other things, marriage law reform and the creation of equal opportunities for women in education and employment. It was the effort to obtain the right to vote, however, that ultimately became the focus of the first-wave feminist movement. To this end, Elizabeth Cady Stanton and Susan B. Anthony founded the National Woman Suffrage Association in 1869. Their struggle was long and hard-fought, but it eventually achieved its objective with the passage of the Nineteenth Amendment to the **Constitution** (page 72) in 1920.

Second-wave feminism emerged in the 1960s, alongside the **civil rights** (page 54) movement and the campaign to end the **war** (page 256) in Vietnam. It soon split into two main branches: the more politically radical one—a product of the broader New Left movement—came to be known as the women's liberation movement, while the second camp fell under the wing of the liberal National Organization for Women (NOW). Founded by Betty Friedan in 1966, NOW became the largest women's organization in the US. The bulk of its energies were directed toward the passage of the Equal Rights Amendment, which ultimately failed to win ratification.

Disillusioned with earlier feminism's focus on issues of relevance to white middle-class women, third-wave feminism addressed questions of race and class, as well as matters of concern to lesbian, gay, bisexual, and transgender communities. It directed attention away from the broad macropolitical demands of its predecessors, focusing on the "micropolitics" of gender oppression instead.

FOREIGN POLICY

Broadly defined, *foreign policy* is the entirety of a state's practices toward other states and non-state actors. Encompassing both long-term and short-term objectives, it may involve relatively minor matters like tariff arrangements, or major issues such as **military** (page 168) intervention.

In the 1960s, foreign policy analysis became a distinct subfield of **international relations** (page 134). Rejecting the largely descriptive approach adopted by opinion journals and historical literature, foreign policy analysts sought to examine their subject matter in an empirically and theoretically rigorous manner. Their viewpoint was influenced by post–**World War II** (page 266) consensus regarding the supremacy of doctrines such as **liberalism** (page 152), rationalism, and **democracy** (page 78); a well-informed citizenry, maintained the analysts, would come to wise decisions about which foreign policies a nation should adopt.

In the **United States** (page 248), foreign policy has become an increasingly remote concern for the **legislative** (page 149) branch of the government. Since the latter half of the twentieth century, representatives in **Congress** (page 69) have focused on formulating legislation of relevance to their own local constituencies. Indeed, as legislative "specialists," they have tended to concede the broader areas of national and foreign policy to the **president** (page 194). Insofar as it is perceived to address the concerns of the nation at large, the executive branch is considered by some to be the most "democratic" branch of the American government.

In general, the presidency has had little difficulty getting Congress to accept its foreign policy proposals, especially those involving military intervention. However, Congress does retain the power to stymie the president when it is dissatisfied with his initiatives. In 2015, for example, President Barack Obama faced staunch opposition from lawmakers over his Joint Comprehensive Plan of Action, which was aimed at curtailing the ability of Iran to develop **nuclear weapons** (page 180). Many disparaged the agreement as an **appeasement** (page 26) maneuver that would ultimately fail to realize its objective.

FREEDOM

See *liberty*.

FREE MARKET

Economists conceive of *free markets* as systems in which the distribution and prices of goods and services are determined by the unrestrained activity of private economic competitors, consumers, and the forces of supply and demand. As their name suggests, free markets are unburdened from intervention on the part of **governments** (page 118), cartels, monopolies, and similar entities. Nonmarket interference of any sort—setting prices or erecting barriers to market entry, for example—is to be strictly avoided; meanwhile, the growth of highly competitive markets and private ownership of businesses is to be encouraged.

Organizationally, free markets are based on the principle of *laissez-faire*—a French term meaning "let things be." Initially adopted by a school of French writers known as the physiocrats, the idea was popularized in the eighteenth century by the Scottish economist Adam Smith. Smith maintained that if individuals are able to freely pursue their own economic interests, the "invisible hand" of market competition will promote **wealth** (page 259) and social prosperity far more effectively than trade restrictions, social welfare programs, or any other measures of state intervention.

As the **capitalist** (page 44) system evolved during the nineteenth century, the principles of free-market economics were increasingly undermined by capitalists themselves. Many large businesses found it economically advantageous to merge with their competitors and form huge trusts, as this enabled them to control prices and coordinate production; competitive market forces thus led to the growth of monopolies. Ironically, state intervention was now necessary to restore and defend the freedom of the market. This was the objective of the Sherman Antitrust Act of 1890 and the Clayton Act of 1914. Later, during the New Deal era, minimum-wage laws, workers' compensation statutes, and other forms of social welfare legislation were instituted to provide economic and social benefits that the free market seemed incapable of delivering on its own. The term "free market" nevertheless remains a well-worn rhetorical tool in US politics.

FRENCH REVOLUTION

The *French Revolution* (1789–1799) brought about profound changes in the political landscape of France and the world at large. A period of radical social and political upheaval, it ushered in the demise of France's *Ancien Régime*, the old feudal class system in which aristocracies ruled over peasantries, and monarchies justified their **absolute** (page 15) powers under the doctrine of **Divine Right** (page 87). Inspired by the **liberal** (page 152) ideals of the European Enlightenment, the Revolution proclaimed "Liberty, Equality, Fraternity" as its slogan. The phrase would later be adopted as the motto for France's new liberal-democratic government. The French Republic became a model for similar governmental arrangements the world over, altering the political climate of regions as far-flung as the Caribbean and the Middle East.

The Revolution was not a single event, but rather a series of revolutionary actions whose origins are multiple and complex. Among them was the disfavor into which France's ruling aristocracy had progressively fallen. The French population was none too pleased, for instance, about the various **taxation** (page 236) schemes the monarchy had imposed to whittle down debt amassed in during the Seven Years' War and the American Revolutionary

(Below) The 1789 Storming of the Bastille marked the beginning of the French Revolution.

F

War. Years of poor harvests and privation had also stoked the flames of popular resentment against the privileged clergy and aristocracy, who had suffered no such hardship.

In a bid to resolve his government's financial crisis, Louis XVI convened a general assembly known as the Estates-General in May 1789. This chamber had three subdivisions: the First Estate, for the clergy; the Second Estate, for the nobles; and the Third Estate, for the common people. Stimulated by the Enlightenment's liberal challenge to the established order, the Third Estate formed a revolutionary National Assembly and invited the other two Estates to participate. The move, which was against the wishes of the king, was the basic trigger of the French Revolution.

On July 14, 1789 members of the Third Estate thronged into the streets of Paris and stormed the Bastille, a medieval prison representing royal authority within the old feudal order. In August, the *Declaration of the Rights of Man and of the Citizen*—one of the modern age's most important legal documents on the question of **human rights** (page 128)—was passed by the French National Constituent Assembly. In October, a women's march descended upon the Palace of Versailles, the seat of Louis XVI's monarchy, protesting the high price and shortage of bread. These events were the first of several that would ultimately result in the demise of feudalism. Although right-wing supporters of the monarchy

1754–1776	*Years of war bring debt and higher taxation*
1789	*Third Estate storms the Bastille;* Declaration of the Rights of Man *is issued*
1792	*Founding of the French Republic*
1793	*Louis XVI and Marie Antoinette beheaded*
1793–1794	*Reign of Terror targets "traitors"*
1799	*Napoleon takes power, bringing Revolution to a close*

sought to foil the major reforms initiated by the newly established liberal assemblies, the rebel cause prevailed. In September 1792, a French Republic was declared after the revolutionaries emerged victorious from the Battle of Valmy.

Several months later, Louis XVI was executed. The king became the first victim of the Reign of Terror, a period of stark political repression launched by the revolutionary Maximilien Robespierre and the **Jacobins** (page 137); during their two-year campaign, tens of thousands of "enemies of the revolution" suffered the same fate as the beheaded king. While ruthlessly brutal, the Jacobins were behind several progressive initiatives,

(Opposite) Following the Storming of the Bastille, the 1793 beheading of Louis XVI signaled victory for advocates of republicanism.

F

including the abolition of slavery in the French colonies and the secularization of French society.

The Reign of Terror lasted until 1794, only to be replaced by another repressive government the following year. In 1799, this government—known as the Directory—was overthrown by **Napoleon Bonaparte** (page 172); this brought the Revolution to a close. Hailed as the hero of the Revolution for his many successful military exploits, Napoleon would eventually establish a centralized republican government called the Consulate; he later became head of the First Empire of France.

The French Revolution's core values of liberty, equality, and fraternity, as well as its successful dissolution of the aristocratic and religious foundations of the state, have been key sources of inspiration for many revolutionary movements since. Among these were the Russian Revolution of 1917, the struggle to end the institution of slavery, and movements on behalf of **civil rights** (page 54), **women's rights** (page 106), and universal suffrage. The written constitutions and parliamentary arrangements of many of the world's governments today have been modeled on the system of liberal **republicanism** (page 206) established by the French Revolution.

(Above) During Robespierre's Reign of Terror, the Jacobins often beheaded members of the aristocracy and other perceived traitors.

FUNDAMENTALISM

Broadly applied, the term *fundamentalism* refers to any standpoint espousing strict adherence to a founding set of doctrines or beliefs. However, it is most commonly employed in reference to religious groups that maintain unwavering fealty to the tenets of their faiths in reaction to social, political, cultural, and economic changes brought on by modernity. Religious fundamentalists adopt literalist interpretations of the theological scriptures and dogmas to which they subscribe, and maintain rigid boundaries between themselves and other members of society. They insist on the "purity" and inviolable correctness of their own doctrinal interpretations, while showing intolerance for competing perspectives.

Religious fundamentalism is currently a global phenomenon, attracting adherents from different cultural backgrounds with different experiences of, and reactions to, the modern world. The first major fundamentalist movements, however, took hold in the **United States** (page 248) in the late nineteenth and early twentieth centuries. Led by Presbyterian theologians, and later by Baptists and adherents of other Christian denominations, the early religious fundamentalists sought to fend off challenges from a new movement of **liberal** (page 152) theology. Liberal theologians promoted a vision of **Christianity** (page 46) relieved of its investment in miracles and the supernatural, and more compatible with the standpoints of modern science, secularism, rationalism, and progressivism.

Politically, religious fundamentalists in the US were relatively restrained throughout most of the twentieth century. However, in the late 1970s, the idea of using politics to defend and propagate established theological doctrines became increasingly attractive to a certain segment of the fundamentalist movement, which proceeded to forge alliances with **conservative** (page 71) Christian Evangelicals. Together, these forces—sometimes referred to simply as the Religious Right—have been a major factor behind the electoral successes of the **Republican Party** (page 206) over the last three and a half decades. Backed by organizations such as the Christian Coalition of America and the American Decency Association, political religious fundamentalists see the moral edicts of the Bible as the normative foundation of America's global preeminence. They argue that this status is now in jeopardy due to liberal policies and cultural attitudes promoting "morally decadent" behaviors: drug use, sexual promiscuity, abortion, divorce, homosexuality, etc. For such fundamentalists, the US's prosperity and success can be assured only through strict adherence to traditional religious values and conservative political ideals such as limited government—a perspective that still constitutes a prominent backdrop of American political discourse.

G

MAHATMA GANDHI

At the forefront of the wave of **decolonization** (page 77) movements that arose in the mid-twentieth century was Mohandas Karamchand *Gandhi*, more commonly known as Mahatma (Sanskrit for high-souled), a physically diminutive man who would become one of the giants of contemporary political history. Gandhi's role as the leader of the Indian movement against British colonial rule, which was based on the principle of **nonviolent resistance** (page 179), helped to inspire **civil rights** (page 54) and social **justice** (page 140) campaigns throughout the world—including the one led by **Martin Luther King, Jr.** (page 141) in the United States.

Gandhi began to press for Indian independence in 1915, when he returned to his homeland after working as a lawyer in South Africa—where he first turned to nonviolent resistance as a strategy for defending the civil rights of that nation's minority Indian community. Back in India, Gandhi drew on his experiences in South Africa to unite farmers, peasants, and urban industry workers in a nonviolent movement against the discriminatory policies and unfair land **taxation** (page 236) laws of the British Raj. In 1921, he became the head of the Indian National Congress, leading the drive to reduce poverty and contest the "untouchable" status of India's *Dalit* caste. He also championed the advancement of women's rights and promoted religious and ethnic tolerance.

Gandhian civil disobedience was based on the principle of *Swaraj*, or self-rule. Gandhi argued that India should be free to determine its own destiny, and that such independence meant forsaking the hierarchal political, economic, bureaucratic, legal, military, and educational institutions that Britain had imposed upon the nation. Two of Gandhi's more well-known anticolonial efforts were the non-cooperation movement of 1920 to 1922 and the Dandi Salt March of 1930. While the march was a direct response to the excessive tax revenue extracted from Indian salt producers by the British Crown, it had a much broader impact: it significantly affected people's perceptions of British rule in India, and attracted many fresh recruits to the cause of Indian independence. Gandhi's support continued to grow over the next decade; by 1942, he was well positioned to launch his famous Quit India Movement, in which he called for the British to undertake an "orderly" exit from India.

The groundswell of resistance to its presence in India eventually proved too much for Great Britain: in August 1947, it granted India its independence. However, the demise of British rule did not unfold in precisely the way that Gandhi had hoped it would. Beginning in the early 1940s, a growing number of Muslim nationalists began to challenge Gandhi's vision of a unified, independent India. Rejecting his ideals of religious toleration and pluralism, they demanded that a separate Muslim nation be created out of the ashes of the toppled British Raj. As a result of their efforts, the British Indian Empire was split into two

Mahatma Gandhi launched the Quit India Movement in 1942, leading millions in acts of nonviolent resistance against the British Raj.

G

independent countries: Hindu-majority India, and the smaller, Muslim-majority Pakistan to its west (with the provincial state of East Pakistan formed at the other end of the subcontinent, to the east of India.) This decision to split up India—to which Gandhi remained opposed—uprooted 10 to 12 million Hindus, Muslims, and Sikhs, forcing them to cross the newly created border between India and Pakistan and take up residence in their newly designated homelands. The result was mass chaos and rioting, in which more than half a million people lost their lives.

Deeply troubled by these developments, Gandhi refused to attend the official Delhi ceremonies celebrating the arrival of Indian independence. He traveled to the affected areas and endeavored to quell the tide of violence. He also undertook several fasts, both to protest the bloodshed and to plead for religious toleration and cooperation between Hindus and Muslims. Gandhi began his final fast in 1948, with the aim of pressuring India into paying back debts that it owed to Pakistan.

Gandhi's conciliatory tone with Pakistan and his overall vision of religious toleration did not sit well with strident Hindu nationalists, who wanted little to do with their new western neighbor. Among them was Nathuram Godse, who, on January 30, 1948, approached Gandhi and assassinated him at gunpoint. Gandhi had already survived five attempts on his life.

In present-day India, Mahatma Gandhi continues to be venerated as the father of the nation. Outside India, he is also widely lauded as a patron of peace and nonviolence. His legacy, however, is often surrounded by idolatry and myth-making, which serves only to undermine the real substance of his political vision. Gandhian nonviolent resistance was not simply directed against the **tyranny** (page 244) of British rule; it was also a call to struggle against exploitation and social injustice, and to end the domination of the weak by the powerful. It would seem that Gandhi's **socialist** (page 224) dream of a pacific, classless society was all but forgotten by the Indian leaders who succeeded him.

GLOBALIZATION

Globalization refers to the process of increasing global integration due to the spread of ideas, **culture** (page 74), technology, **trade** (page 242), and investment across national borders. The political theorist David Held has set forth a widely cited definition of globalization as the set of "those spatial-temporal processes of change which underpin a transformation in the organization of human affairs by linking together and expanding human activity across regions and continents."[8] This phenomenon is arguably nothing new; some have even suggested that it has been taking place since the advent of the first human communities. However, what *is* unique about the present moment is the scale and rapidity at which it is unfolding.

The first use of the term "globalization" has been credited to Theodore Levitt, who employed it in an article for the *Harvard Business Review* in 1983. Since then, economists and business writers have employed it to home in on certain developments that older terms like "internationalization" and "cosmopolitanism" overlook.

Globalization, it is argued, is currently being promoted by rapid technological advances (particularly in the fields of communications and transportation) and shifts in international economic policy (notably, the deregulation of global markets and the relaxation of international trade barriers). The advent of jet planes, fiber-optic cables, satellite communications, and the Internet, on the one hand, combined with a **neoliberal** (page 176) consensus about the propriety of free trade, **privatization** (page 198), and competitive markets, on the other, sets present-day globalization apart from earlier movements toward international integration. These changes have vastly expanded the flow of information, money, goods, and services across international borders, linking nations, people, private businesses, and nongovernmental organizations together in increasingly larger and well-integrated social and economic networks.

Some economists have credited the **United States** (page 248) with pushing the process of globalization forward. They argue that, were it not for America's sponsorship of a deregulated international market overseen by financial institutions like the World Bank, the International Monetary Fund, and the World Trade Organization, integration might well have been confined to regional blocs rather than extended throughout the far corners of the globe.

Defenders of globalization have been quick to underscore its many presumed advantages, including its tendency to break down parochial prejudices and promote awareness of different cultural perspectives. Some have also credited globalization with fostering economic growth, market efficiency, and democratization. Critics argue that, in tearing down barriers to trade and investment, globalization compromises the occupational security of workers in developed nations: employers shift jobs to "external markets" in developing countries, where **labor** (page 143) costs are lower. At the same time, globalization encourages workers in the developing world to emigrate to the developed world as they seek to enhance their economic prospects. Some have claimed that, rather than promote solidarity among the international working class, this process serves only to pit sectors of the global workforce against each other. Many critics also note that the economic gains of globalization are not evenly distributed, and that **wealth** (page 259) is becoming increasingly concentrated in the hands of a small group of powerful business and financial **elites** (page 94). Others have charged globalization with contributing to a worldwide environmental crisis, undermining public health, destroying indigenous traditions and cultures, and threatening the **sovereignty** (page 226) of the world's nation-states.

G

GOVERNMENT

The political system that administers and regulates the affairs of a nation or community is known as a *government*. Throughout human history, governments have assumed countless incarnations. For the last two millennia, terms of Greek and Roman derivation such as **aristocracy** (page 30), **oligarchy** (page 182), and **democracy** (page 78) have been used to describe their most common varieties. All

The US Capitol in Washington, DC, is home to Congress, making it a centerpiece of the country's government.

governments have the power to determine, assess, and implement the laws under which the nation is ruled. They differ, however, with respect to how this is to be achieved. In an **absolute** (page 15) monarchy, for example, the lawmaking, law-interpreting, and law-enforcing powers of the government are consolidated within a single entity, whereas a **republican** (page 206) state divides them among different governmental branches.

Throughout history, governments have been targeted by various political movements seeking to either alter their institutional composition or overturn them entirely. Indeed, they do not operate statically or in isolation from the rest of society: they are dynamic entities that intersect with the cultures, traditions, and personal lives of people within and outside their own borders. Accordingly, as a field of study, government is not simply of concern to political scientists, but also to anthropologists, economists, sociologists, historians, and philosophers.

GREEN MOVEMENT

See *environmentalism*.

GUN CONTROL

Gun control is one of the more contentious political issues in the United States today. There has been no shortage of high-profile incidents involving privately-owned guns in recent decades, including mass shootings and assassinations at gunpoint. Such events have heightened calls for stricter controls on the production, sale, distribution, and possession of firearms. In response, conservative **lobby** (page 158) organizations such as the National Rifle Association (NRA) have attributed the misuse of firearms to a lack of personal responsibility on the part of their users; the mere possession of a gun is said to have little bearing on the ends to which it is ultimately put. The NRA sees restrictions on gun ownership as infringements on individual **liberty** (page 155) and the Second Amendment of the US **Constitution** (page 72), which grants citizens the right to "keep and bear arms." Gun control advocates insist that the widespread availability of firearms does, in fact, contribute to higher rates of homicide, gang warfare, robbery, and other violent crimes. They note that the incidence of such offenses is higher in countries like the United States, where gun control laws are relatively lax, than in countries like Germany and the United Kingdom, where gun ownership is more tightly regulated.

H

HABEAS CORPUS

Habeas corpus ("You shall have the body," in medieval Latin) is a formal written order, or writ, which enables those who believe they have been unlawfully imprisoned—or those acting on their behalf—to petition for relief. Writs of *habeas corpus* are addressed to the officials in whose custody a prisoner has been placed, enjoining them to present proof of the legality of the detention before a court. The court is obliged to release the prisoner if it determines that the custodian has acted beyond his or her legal authority.

Habeas corpus is an important procedural remedy against possible abuses of state power, but it is not without its limitations. It protects one from being detained unlawfully, but it does not shield one from the abridgement of other legal entitlements, such as the right to a speedy trial before a jury of one's peers. Governments have sometimes cited national crises or emergencies as legitimate grounds for suspending *habeas corpus*. During the American **Civil War** (page 58), for example, President **Abraham Lincoln** (page 156) denied those detained by Union forces the writ of *habeas corpus*, in light of the threat that Confederate rebels posed to the continued existence of the US Republic.

HEALTH CARE

Today, *health care* systems have been established in most of the world's nations. Such systems provide medical services for the prevention and treatment of diseases and the promotion of physical and mental health. In recent years, health care has been the subject of a heated political debate in the **United States** (page 248), which has raised questions about how it is to be organized, financed, and delivered. Should it be provided by private practitioners or large corporate organizations? Should it be paid for by individuals, private insurance companies, or **social insurance** (page 223) programs? These questions remain far from settled.

The nature of health care in the US has changed dramatically since the founding of the **republic** (page 205) almost two and a half centuries ago. Early health care in America was largely the province of general practice physicians, who treated diverse patient populations suffering from an equally diverse range

Health care is often a battleground between those who deem it a government responsibility and those who see it better left to the workings of the free market.

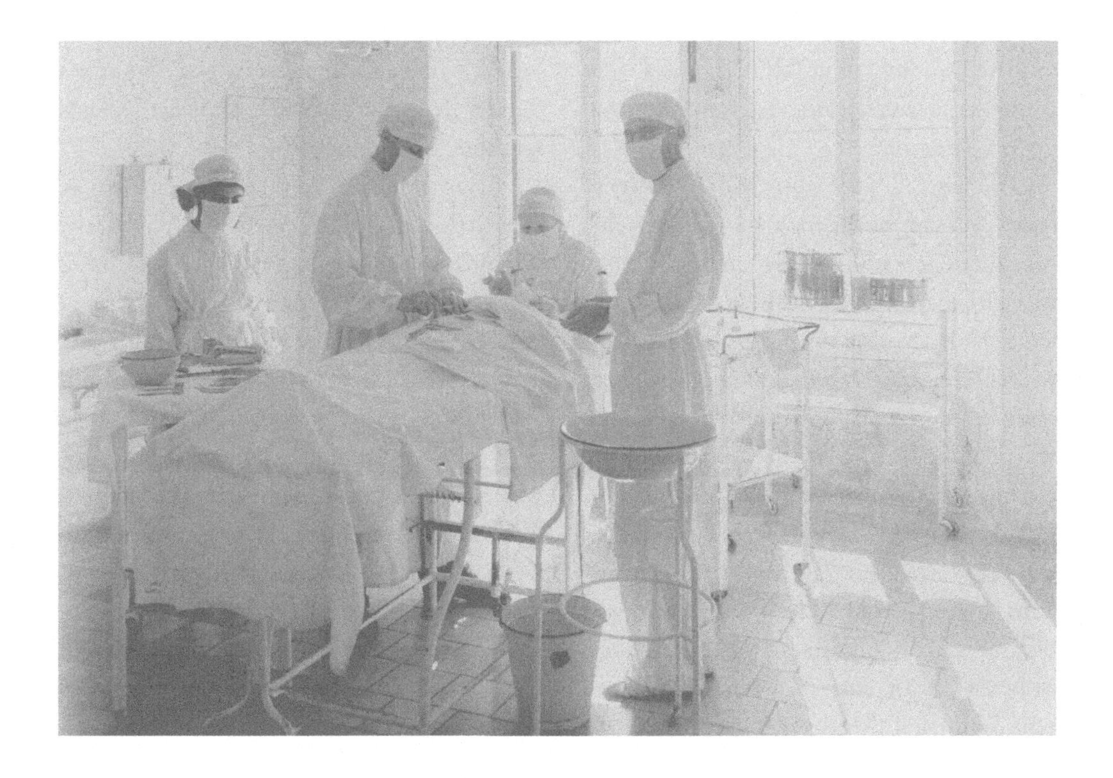

of ailments. They were typically solo practitioners who made house calls or welcomed patients in their own homes. Meanwhile, patients generally paid for their treatment out-of-pocket, on a fee-for-service basis. In the late nineteenth century, technological advances in the fields of surgery and bacteriology helped enhance physicians' institutional and cultural authority. Their small home offices were supplanted by large modern hospitals, whose number jumped from 661 in 1875 to around 7,000 in 1930. Most of them were clustered in large metropolitan areas. At first, hospital-based health care was organized according to a two-tiered system: paying patients were seen in private rooms, while "charity" cases were consigned to large, wide-open wards housing up to 40 patients.

The period following **World War II** (page 266) saw the decline of the general "solo" practitioner and the rise of specialty and subspecialty medicine, biomedical research, and large pharmaceutical and medical supply companies. The social reforms of the New Deal era instilled in many the belief that health care was not simply a privilege to be enjoyed by the wealthy, but a fundamental right of all citizens. Consistent with the principles of **free-market capitalism** (page 108), private medical insurance companies like Blue Cross/Blue Shield became the conduit through which more and more Americans entered the health care system. However, the **government** (page 118) did establish two major insurance programs to assist vulnerable populations: Medicare (for citizens over the age of 65) and Medicaid (for the poor). These two programs were also responsible for ending racial segregation in US hospitals, as institutions that carried on with the practice were no longer eligible to receive federal payments.

Despite these advances, numerous problems continue to plague the American health care system. Some of its deficits include fragmented services caused by overspecialization; an emphasis on disease treatment rather than disease prevention; and a high level of **bureaucratization** (page 43), which some studies have shown to be two to four times higher than those of the health care systems of other Western nations.

Championed by President Barack Obama, the Affordable Care Act was passed by **Congress** (page 69) in 2010 with the aim of reforming the troubled US health care system. Under the law, citizens without health care coverage (of which there were an estimated 48 million in 2012) are required to subscribe to a modestly subsidized, means-tested private health insurance plan. The decentralized scheme gives each state the option of running its own health insurance "marketplace." Some view the law as indicative of the US government's preference for market-based (rather than state-based) solutions to national social problems.

HEREDITARY PRINCIPLE

Under the *hereditary principle*, the leadership of a state is passed down from one family member to another. The model is most commonly found in monarchies, where the crown is usually transferred to successive generations of the same royal family. However, it may also operate in **despotic** (page 83), non-monarchical governments: North Korea, for example, has been ruled by three generations of the Kim dynasty since 1948.

Advocates of the hereditary principle claim it assures continuity in the national government, placing power and **wealth** (page 259) in the hands of a single family line that can predictably manage state affairs. Societies led by successful royal dynasties, they say, are highly stable and often garner a significant amount of popular support. Critics note that the hereditary principle may be relatively innocuous in countries such as the United Kingdom, where the royal family holds no real political power; however, genuine hereditary rulers, unconstrained by **democratic** (page 78) mechanisms such as **elections** (page 92), tend to maintain traditional institutions that serve their own interests at the expense of the larger society's. In this view, the hereditary principle is poorly equipped to guard against abuses of state power.

HIERARCHY

The term *hierarchy* refers to the ranking of positions of authority within a governmental or **bureaucratic** (page 43) organization. Hierarchies are typically accompanied by a well-integrated system of command and control. Power is transferred downward from a central authority to a series of increasingly subordinate positions, each of which is answerable to the level immediately above it. Social scientists use the word "nestedness" to describe hierarchical structures: each level is organized into units that are in turn divided into subunits, with the same pattern repeating down to the bottom—much like a Russian Matryoshka doll. Hierarchies are highly formalized: at each level the roles, relationships, and behaviors of those involved are constrained by an established set of rational-legal rules. They also entail a highly specialized division of **labor** (page 143), obliging each unit to adhere to its own prescribed tasks.

Hierarchies are common features of modern life, often credited with increasing the efficiency of the organizations in which they operate. Some observers object to their unequal power relations and anti-**democratic** (page 78) decision-making processes, which, they argue, contribute to a loss of individual **autonomy** (page 33) and creativity.

ADOLF HITLER

Arguably the most notorious political figure of the twentieth century, *Adolf Hitler* is associated with some of the most barbaric crimes in human history. Born in Austria in 1889, Hitler rose to power in Germany in the 1920s as the head of the Nazi Party (National Socialist German Workers Party). He was imprisoned in 1923 on charges of attempting to overthrow the Weimar Republic—the German government at the time—in a failed coup known as the "Beer Hall Putsch." He was convicted of treason and remanded to Landsberg Prison. It was there that he wrote his infamous political pamphlet, *Mein Kampf* ("My Struggle"). The manifesto, which was widely distributed across Germany, is a rambling ideological attack on Jews, communists, and other racially and politically inferior "undesirables"—all presumed threats to the superior "Aryan race" and the National Socialist movement.

H

After his release from prison in 1924, the highly charismatic Hitler continued to propagate many of the **anti-Semitic** (page 23) and anticommunist views outlined in *Mein Kampf*. His rhetoric was warmly received by many Germans, as it offered them scapegoats for the economic miseries of the Great Depression and the aftereffects of Germany's involvement in **World War I** (page 262). In the elections of 1933, the Nazi Party captured the largest number of seats in the Reichstag (the German parliament), allowing Hitler to ascend to the office of Chancellor. The following year, he was installed as the *Führer* (or leader) of the Third Reich, giving his Nazi Party **totalitarian** (page 240) control of the government. Hitler immediately set out to rid Germany of its Jewish population, and to capture territory from Poland and other surrounding nations from which millions of ethnic Germans hailed. This effort, along with improvements to the German economy, won him substantial popular support.

Hitler and the National Socialists thus faced little domestic opposition as they embarked upon a systematic program of genocide, which continued until the end of **World War II** (page 266). Known now as the Holocaust, this campaign resulted in the imprisonment, enslavement, and extermination of nearly six million Jews and millions of others, including communists, Gypsies, homosexuals, and Jehovah's Witnesses—all of whom the Third Reich found guilty of being *Untermenschen* ("sub-humans"). Hitler's Nazi regime has been held responsible for the deaths of an estimated 19.3 million people.

(Opposite) After being appointed German Chancellor in 1933, Adolf Hitler went on to orchestrate the mass killings of more than 19 million people.

HOMELAND SECURITY

The term *Homeland Security* entered the American political vocabulary in 2002, when **Congress** (page 69) passed the Homeland Security Act in response to the September 11, 2001 **terrorist** (page 238) attacks on New York City and Washington, DC. The law resulted in the creation of a new cabinet agency known as the Department of Homeland Security (DHS). Its stated mission is to protect the population, territory, infrastructure, and **sovereignty** (page 226) of the **United States** (page 248), and to "ensure a homeland that is safe, secure, and resilient against terrorism and other hazards."

The Department of Homeland Security reorganized 187 federal agencies—including the Federal Emergency Management Agency and the Department of Immigration and Customs Enforcement—and brought them under a single central authority, the largest such body in the world today. Despite the enormous scope of the DHS, many homeland security operations remain under the control of other federal departments—notably, the Central Intelligence Agency, the Federal Bureau of Investigation, and the Department of Defense.

As a concept and as an institution, the idea of homeland security has been criticized on a number of counts. Some argue that, in attempting to carry out its mandate to protect American citizens from possible terrorist threats, the DHS has engaged in activities inconsistent with the principles of the US **Constitution** (page 72), and particularly the **Bill of Rights** (page 37): taking advantage of powers granted to the **government** (page 118) under the 2001 USA Patriot Act, the DHS has at times abrogated the **civil rights and liberties** (page 54) of US citizens, including the right to privacy and the right to be protected from indiscriminate searches and seizures.

Some add that America's homeland security policies have flouted principles of **international law** (page 133). For example, under the administration of President George W. Bush, the US government sought to exclude "enemy combatants" captured by **military** (page 168) force from the Geneva Convention's international norms governing the treatment of wartime prisoners. In this context, many saw the concept of homeland security as a means of providing ideological legitimation for the subjection of detained terrorism suspects to "extraordinary rendition" techniques; they argued that the US should abide by the treaty, even though it was not a signatory to all of its portions.

Some have also questioned whether the billions of tax dollars spent on homeland security have been necessary to achieve America's antiterrorism objectives, and whether the symbolism of a Department of Homeland Security has been more important to the US government than the efficacy of its operations.

HOUSE OF REPRESENTATIVES

Along with the **Senate** (page 212), the *House of Representatives* is one of the two chambers that comprise the United States **Congress** (page 69). Its main responsibility is to formulate national legislation. The House and the Senate deliberate and vote on proposed legislation independently; bills that pass both chambers are then sent to the president, who may either veto them or sign them into law. While both arms of Congress are equally responsible for making federal law, the **Constitution** (page 72) grants members of the House (known as Representatives or Congresspersons) certain powers that their counterparts in the Senate lack: they can propose revenue-raising bills, initiate impeachment proceedings against government officials (which are then moved to the Senate for trial), and elect the president if no candidate receives a majority of votes in the Electoral College.

The number of Representatives assigned to each state is determined in proportion to its population. Accordingly, populous states like California have many Representatives, while less populous states such as Wyoming have only one (the minimum number that each state must possess). There are a total of 435 voting members in the House, along with six non-voting members. The proceedings of the chamber are presided over by the Speaker of the House. The Speaker is customarily the leader of the House Democratic Caucus or the House Republican Conference, depending on which party has the majority of votes needed to elect its candidate to the post.

Under the Articles of Confederation that preceded the Constitution, Congress was organized as a one-chambered body, with only one vote allocated to each state. This worried James Madison and other framers of the Constitution: having a single chamber representing the citizenry at large—a "People's House," as they called it—left the property of wealthy landowners vulnerable to appropriation by the propertyless majority, whom Madison characterized as having a "rage for paper money" and similar "wicked projects." To protect the property rights of the minority against the **tyranny** (page 244) of the majority, Madison proposed a two-chambered solution, placing the more democratic institution of the House in a subordinate position to an upper house, or Senate. He envisioned the Senate as a more deliberative body that would guard against the eruption of mass sentiments. His proposals were eventually incorporated under Article One of the Constitution, which established the present two-chambered Congress.

President Obama addressing Congress about his health care reform bill, which needed approval by both the House and the Senate to become law.

HUMAN RIGHTS

The term *human rights* has come into popular usage only relatively recently. The first major modern statement on the concept was the *Declaration of the Rights of Man and the Citizen* of 1789, the founding legal document of the **French Revolution** (page 109). The declaration averred that all men are naturally free and protected equally under the law.

However, the idea that the law or a lawgiver should determine and defend the legal rights of the members of a political community dates back to antiquity. According to some authors, there is evidence of certain human rights protections in the Code of King Hammurabi, who ruled Babylonian civilization almost 4,000 years ago. Later, in the fifth to first century BC, the Roman Republic guaranteed its citizens the right to hold public office, formulate legislation, administer criminal **justice** (page 140), and participate in elections. In so doing, it laid the normative foundations for modern principles of justice and the protection of every human being's inherent dignity.

The contemporary notion of human rights arose from the framework of international organizations and covenants created upon the establishment of the **United Nations** (page 245), or UN, in 1945. As worked out by the UN, human rights law encompasses two broad areas of concern. The first is the realm of humanitarian law, which the UN has attempted to codify through initiatives like the 1949 Geneva Convention on the Prevention and Punishment of the Crime of Genocide, and the establishment of the International Criminal Court in 1998. The second concerns the idea of fundamental human rights, a concept developed in the UN's 1948 *Universal Declaration of Human Rights* (UDHR). In its first article, the UDHR asserts that "all human beings are born free and equal in dignity and rights. They are endowed with reason and conscience and should act towards one another in a spirit of brotherhood." In subsequent articles, the UDHR delineates three main categories of basic human rights: political and **civil rights** (page 54), socioeconomic and security rights, and the rights of minorities and other vulnerable populations. To help nation-states defend and advance human rights, numerous international treaties have been enacted under UN auspices; they include the International Covenant on Civil and Political Rights and the Convention on the Rights of the Child. Unlike the UDHR, they have not been affirmed by all UN member states.

I

IMMIGRATION

The process by which nonresidents enter a nation and settle permanently or temporarily as residents is known as *immigration*. Its flip side is emigration, the process of leaving one's country of origin for another. Immigration is often motivated by unfavorable circumstances in the immigrant's home country, such as lack of employment opportunities, **poverty** (page 193), natural disasters, political persecution, and racial, ethnic, or religious discrimination.

Today, the **governments** (page 118) of **sovereign** (page 226) nation-states decide which immigrants to admit and how to integrate them into their newly adopted societies. The idea that the right to immigrate should not be absolute, but rather subject to conditions imposed by the host country, was defended by Enlightenment philosophers like Immanuel Kant. Kant argued that all sovereign states are obliged to extend the right of "hospitality" to foreigners seeking to enter their borders, but with certain stipulations. For example, the would-be immigrant must be a citizen of another nation-state, behave peaceably in the host country, abide by its laws and **taxation** (page 236) policies, and give it something in return. In Kant's view, opening up national borders without any such conditions would serve only to invite the prospect of a "war of each against all."

The question of which conditions, if any, should limit the right of immigration remains the subject of much debate. A key point of contention concerns the fact that immigration is often attempted by people in desperate economic circumstances. In many contemporary Western societies there is a popular perception that immigrants, particularly "undocumented" immigrants from poor countries, do little more than "steal" jobs from the existing citizenry. Anti-immigration rhetoric is also often tinged with ethnocentric or **racist** (page 200) assumptions—for example, the belief that immigration dilutes the host nation's "authentic" cultural and linguistic traditions and its demographic makeup. Such views have been attributed to (and denied by) Great Britain's UK Independence Party, for example. They have also been voiced by the **Tea Party** (page 237) and other right-wing political movements and government officials in the **United States** (page 248).[9] For their part, supporters of immigration argue that it has many benefits: it enables countries to fill employment vacancies in certain sectors of the job market; promotes a cosmopolitan exchange of ideas and cultural traditions across national borders; and offers relief to refugees, asylum seekers, and others facing dire economic and political circumstances in their home countries.

Millions of European immigrants arrived to the United States through Ellis Island, near the famed *Statue of Liberty*.

I

IDEOLOGY AND POLITICS

One of the most important and influential accounts of the relationship between *ideology and politics* was set forth by Niccolò Machiavelli, the first great theorist of modern **statecraft** (page 230). In his 1513 book *The Prince*, Machiavelli contends that the ruler must be under no illusions about the basic purpose of his regime: to acquire, maintain, and expand power. If he is to be successful, however, the prince must conceal this objective from his subjects, and persuade them that he is ruling in accord with their interests. He should *appear* to be just, humane, religious, and so forth, while never forgetting that he is something else entirely.

If they are convinced of the yarns he has spun, the people will consent to his rule and grant it legitimacy. Potential challenges to the prince's authority will thus be averted, leaving him free to pursue his own objectives in a climate of social stability. Machiavelli's claim that success in politics is dependent upon throwing an ideological veil over the state's underlying relationships of power and domination had an enormous impact on the development of Western political thought, influencing traditions from *Realpolitik* (or political realism) to **Marxism** (page 166).

Niccolò Machiavelli, born in 1469, believed that great statesmen must control their subjects not only through physical force but also through ideological manipulation.

IMPERIALISM

The concept of *imperialism* has attracted the attention of writers from numerous disciplines, including historians, political theorists, and cultural critics. Emerging in the literature in the second half of the nineteenth century, it refers to a situation in which powerful **states** (page 229) establish and extend political control over distant territories. These territories are transformed into colonies, which are governed from an imperial metropolitan center for direct or indirect economic benefit. Today, critics often use the term "imperialism" rather loosely, applying it to any foreign policy agenda viewed as expansionist, aggressive, and oriented toward political, economic, and cultural domination.

I

Although empires with a center of supreme command have been part of the world's political landscape since antiquity, the word "imperialism" is generally reserved for the period of **colonial** (page 61) rule that arose in the eighteenth century. At this time, **capitalism** (page 44) took hold as the prevailing economic system of Western nation-states, affording them tremendous economic and **military** (page 168) advantages. With the aid of these resources, the Western powers adopted and pursued formal policies of acquisition, annexation, and administration of overseas territories. Between 1880 and 1914, much of the world had been brought under the direct political control or influence of the imperialist nations of Europe—notably Great Britain, Germany, the Netherlands, France, and Belgium. Imperialist domination of colonized territories (which entailed the unequal distribution of political and economic resources) was legitimized by an attendant ideological worldview: imperialist regimes portrayed themselves as intellectually and morally superior, and destined to bring "civilization" to the "backward," "racially inferior" populations and cultures over which they ruled.

In the 1890s, many commentators began to associate imperialism with a new stage in the development of the international capitalist order. Leaving behind an earlier era in which the economy was based largely on **free-market** (page 108) principles, imperialism was characterized by active collaboration among the European powers. At the Berlin Conference of 1884, for example, German leader Otto von Bismarck suggested parceling out colonial rule over Africa to assure European control of the continent. Meanwhile, drawing on the insights of the **liberal** (page 152) writer John A. Hobson, the **Marxist** (page 166) theoretician and **Bolshevik** (page 41) leader Vladimir Lenin developed a portrait of imperialism as a new, "higher" phase of capitalism. His analysis generated a vast body of literature, to which Nikolai Bukharin, Rudolf Hilferding, Rosa Luxemburg, and other Marxist writers also contributed.

INEQUALITY

Inequality refers to a situation in which rewards or opportunities are distributed unevenly among different groups or classes, or among different individuals within a particular group. It may be mandated by law or fostered by prevailing institutions, social practices, or systems of belief. In whatever guise, inequality has been and continues to be a feature of all human societies. The question of whether it is unavoidable has generated much debate among **liberals** (page 152), **Marxists** (page 166), and proponents of other political perspectives.

Most liberals concede that in a **free-market** (page 108) economy, life chances, wealth, social privileges, and leverage over the political process will be distributed unequally; at least some level of inequality is, for them, an acceptable cost to bear in view of the general economic growth and prosperity to which **capitalism** (page 44) gives rise. Some also note that, despite their doctrinal commitments against it, both former and current **communist** (page 64) regimes have succeeded in producing novel forms of inequality. Yet many Marxists refuse to view such avowedly communist systems as exemplars of their ideal, and insist that inequality between socioeconomic classes is neither a necessary nor a desirable feature of human society.

INTERNATIONAL LAW

The eighteenth-century thinker Jeremy Bentham is credited with coining the term *international law* to refer to the system of legal rules that govern relations between sovereign nation-states. Over the years, his description has been broadened considerably, bringing legally recognized international organizations and some individuals under its scope. Moreover, international law is no longer just a collection of legal regulations as Bentham conceived of it, but rather an evolving, complex body of norms, principles, and practices.

As an independent order situated outside the legal systems of individual states, today's canon of international law deals not only with traditional issues like war, peace, and diplomacy, but also with issues such as **human rights** (page 128), trade, and space law. Although it is an expressly legal framework, its development has been shaped in important ways by ethical arguments and principles.

International law should be distinguished from international comity, whose principles oblige nation-states to extend certain diplomatic courtesies to one another on terms that are not legally binding; the same can be said of non-binding resolutions issued by the **United Nations** (page 245) General Assembly.

INTERNATIONAL RELATIONS

International relations (IR) is an academic discipline that examines relationships among nations, nongovernmental organizations, multinational businesses, and other international actors. In the continental European and British academy, IR is a separate interdisciplinary field; in the **United States** (page 248), it constitutes a subfield of political science. Political analysis is often concerned with the institutional structures, principles, and behavior of **sovereign** (page 226) states—entities that are usually recognized as having the authority to exercise the force of law within their national borders. In contrast, IR considers relationships among actors operating in an environment where there is no common superior authority—a climate that some have likened to **anarchy** (page 22).

There is much debate within IR regarding how to analyze what is being studied (methodology) and how to understand and interpret it (epistemology). Many international relationists subscribe to positivist epistemological approaches, meaning that they attempt to scientifically determine whether the hypothetical models they have developed are predictive of the behavior of international actors. Other analysts, known as interpretivists, focus on understanding rather than predicting interactions among different international players. A third group rejects both approaches, arguing that they do little more than uphold the legitimacy of existing global power structures. Known as post-positivists, they aim to disarticulate such structures and liberate the disadvantaged groups currently trapped within them.

Post-positivist IR is part of a broader philosophical movement known as "critical theory," which also encompasses schools of thought such as poststructuralism, **feminism** (page 106), and neo-**Marxism** (page 166). Neo-Marxist IR examines how the global economy's **free-market** (page 108) forces help create structural inequality between nation-states and other international entities. Some neo-Marxists, drawing on the work of the early-twentieth-century theorist Antonio Gramsci, are particularly attentive to the role of "consent" in legitimating and sustaining international power relations: they argue that the free market endures because a belief in its propriety is fostered among individuals and groups, including those who are most adversely affected by its operations.

IRANIAN REVOLUTION

The 1979 overthrow of Iranian leader Mohammad Reza Shah Pahlavi (or simply, "the Shah") was a pivotal event in contemporary Iranian history; it significantly impacted the political climate of Iran and the broader Persian Gulf region.

The movement to depose the Shah first gained momentum in October 1977, when his opponents launched a civil resistance campaign. It was fueled by widespread dissatisfaction with the Shah's close ties to Western nations such as the United States, which were moving Iranian society in an increasingly secular direction. There were also complaints about the regime's inept economic policies, corruption, human rights violations, and indifference to social justice. The tide of civil unrest reached its peak during the summer and winter of 1978, with a series of nationwide strikes and public demonstrations against the Shah. Under the pressure of this public outcry, the ruler fled Iran in January 1979.

The removal of Iran's last Persian monarch created a political vacuum that was soon filled

Demonstrators gather on the eve of the 1979 Iranian Revolution in Tehran's Shahyad Square, which was renamed Azadi—Freedom—Square shortly after.

I

by the Grand Ayatollah Ruhollah Khomeini, who returned from a fifteen-year-long exile to become the Supreme Leader of the Islamic Republic of Iran in December 1979. With the Ayatollah at the helm, the Shah's pro-Western, secular, and semi-**absolutist** (page 15) monarchy was overturned. It was replaced by an anti-Western, theocratic-**republican** (page 206) constitution based on a set of religious principles known as the Guardianship of the Islamic Jurists.

The impact of Khomeini's Shia version of Islamic revival was felt far beyond the borders of Iran. The regime's attack on capitalism and Western (particularly American) meddling in Iranian affairs garnered international attention, as did its support for non-Muslim revolutionary movements in countries such as Nicaragua, Northern Ireland, and South Africa. In the Muslim world, the triumph of the Iranian Revolution was greeted with enthusiasm, inspiring a successful Islamic insurgency movement in Lebanon and similar (but ultimately unsuccessful) campaigns in Saudi Arabia, Egypt, and Syria.

Not long after its founding, Khomeini's regime became embroiled in the Iran–Iraq War. Instigated by Iraq, which sought to clip the wings of the Ayatollah's newly launched Islamic Revolution, this eight-year-long conflict resulted in hundreds of thousands of deaths on both sides of the border. While it did not produce the hoped-for overthrow of Saddam Hussein's Sunni-Muslim-dominated government in Iraq, most Iranians strongly supported it. It helped cement national unity and heighten the devotion of revolutionary groups intent on advancing the cause of Islamic revival.

Today, the legacy of the Iranian Revolution remains disputed. Some observers applaud Iran's Islamic government for rectifying many of the social problems that plagued the country during the Shah's reign. For example, after the Revolution, illiteracy and infant mortality rates decreased significantly, and the quality of education and health care for the poor improved. For critics, these advances pale in comparison to the prevailing climate of political repression for which the Iranian regime is responsible. Although they are now found in greater numbers at universities and in the civil service sector, women continue to face systematic discrimination in Iran. Non-Muslim minorities are also denied equal rights. Members of the Baha'i Faith, labeled as "heretics" and "subversives," have been subject to particularly pronounced political persecution and human rights abuses. In addition, under the authority of the Ministry of Culture and Islamic Guidance, Iran's media are tightly controlled and subject to strict, religion-based censorship.

J

JACOBINS

The **French Revolution** (page 109) of 1789 through 1799 aimed to overthrow the feudal aristocracy that had ruled France throughout the Middle Ages. At its forefront was the *Jacobin* Club, a group of revolutionaries who took their name from the Dominican convent in Paris where they met. While it was not the only revolutionary organization in France, it was certainly the most radical.

The Jacobins joined a group of rebellious peasants and urban laborers known as the *sans-culottes* to demand social and economic equality, as well as popular democracy. They gained a significant number of seats in the upper chamber of the French Assembly, which earned them the nickname "The Mountain." Aided by the *sans-culottes* and under the leadership of Robespierre, the Jacobins instituted the notorious Reign of Terror: they employed violent measures—including beheadings—to crush those opposed to the ideals of the new French Republic.

In contemporary France, the word "Jacobin" is sometimes used to describe one who supports centralizing the authority of the government and giving it extensive powers to intervene in private affairs.

JESUS

In addition to being the principal figure of Christianity, *Jesus* of Nazareth has had a profound influence on the development of the politics, arts, and culture of Western civilization. Most contemporary scholars view his existence as a historical reality.

Although many aspects pertaining to the life and times of Jesus have been disputed for millennia—both within Christianity and outside of it—most Christian denominations concur on at least a few basic points. They believe Jesus is the Son of God, sent to Earth in order to liberate its people from bondage and oppression. They also claim he lived in the town of Nazareth in Galilee (now in northern Israel), where he assumed the role of a Jewish rabbi and wandering preacher. Most Christians also believe that he was conceived by his mother Mary through the agency of the Holy Spirit. They add that he was crucified in Jerusalem under the orders of Pontius Pilate, the Roman prefect, and that he will return to Earth upon the coming of the apocalypse—the final and complete destruction of the world. For most Christians, acceptance of Jesus as their Lord and Savior enables them to befriend God, who will then judge them favorably upon their deaths and offer them eternal salvation.

The story of Jesus's life as recounted in the Bible's New Testament has left an indelible mark on Western culture, serving as the inspiration for many of its artistic masterpieces—notably during the Renaissance era. Over the millennia, Jesus's name has been called upon to promote various political agendas. In the late Middle Ages, the European monarchs endeavored to justify their **absolutist** (page 15) rule by proclaiming themselves his disciples and invoking the authority

Jesus of Nazareth has been taken up as a symbol of both the oppressed and the powerful over the course of human history.

of **divine right** (page 87). In the contemporary era, many conservative evangelical Christians see the growing militarization and nuclearization (see **nuclear weapons**, page 180) of the modern state as a harbinger of Jesus's Second Coming. They also find support for their highly conservative views on sexuality, marriage, and family life in their interpretation of his teachings.

On the other side of the political spectrum, adherents of movements such as liberation theology view Jesus as an egalitarian reformer; an advocate for social **justice** (page 140) and **human rights** (page 128). They point to a variety of his moral teachings, such as the Parable of the Good Samaritan, in which he instructs his followers to worship God without prejudice or violence, and to offer comfort to those afflicted by hunger, disease, and poverty. Many Christians have understood such claims as validations of the contemporary **Welfare State** (page 259), which offers protections and benefits to the elderly, the sick, the poor, and other disadvantaged communities.

Jesus's call to "Render unto Caesar the things that are Caesar's, and unto God the things that are God's" (Matthew 22:21) has likewise been of great political significance, sparking a wide-ranging debate about the relationship between Church and State. Some Christians have interpreted Jesus's admonition as a defense of the separation of the two. Others read the plea to "Render unto Caesar" as an argument against supporting governmental policies that are inconsistent with Jesus's moral ideals. The American Quakers, for example, appeal to it in order to justify withholding taxes from governments that would use them to wage war and kill innocent people.

Another pronouncement with profound political implications is Jesus's so-called Golden Rule: "Do unto others as you would have them do into you." Here, Jesus rejects the idea of using others as mere means for one's selfish ends. The Golden Rule was incorporated into the secular political philosophy of Immanuel Kant and other thinkers of the European Enlightenment, at which time it also became the basis for modern **liberal** (page 152) ideals such as equality.

Liberal John Stuart Mill saw Jesus's Crucifixion as a cautionary tale against the **tyranny** (page 244) of majority rule. In his book *On Liberty*, Mill cites the popular support for the Roman religious establishment's execution of Jesus as an argument against the suppression of minority opinion. The right to free speech must always be universal, as the truth is oftentimes on the side of the marginalized.

JUSTICE

Justice can be described as a situation in which the **rights** (page 208) of all individuals are equally protected and each person is equally respected; a certain moral quality of individuals and political institutions is necessary to achieve this outcome. This rather loose definition, however, fails to encapsulate the wide-ranging debates about justice that have animated political philosophy since antiquity. For the ancient Greeks and the theologians of medieval **Christianity** (page 46) and Islam, justice sat alongside wisdom, courage, and moderation as one of the cardinal **virtues** (page 255). In *The Republic*, Plato argued that a society would obtain justice when its social classes and the elements of each individual's soul were rightly ordered. In his *Nicomachean Ethics*, Aristotle portrayed general justice as a situation in which one deploys all of the virtues in the treatment of other persons, thereby distinguishing it from particular justice, which involves the fair exchange and distribution of wealth, honors, and other goods. His account was taken up by later philosophers, who differentiated between justice oriented toward reciprocation and the rectification of harms (commutative justice) and justice aimed at the allocation of commonly held goods (distributive justice).

In the modern era, the *social contract* theorist Thomas Hobbes claimed that individuals are incapable of achieving justice in their "natural state" of absolute **freedom** (page 107). In order to preserve their lives and property, they are rationally compelled to surrender some of their rights to an all-powerful sovereign. Utilizing the coercive power of civil **law** (page 147), the **state** (page 229) then makes them behave justly. In a similar vein, John Locke insisted that the state facilitates justice by constraining citizens whose actions infringe upon others' natural rights to life, liberty, and property. However, unlike Hobbes, he sought to limit the state's authority over individuals' private affairs.

In his 1971 book *A Theory of Justice*, the American philosopher John Rawls proposed an account of justice as "fairness." In his model, justice is obtained when individuals determine a society's governing principles behind a procedural "veil of ignorance"—that is, as if lacking knowledge of certain biographical facts about themselves, such as their social status and strength. As elaborated in *A Theory of Justice* and modified in later texts, Rawls's account of justice continues to exert an important influence on contemporary thinking about the question of justice.

J

K

MARTIN LUTHER KING, JR.

Martin Luther King, Jr. was the most renowned leader of the movement for **civil rights** (page 54) that arose in the United States in the 1950s and 1960s. King's movement helped abolish legalized racial segregation in the American South, an institution colloquially known as Jim Crow. It also pressured federal lawmakers into passing the landmark Civil Rights Act of 1964 and the Voting Rights Act of 1965.

In 1954, King became a Baptist minister in Montgomery, Alabama, and a year later earned a doctorate in theology. Inspired by **Mahatma Gandhi**'s (page 114) **nonviolent resistance** (page 179) movement against colonial rule in India, as well as by the tenets of his own Christian faith, the twenty-six-year-old King was at the forefront of the 1955 Montgomery Bus Boycott. The boycott sparked a civil suit before the US Supreme Court, and resulted in a local ordinance that desegregated the Montgomery bus system in 1956. This victory was greeted by a violent backlash on the part of the city's white establishment.

Undaunted, King helped found the Southern Christian Leadership Conference (SCLC) in 1957. As the organization's first president, he continued to struggle against racial segregation in the face of violent opposition. In 1963, he led demonstrations in Birmingham, Alabama, and a march on Washington—the site of his famous "I Have a Dream" speech—and in 1965, he participated in the Selma protests. These events, among others, brought the civil rights cause into the media spotlight and drew legions of blacks and white sympathizers into the movement.

Towards the end of his life, King broadened the focus of his struggle: he spoke out against the war in Vietnam and called for a Poor People's Campaign to eliminate poverty. He thus began to build a broad-based movement of social **democracy** (page 78), and to question the legitimacy of America's ruling power structure. Those in charge of that structure sensed the threat he posed; under orders from Attorney General Robert F. Kennedy, and alleging that King's movement had been infiltrated by **communists** (page 64), the Federal Bureau of Investigation (FBI) began to secretly record his and other SCLC leaders' telephone conversations. FBI Director J. Edgar Hoover attempted to use some of the personal details collected in the wiretaps to discredit King and remove him from the movement's leadership. King was assassinated in Memphis, Tennessee, in 1968, sparking riots in many cities throughout the US.

K

Martin Luther King, Jr. (left) at a meeting with President Lyndon B. Johnson (right), whom he was able to pressure into passing the 1964 Civil Rights Act.

L

LABOR

Labor occurs when human beings apply their physical and mental energies toward the production of something, be it a material good, a service, or an idea. Regardless of the context in which it takes place, all labor uses time, consuming at least part of the days, and ultimately part of the lifetimes, of those who engage in it. Unlike play, labor is generally not perceived as an end in itself: it is meant to generate a product, especially a product that becomes available to others and useful for the reproduction of the community.

Throughout human history, societies have devised numerous systems of labor. In ancient Greece and Rome, for example, skilled and unskilled slaves were utilized in agriculture and manufacturing. In the feudal economy of the Middle Ages, aristocratic landlords granted protection to peasant farmers and gave them the right to use their land as a means of sustenance. In exchange for these privileges, peasants were obliged to pay the **aristocracy** (page 30) with both goods and services. This arrangement was enforced not only by the aristocratic landowners, but also by the executive and judicial authority of the **state** (page 229). Under feudalism, areas that were not under the direct rule of the aristocracy were known as free cities. It was here that laborers in the manufacturing crafts (blacksmiths, stonemasons, shoemakers, and so on) went to ply their trades. To protect their interests, they organized themselves into guilds. However, the fate of the guild worker remained in the hands of the powerful guild masters, who alone had the authority to promote apprentices to the master level. Accordingly, despite being situated in the free cities, guild craftsmen managed only to free themselves from the rule of the aristocracy; their labor was still anything but "free."

In the eighteenth century, the terms of production began to shift: small-scale trades and feudal agriculture began to give way to a new, industrialized system. Unlike the older labor schemes, industrial manufacturing added novel features to the production process, including a highly specialized division of labor. The British economist Adam Smith could

L

only marvel at how, in the modern factory, the manufacture of a single pin involved an array of different workers, each making his own specific contribution towards the achievement of the final product. The process of production was also revolutionized by a technological innovation: the industrial machine. The first modern industrial steam engine, patented by James Watt in 1781, enabled factory owners to increase productivity rates and move the industrialization process forward apace.

Known as the Industrial Revolution, this period saw a massive exodus of peasants from the rural countryside to large towns and cities, where they found work as unskilled workers in newly constructed manufacturing plants. Released from their ties to the old feudal landowners, they were now bound by different terms of employment: in exchange for their labor, they were given wages. The peasantry of feudal Europe was thus transformed into a new working class, while control over the process of production was wrested from the feudal aristocracy and consigned to a new class of modern factory owners.

The analysis and criticism of the **capitalist** (page 44) system of production became the life's work of the nineteenth-century German thinker Karl Marx. Marx sought to demonstrate how, under capitalism, laborers remain estranged from the conditions and product of their labor. He argued that in the capitalist system, a small class of **property** (page 199) owners controls the means of production, depriving workers of the capacity to direct the labor process themselves. Mechanized, routinized, and host to a highly specialized division of labor, capitalist production compels the worker to increase his output while relieving it of all creativity. Although labor is always a social process, the social relations between workers now take the form of "relations between things": the worker is reduced to the level of the very commodities he produces. Capitalists appropriate these commodities and put them up for sale on the market, where they confront their producers "as something hostile and alien." Moreover, capitalists must retain some portion of the value generated by the workers in order to revolutionize the means of production, generate more surplus, and reproduce themselves as a class. Marx's analysis of the inherently exploitative nature of labor under capitalism has inspired numerous movements for both reform and radical transformation of the capitalist system.

(Opposite) Industrialization gave rise to the proletariat, or wage workers, which theorists like Karl Marx believed to be the basis for a communist revolution.

LAND

In politics, the term *land* encompasses much more than the simple idea of the ground beneath one's feet. It may refer, for example, to the physical territory over which nation-states declare the **right** (page 208) of **sovereignty** (page 226); to **property** (page 199) over which individuals claim private ownership rights; to a resource partially available to the **state** (page 229) for the construction of public infrastructure; to a resource controlled entirely by the state; or to one of the principal factors of the **free-market** (page 108) economy, along with capital and **labor** (page 143).

Throughout much of human history, landownership has been linked to social prestige. In medieval Europe, for example, land was awarded to feudal **aristocrats** (page 30) on the basis of their social status and rank. In owning land and passing it down to succeeding generations according to the **hereditary principle** (page 123), the aristocracy gained control over the process of production; it also acquired political power. In the late eighteenth century, with the advent of **capitalism** (page 44) and its attendant **republican** (page 206) policies, the aristocracy was compelled to relinquish its economic and political authority. Although sovereignty was now assumed to reside with the citizenry, land continued to be a factor in the retention of political power: full franchise rights (the right to vote and the right to hold public office) were initially extended only to landowners. It was not until the late nineteenth century, with the implementation of universal male suffrage, that landownership was abandoned as a criterion for full and equal citizenship.

The question of how land itself is to be utilized remains a controversial subject. In his 1689 text *Two Treatises of Government*, John Locke portrayed land (along with the earth's other natural resources) as available for private appropriation by those who labor upon, and thus modify, it.[10] He saw the possession of private property and individual **liberty** (page 155) as coextensive natural **rights** (page 208)—a perspective that was eventually incorporated into the founding legal documents of most modern constitutional republics. Over the centuries, large corporations and private industries have wielded their legal property rights to acquire land and further their own economic interests. This has often resulted in significant damage to the land in question and costs to the communities that depend on it, leading some to doubt the propriety of private landownership.

LAW

Simply put, a *law* is a rule of conduct, prescribed by a **sovereign** (page 226) **state** (page 229), to which citizens are obliged to adhere. Failure to obey the law generally leaves the lawbreaker liable to some sort of sanction or punishment commensurate with the severity of the violation. Throughout history, numerous systems of law have been devised, from the ancient Babylonian Code of King Hammurabi to the **Napoleonic** (page 172) Codes of the modern era. The law has become the principal mechanism by which political orders govern their members.

The question of why laws are necessary in the first place figured prominently in the discourses of Enlightenment political philosophy. Echoing the views of many other thinkers of his era, James Madison opined that the law is needed because men are not "angels," but rather are naturally self-interested, competitive, and inclined to pursue their affairs in isolation from one another. This portrait of human nature had already been advanced by the Late Renaissance thinker Niccolò Machiavelli, and endorsed in the seventeenth century by the founder of modern **liberalism** (page 152), Thomas Hobbes. Hobbes argued that man's "natural state" is one of absolute **freedom** (page 107), but that said freedom comes at a terrible cost: with no laws to constrain them, men are destined to destroy one another. For Hobbes, the purpose of the law is to allow people to exercise only *some* of their natural **rights** (page 208), so that a peaceable and moral civilization can be established. The law is thus a fundamentally coercive instrument predicated on the abridgement of human freedom. Citizens agree to be bound by the state's laws out of a rational fear for the chaos and bloodshed that would arise in their absence.

This idea of the law has been challenged by many thinkers. The philosophers Jean-Jacques Rousseau and Immanuel Kant, for example, claimed that the properly constituted law does not issue from an authority external to the citizenry; rather, it is a product of the citizens' deliberations about the universal rules to which they are to be bound. Kant, for one, insisted that the law cannot be construed as rational unless the citizens themselves determine, under the authority of their own free wills, which maxims are to become absolute. Freedom, argued Kant, is nothing more than obedience to one's self-prescribed laws.

LEAGUE OF NATIONS

The *League of Nations* (LN) was an international governmental body established in 1920 during the Paris Peace Conference, which concluded **World War I** (page 262). It was the first global organization to adopt world peace as one of its principal objectives. Echoing the ideals of Immanuel Kant, it insisted that future wars could be prevented only if nation-states arranged themselves in a cosmopolitan confederation, enjoyed mutual security, were committed to disarmament, and agreed to cooperate with one another to resolve contested issues. Among other things, League members were also required to abide by certain international standards regarding the treatment of laborers, indigenous communities, ethnic minorities, and prisoners of war.

The League's emphasis on peaceful dispute resolution marked a major shift from the previously belligerent diplomatic climate. However, lacking a military force of its own, the LN was powerless to enforce any of its resolutions. It ultimately proved incapable of preventing the onset of **World War II** (page 266), thus failing to fulfill its principal aim. It was dissolved in 1946 and replaced by the **United Nations** (UN) (page 245), which incorporated several of its agencies and organizations.

The first assembly of the League of Nations, held in 1920 in Geneva. The League was replaced by the United Nations in 1946.

LEGALISM

Legalism was the theoretical basis for China's first imperial regime, the Qin dynasty of 221 to 206 BC. Developed by philosopher Han Fei, its basic aim was to promote the "rule of **law**" (page 147) as both an ethical system and a pragmatic means of shaping the political life of society. Because it criticized the Confucian idea of "rule by virtue" and postulated a kind of **utilitarianism** (page 252), the doctrine was favored by China's new middle-class landowners.

Legalism consists of three main principles. *Fa*: The legal code must be clear, well-publicized, and equally binding upon all; the law, rather than the ruler himself, should serve as the foundation of the state. *Shu*: The ruler must enforce the law and employ special techniques to assure that administrators will not abuse their positions. *Shi*: The power and authority of the **state** (page 229) resides in the office, not the person, of the ruler, who must exercise "non-action" to enable the natural order of things to unfold.

Legalist regimes remained vulnerable to despotic rule, since, in contrast to modern **republican** (page 206) forms of government, they lacked a mechanism to check their centralized authority and guard against abuses of state power.

LEGISLATURE

The branch of the government that is responsible for making laws is known as the *legislature*. The legislature is normally part of the national government; however, in a **federalist** (page 105) system, smaller lawmaking bodies may also be established at the regional or state level. In **liberal** (page 152) theory, legislatures are said to be the basis of popular **sovereignty** (page 226): the laws they make are intended to reflect the will of the people, with whom the authority of the state ultimately resides. Elected by popular vote, legislators are charged with representing their constituents and formulating laws consistent with their interests.

Two basic types of legislature are employed in contemporary representative **democracies** (page 78). In the first, the authority of the legislative branch is clearly distinguished from that of the executive; such is the case in the **presidential** (page 194) democracy of the **United States** (page 248), for instance. In **parliamentary democracies** (page 189) such as the United Kingdom's, on the other hand, the executive is chosen by (and accountable to) the legislative branch.

A legislature consisting of only one chamber is unicameral; those with two chambers are bicameral. Both Great Britain, with its House of Lords and House of Commons, and the US, with its **Senate** (page 212) and **House of Representatives** (page 126), have bicameral legislatures. The US House has members from congressional districts within

L

each state (determined by population size), and the Senate consists of two representatives from each state (regardless of population size). The framers of the US **Constitution** (page 72) believed that, consistent with the principles of federalism, the two legislative chambers would check and limit one another's authority. They also felt that Senators would be more mindful of the interests of wealthy property owners than their counterparts in the House.

Prior to assuming their modern form, legislatures were constituted on different terms: the representatives of the old English Parliament, the Estates-General of France, and the Diet of the Holy Roman Empire, for example, were selected on the basis of the class or estate to which they belonged. This resulted in a lower house representing the middle classes, and an upper house representing the clergy and the nobility. These earlier bicameral structures were carried over into modern bicameral legislatures, but without social status or rank as criteria for selection.

L

LIBERAL DEMOCRACY

Liberal democracy is a form of representative **government** (page 118) that arose in the late eighteenth century from the ruins of Europe's old feudal orders. Inspired by Enlightenment ideals, liberal democracies regard the consent of their people—rather than God's will or the social status of their political leaders—as the basis of their legitimacy. Contemporary liberal-democratic orders have established a number of institutional mechanisms to assure that governmental actions remain anchored in the will of its citizenry. Among them, competitive multiparty **elections** (page 92) serve two main purposes: they allow citizens to both select the officials who will presumably best represent their interests, and to make their public policy preferences known to the government. Liberal democracies also enshrine the **separation of powers** (page 216) doctrine, which parcels out political authority among different governmental branches with specific designated functions. Rather than being concentrated in the hands of a single political entity (a king or a president, for example), a government with divided powers is said to be well positioned to "check and balance" itself against abuses of state power.

As its name suggests, liberal democracy aims to protect the **liberties** (page 155) and **rights** (page 208) of the individual. Civil rights, such as the right to a fair trial, are usually safeguarded through legal constitutional guarantees; civil liberties, such as the freedoms of speech and public assembly, sprout from the government's resolve to relieve people from undue interference in their private actions.

Following the collapse of the **Soviet Union** (page 226) in 1991, liberal democracy became the world's predominant governmental form. Despite the apparently near-universal acceptance of its legitimacy and permanence, it is not without its critics. Some argue that its founding principles—which aver that all who participate in political life do so on a completely free and equal basis—are at odds with the reality of political processes. They contend that those processes are in large measure controlled by powerful economic and political **elites** (page 94), which squeeze out the voices of those without such resources. For some, the policies of liberal-democratic governments are thus less a reflection of the will of the people than the will of those who are able to wield the political system in the service of their own narrow interests.

Elections are the centerpiece of liberal democracies, allowing officials to be held accountable by citizens.

LIBERALISM

Like all political philosophies, *liberalism* addresses the question of how to found and structure the political order. It emerged in seventeenth-century Europe, fueling an allied political movement that ultimately toppled prior religious and **absolutist** (page 15) forms of government in the continent. Although liberalism has developed in a variety of directions over the ensuing centuries, several basic claims are common to all its strains. Most critically, it is invested in the individual's fundamental **rights** (page 208) and **liberties** (page 155). The latter can be legitimately abridged only under special circumstances, the details of which continue to be debated. In any case, they should take precedence over the traditions, beliefs, and customs of the larger community. A number of associated theories of human nature are advanced in support of this thesis.

L

The seventeenth-century **social contract** (page 221) theorist Thomas Hobbes is generally recognized as being the founder of modern liberalism (though he himself did not employ the term). According to his philosophical anthropology, individuals in the "natural state" are constitutively free and equal; they may apply their own wills to shaping the direction of their lives. This view of human nature stands in stark contrast to the Catholic Church's doctrine of predestination, which views the fate of the individual as preordained by God.

For Hobbes, however, allowing people to exercise free will without any constraints would leave them in a state of perpetual insecurity—a "war of each against all" in which every individual would pursue his or her self-interests at the expense of everyone else's. The **state** (page 229) exists for no other reason than to prevent such a war. In exchange for peace and security, Hobbes argued, people will rationally agree to surrender some of their natural rights and freedoms to an all-powerful **sovereign** (page 226), whose task is to implement the natural law on their behalf. In maintaining that this sovereign's authority derives not from God but from the people, Hobbes breaks with the **divine right** (page 87) doctrine. Although the powers of the Hobbesian ruler are absolute, he is justified in constraining the private will only when its free exercise threatens the aims of the social contract—where the sovereign law is silent the individual remains free.

John Locke, the next great thinker within the social contract tradition, endorsed both Hobbes's view of humans as naturally free and equal, and his critique of rule by divine right. He did, however, dispute Hobbes's case for monarchical absolutism: he argued for severely limiting the scope of the state, such that it is no longer positioned to keep the people in "awe" of the ruler's authority. For Locke, the state's primary purpose is to defend the individual's right to **property** (page 199)—the right to acquire and accumulate goods and the right to liberty are tightly intertwined in his conception of human selfhood. Many of Locke's proposals were incorporated into the founding legal documents of the representative **democracies** (page 78) established in the late eighteenth century, including the **Constitution** (page 72) of the **United States** (page 248).

At that time, the liberal portrait of an individual who is inherently free and motivated by self-interest was also assimilated into the theories of **free-market** (page 108) economics advanced by British authors like Adam Smith, David Ricardo, and Thomas Malthus. Such a portrait fit nicely into their accounts of the **anarchic** (page 22), nature-like operations of the **capitalist** (page 44) market.

Another especially notable contributor to the philosophy of liberalism was the nineteenth-century thinker John Stuart Mill. In his 1859 text *On Liberty,* Mill mounted a robust defense of three fundamental freedoms: the freedoms of speech, public assembly, and individual taste. He argued against the **tyranny** (page 244) of majority rule and insisted that those with minority and dissenting opinions should not merely be permitted to air their contrarian views publicly—they in fact had a moral obligation to do so. To Mill, the state is justified in restraining the individual's basic freedoms only in instances where harm to others results from their expression.

In the twentieth century, one of the most important contributions to the liberal tradition was John Rawls's 1971 book *A Theory of Justice*. Rawls attempted to defend the propriety of the state's role in providing for the social welfare without abrogating the fundamental rights and freedoms of the individual. Rawls's conception of "justice as fairness" was challenged by numerous competing perspectives, including **communitarianism** (page 68).

(Above) Seventeenth-century political theorist Thomas Hobbes believed that government was necessary to maintain peace among self-interested individuals.

LIBERTARIANISM

Like **liberalism** (page 152)—a political doctrine with which it is sometimes confused—*libertarianism* defends the idea that people are naturally free and have a right to enjoy their **liberty** (page 155) without undue **government** (page 118) interference. The two philosophies fundamentally disagree, however, on what counts as such an interference. Classical liberals such as Thomas Hobbes give the **state** (page 229) ample authority to restrain the private will in cases where its free exercise threatens to compromise civil peace and stability. By contrast, libertarians argue that the government should intervene in private affairs as little as possible, so that each individual may enjoy a maximum level of freedom and decisional **autonomy** (page 33).

Libertarians are therefore more invested in government inaction than in government action. They give primacy to individual judgment, and are highly skeptical of state authority and coercive social institutions. They contend that, whenever the state applies the force of **law** (page 147), it gains control of people's bodies and lives in a way that deprives them of their dignity. By surrendering some of their natural **rights** (page 208) to the government, they argue, people risk being robbed of their creativity, spontaneity, and capacity to direct their lives as they see fit. While libertarians recognize that individuals must sometimes cooperate with one another, they maintain that such cooperation should take place voluntarily, not through the state's external imposition.

The libertarian argument for the maximization of individual freedom and minimization of state coercion has proved attractive to thinkers of various political stripes. Many contemporary libertarians fall on the right side of the political spectrum, at least with respect to economic issues: they advocate for the protection of private **property** (page 199) rights and for minimal government interference in the **free market** (page 108). Such libertarians tend to be more progressive on social issues, however, arguing against governmental surveillance of private communications and in favor of the rights of individuals to adopt nontraditional identities. Libertarian **socialists** (page 224), for their part, advocate for the abolition of **capitalism** (page 44) and cooperative ownership of the means of production, but on terms that would assure a maximum degree of human freedom.

LIBERTY

Political philosophers have approached the idea of *liberty* from many different angles. However, one useful schematization of the concept was offered by the German Enlightenment thinker Georg Wilhelm Friedrich Hegel. Hegel distinguished among three basic types of liberties: moral (the freedom of individuals to make moral choices); civil (the freedom that individuals exercise within civil society, such as the freedom to express thoughts and opinions); and political (the freedom that individuals enjoy in relation to the state, such as the freedom to assemble publicly). This is a decidedly modern model of liberty, for, in contrast to the conceptions that prevailed in pre-modern Europe, it applies to individuals rather than communities or social relations.

Hegel's account also illustrates how far the modern understanding of liberty has departed from that of the ancients. In antiquity, the Greeks saw the divide between free persons and slaves as one imposed by nature—liberty cannot be extended to those who do not possess it naturally. Free individuals at the time had the **right** (page 208) to own those considered to be slaves by nature; likewise, politically free communities could control those who lacked such freedom. For Aristotle in particular, liberty also entails equal political rights and the freedom to participate in political affairs—at least for adult males who possess reason and the ability to administer **justice** (page 140).

British author Thomas Hobbes was the first great theorist of the prevailing modern idea of liberty. He argued that the individual is free whenever he is relieved of impediments that hinder him from exercising his will as he sees fit. According to Hobbes, the freedom to act without constraint is humans' natural condition. There is only one rational justification for renouncing some portion of one's liberty and subjecting oneself to the legal obligations and constraints of civil society: to secure the natural right of self-preservation, which is imperiled when all are free to do as they will. Although modified in many different ways, Hobbes's conception of liberty as an absence of external constraints became the basis of the political doctrines of modern **liberalism** (page 152).

ABRAHAM LINCOLN

The political legacy of *Abraham Lincoln*, the sixteenth president of the United States, extends well beyond the country in which he lived and died. Lincoln oversaw one of the most turbulent periods of American history, a time of social crisis and violent struggle over the basic political direction of the nation. Under his leadership, America emerged from the **Civil War** of 1861 to 1865 (page 58) with its **republic** (page 206) of federated states intact and its chattel slavery system abolished.

The Kentucky-born Lincoln studied law as a young adult and went on to become a practicing attorney. From 1834 to 1846, he served four successive terms in the Illinois House of Representatives. These were immediately followed by a two-year term as US Congressman in Capitol Hill. A committed member of the Whig Party, Congressman Lincoln advocated for the modernization of American industry and banking, and for improvements in the nation's railway system; he also opposed the Mexican–American War—a position that did not sit well with voters in his home state of Illinois. Lincoln chose not to run for a second term in Congress, but reentered the political fray in 1854 as a leader of the newly formed **Republican Party** (page 206). In 1858, he ran against Democrat Stephen A. Douglas for a seat in the US Senate. Although he lost, his widely publicized debates with Douglas solidified his reputation as an orator and a firm opponent of slavery.

The Republican Party nominated Lincoln for president in 1860. He was once again opposed by Democrat Stephen A. Douglas, and also by Southern Democrat John C. Breckinridge and Constitutional Union Party candidate John Bell. Lincoln won handily in the North, but his anti-slavery positions drew in few votes from the Southern slaveholding states. Nevertheless, he defeated his rivals and assumed the presidency in 1860.

He had yet to set foot in the White House before seven Southern states formed the Confederate States of America, calling for secession from the Union and the preservation of slavery. In April 1861, the Confederate States Army opened fire on a Union garrison at Fort Sumter in South Carolina, a signal that a civil war was officially under way.

Worried that Southern troops might descend upon Washington, Lincoln imposed martial law in Maryland and authorized the suspension of the writ of **habeas corpus** (page 120), an order that was at one point extended to the nation at large. Under Lincoln's wartime measures, Union adversaries could be detained without a hearing, civilians could be tried in military courts, and the freedoms of speech and the press were at least partially curtailed.

Lincoln understood such steps to be merely temporary evils, required to reunite the nation and abolish slavery. He made a number of other critical moves in this regard, including his celebrated Emancipation Proclamation of 1863, his deployment of the US Army to safeguard freed slaves, and his support of the Thirteenth Amendment to the US Constitution, the aim of which was to permanently outlaw slavery.

In addition to these efforts, Lincoln is remembered for his ardent defense of individual **liberty** (page 155), equal rights, **republicanism** (page 206), and **democracy** (page 78)—ideals that he propounded in his famous Gettysburg Address of 1863. During postbellum Reconstruction, he tried to reconcile both sides of the bitter conflict. On April 15, 1865, just six days after Confederate General Robert E. Lee surrendered to Union General Ulysses S. Grant, Lincoln was assassinated by John Wilkes Booth, a partisan of the Confederate cause.

(Right) Abraham Lincoln declared millions of slaves free in his 1863 Emancipation Proclamation, setting the stage for the Thirteenth Amendment of the Constitution.

LOBBYING

The process by which individuals and organizations endeavor to persuade government officials to implement laws that benefit their interests is known as *lobbying*. The term "lobby" originated in the mid-seventeenth century: at this time, members of the English Parliament were often approached for favors in a large anteroom, or lobby, adjacent to the floor of the House of Commons. Those making the requests came to be known as "lobby agents" (or "lobbiers," and later "lobbyists," in the **United States**, page 248). The right to lobby is upheld by the constitutions of most contemporary representative **democracies** (page 78). The First Amendment to the US **Constitution** (page 72), for example, grants citizens the right "to petition the Government for a redress of grievances."

Organizations that typically engage in lobbying include private corporations, trade unions, and civic groups. Lobbying may be carried out by members of the group itself; however, it is more commonly entrusted to hired professionals. In pursuing their objectives, lobbyists employ a variety of strategies and techniques: they may present their cases before legislative committees; approach, or "buttonhole," government officials in public or private contexts; or barrage lawmakers with letters, campaign materials, emails, and telephone calls.

According to proponents of the theory of democratic pluralism, lobbying expands the scope of political participation by opening it up to a wide variety of groups and individuals. Democratic pluralists view lobbying as an even more important marker of a state's democratic legitimacy than **elections** (page 92) (which are, after all, only intermittent expressions of public sentiment). In their view, it is a mechanism for resolving conflicts among often diverse and competing political opinions. It provides lawmakers with the information they need to accurately assess the potential impact of proposed legislation, and to make judicious policy decisions on that basis. Moreover, by provoking competition among different interest groups, lobbying establishes a system of checks and balances; this assures that no single group retains a monopoly on the political decision-making process.

Critics have rejected this portrayal of the lobbying process, claiming it is based on the false assumption that competition among lobby groups takes place on a level "playing field." They argue that the ability of lobbyists to sway the political process is proportional to their resources—notably money and time. Lobby groups representing powerful corporate and financial **elites** (page 94) have indeed been shown to be the most successful. Meanwhile, lobbyists for less powerful groups—for workers, **civil rights** (page 54) organizations, and the poor, for example—lack the financial wherewithal that would enable them to fully participate in the supposedly "free and fair" lobbying competition.

In the US, numerous legislative efforts have been made to curb powerful elites' ability to work the lobbying system in their favor. These initiatives date back to the Tillman Act of 1907, which prohibited banks and corporations from making monetary contributions to national electoral campaigns. Further restrictions were imposed by the 1946 Federal Regulation of Lobbying Act, which requires congressional lobbyists to reveal information about themselves and those for whom they work to **Congress** (page 69). The constitutionality of this Act was challenged in the 1954 Supreme Court case *United States v. Harriss;* the Court allowed the law to stand, but limited its scope and application. Despite these modifications and the passage of several subsequent statutes dealing with special types of lobbying, the 1946 Act remains the only comprehensive piece of federal legislation designed to regulate the practice.

In 1995, Congress attempted to close loopholes in the 1946 law by passing the Lobbying Disclosure Act. Many critics contend that these reforms, which were aimed at holding lobbyists to a higher standard of accountability, have done little to curb the political influence of powerful economic groups: political action committees controlled by lobbyists are still able to make substantial financial contributions to congressional candidates' campaign committees. For critics, then, legislation continues to be shaped in accord with the interests of large corporations and other well-heeled sectors of society. Some have proposed public financing of political campaigns as a solution. They argue that taking private money entirely out of the equation would deprive wealthy lobby groups of one of their main tools of influence over the lawmaking process.

M

MAGNA CARTA

The *Magna Carta* (or "the Great Charter") is a political and legal document to which King John I of England consented in 1215. The Archbishop of Canterbury drafted it in the hope of resolving a longstanding dispute between the king and a group of rebellious barons, who wished to free themselves from his control and limit his powers. The Charter granted the barons and the clergy certain liberties and protections, and committed the monarchy to governing the towns by due process of law.

Over the centuries, the document was woven into the fabric of political life, influencing both England's and other nations' political systems—the American colonists, for example, appealed to it when drafting the US **Constitution** (page 72). But the *Magna Carta*'s role in shaping modern **democracies** (page 78) and legal principles such as **habeas corpus** (page 120) should not be exaggerated. Despite anticipating **liberalism**'s (page 152) defense of individual **liberty** (page 155) and its attack on **despotism** (page 83), the *Magna Carta* was aimed not at supporting the rights of ordinary citizens, but at maintaining the pillars of feudal society: the monarchy, the **aristocracy** (page 30), and the church.

NELSON MANDELA

Often referred to as the father of his nation, *Nelson Mandela* served as the first democratically elected black president of South Africa from 1994 to 1999. He was born in 1918 in Mvezo, Eastern Cape Province. As a young adult, he immersed himself in anticolonial politics and became a founding member of the Youth League of the African National Congress (ANC). At the age of thirty, he was confronted with the rise of the National Party (NP), which assumed power in 1948 and established the system of legalized racial segregation known as **apartheid** (page 24). Mandela was soon at the forefront of several anti-apartheid initiatives, including the ANC's 1952 Defiance Campaign. He was arrested numerous times on the charge of sedition, and both he and other ANC leaders were put on trial for (and ultimately acquitted of) treason.

Throughout the 1950s and 1960s, the apartheid government resorted to arrests, harassment, and armed conflict to silence dissidents. The climate of violent political repression—epitomized by the 1960 Sharpeville Massacre—helped to radicalize the anti-apartheid movement. Mandela,

Nelson Mandela was imprisoned for 27 years for opposing apartheid, going on to become South Africa's first black president after his release in 1990.

M

who had become a member of the banned South African Communist Party (SACP), was no longer prepared to embrace a strategy of **nonviolent resistance** (page 179). He and the ANC were now convinced that success depended on armed resistance and militarization. In 1961, allied with the SACP, Mandela established a militant group known as Umkhonto we Sizwe and embarked on a sabotage campaign against the Afrikaner minority government. In 1962, he was found guilty of sedition and sentenced to life in prison.

Mandela's incarceration lasted twenty-seven years, the first eighteen of which were spent at a jail on Robben Island. Throughout his confinement, calls to free him were raised the world over and developed into an international campaign. By the late 1980s, the apartheid government was facing a rising tide of resistance from within, and the pressure of economic sanctions from without. Sensing that his regime's days were numbered, South African President F.W. de Klerk released Mandela from prison in 1990. He then invited him and other anti-apartheid leaders to participate in diplomatic negotiations, which led to an agreement to hold multiracial elections. Mandela stood for president in 1994, winning the office easily and bringing the ANC into political power for the first time.

As president, Mandela helped develop a constitution for the new Government of National Unity, and invited other political parties to join his cabinet. To help his nation come to terms with the past forty years of government-sponsored violence and human rights abuses, Mandela founded the Truth and Reconciliation Commission. Although his liberal economic policies did not depart significantly from those of de Klerk, his administration made important strides toward curtailing poverty, improving healthcare services, and changing the existing laws regarding land ownership.

In 1999, Mandela was replaced as President of South Africa by his deputy, Thabo Mbeki, after refusing to stand for a second term. He then undertook various diplomatic and humanitarian initiatives, including efforts to fight poverty and HIV/AIDS. At a well-publicized trial in 2000, he served as a mediator between the United Kingdom and Libya, two of whose nationals had been charged with the 1988 bombing of Pan Am Flight 103.

Mandela died in 2013, ten years after receiving the Nobel Peace Prize for his lifetime's work as a campaigner for social **justice** (page 140) and a leader in the struggle against apartheid.

MAO ZEDONG

Mao Zedong (also Tse-tung) was the Chairman of the Central Committee of the Communist Party of China. He assumed this position in 1945, leading the Communist Revolution that resulted in the establishment of the People's Republic of China in 1949. After the Revolution, Mao endured as Communist Party Chairman until his death in 1976. Although he is generally regarded as one of the most important political figures of the twentieth century, his pivotal role in the complex history of revolutionary and post-revolutionary China is poorly understood by many Westerners.

1893 *Born in Hunan province*

1921 *Cofounds Communist Party of China*

1943 *Becomes Chairman of the CPC*

1949 *Founding of the People's Republic of China*

1966 *Launches Cultural Revolution*

1972 *Holds talks with US President Nixon*

1976 *Dies in Beijing*

Mao Zedong was born to a prosperous farmer in 1893 in Shaoshan, a city situated in the east-central region of China's Hunan province. It was not long before a rebellious spirit began to emerge in him: influenced by the tumultuous political upheavals that shook China in the early twentieth century (notably the Xinhai Revolution of 1911 and the May Fourth Movement of 1919), Mao was drawn to the causes of Chinese nationalism and anti-imperialism. His early ideological convictions set the stage for his later turn to **Marxism**-Leninism (page 166), a doctrine to which he was exposed while employed as a library assistant at Peking University. Soon thereafter, in 1921, he joined Chen Duxiu and Li Dazhao in founding the Communist Party of China (CPC).

Like Vladimir Lenin, the leader of the Russian Revolution, Mao sought to adapt and apply Marxist thought to the conditions of a largely rural nation still steeped in the traditions and practices of a preindustrial, feudal economy. While Karl Marx and Friedrich Engels claimed that the Communist Revolution would be led by the urban industrial workers of the most advanced capitalist societies, Mao argued that in China the revolutionary elite had to be drawn from the mass numbers of peasants dwelling in the nation's countryside.

Mao helped establish the Chinese Red Army and played a critical role in the Chinese Civil War, which pitted the forces of the CPC against those of the ruling Kuomintang Party (KMT). The war found Mao at the forefront of a series of military retreats known collectively

as the Long March. Surprisingly, these withdrawals helped to cement Mao's reputation as an astute military leader, ultimately catapulting him to the Chairmanship of the CPC in 1945. With Mao at the helm, the CPC ended the twenty-one-year reign of the KMT, seizing political power and bringing the People's Republic of China into existence in 1949.

Over the course of the next twenty-seven years, Mao solidified his place in both Chinese and world history. Under his leadership, agricultural lands were appropriated from wealthy landlords and placed under tight governmental control. Mao's early land reform efforts were precursors of a later crusade known as the Great Leap Forward. Initiated in 1957, this campaign sought to replace the agrarian base of the Chinese economy with a modern, industrial one. The Great Leap Forward was later blamed for creating widespread food

Mao Zedong, the son of a peasant farmer, believed that in nonindustrialized countries, a communist revolution would come from the countryside.

shortages and leading to the deaths of millions of people, mainly in the impoverished interior regions of the country.

In 1966, Mao launched another controversial initiative: the Great Proletarian Cultural Revolution. This program, which would last ten years, sought to place Mao's ideas at the core of the CPC's ideology, while extinguishing various "counter-revolutionary" elements within Chinese society: capitalists, remnants of the old feudal order, and even some senior officials of the CPC itself. During the Great Proletarian Cultural Revolution, many well-known historic artifacts, cultural relics, and religious landmarks were destroyed. The period also witnessed the rise of a Mao "personality cult," characterized by fierce loyalty to the Chairman and his teachings (known as "Mao Thought") on the part of groups such as the military, urban laborers, and the Red Guards—paramilitary units organized by legions of Chinese youth.

The historical legacy of Chairman Mao remains controversial. His initiatives and political vision, some have argued, were responsible for transforming China from an archaic agrarian society into a major industrial superpower. Mao is also said to have rooted out imperialism, bettered the living and working conditions of women, and substantially improved the quality of education and health care throughout China. Further, by hosting talks with President Richard Nixon in 1972,

Mao's pivotal role in the complex history of revolutionary and post-revolutionary China is poorly understood by many Westerners.

Mao helped to normalize relations between China and the United States, easing the political tensions that had built up between the two nations during the Cold War. For his critics, such successes amount to little in light of the spectacular deluge of death and destruction that Mao unleashed upon his own nation. His regime has been accused of systematic human rights violations and of causing the deaths of up to seventy million people due to famine, forced labor, and political executions.

MARXISM

Developed in the mid-nineteenth century by German thinkers Karl Marx and Friedrich Engels, *Marxism* is both a critique of philosophy and a program for the radical transformation of **capitalism** (page 44). Marx (the more prolific author of the pair) drew on the major theoretical traditions of his day—notably British political economy, the British Chartist movement for universal male suffrage, French **utopian** (page 252) **socialism** (page 224), and German idealism. Rather than deny philosophy, he criticized its investment in the abstract interpretation of fact and aimed to reconfigure it into a discipline that could change the world and the human consciousness of it.

M

To this end, he claimed that any analysis of a society's prevailing ideas must begin with an examination of its material conditions. He argued that in each major historical epoch, the reigning conceptions are rooted in relations of production, and that the history of human society is the history of dominant and subordinate classes. The class that controls the means by which society is reproduced shapes the world in accordance with its own material interests; meanwhile, those who lack control over the means of production remain estranged from their own laboring activity, the surplus of their labor, and their relations with themselves and the natural world.[11]

Marx argued that such alienation is at its height under capitalism, which is divided into two main classes: the capitalist class and the working class. As the first mode of production in human history to institutionalize self-sustaining economic growth, capitalism promotes the rapid expansion of industry, science, and technology; it also champions, in its founding political doctrines, the ideals of **liberty** (page 155) and equality. But these principles operate at the level of ideology, serving only to legitimize and reproduce the existing conditions of "unfreedom."

Thus, thinks Marx, while capitalism creates the material and conceptual bases for true human emancipation, the latter can only be realized by uprooting the system and replacing it with a classless, **communist** (page 64) alternative; this will allow all human beings to control the terms under which their lives are reproduced. Moreover, the industrial working class is the historical agent destined to carry forth this emancipatory project.

Since Marx's death in 1883, his theories have been adapted and modified by many neo-Marxist traditions, and put into practice by various avowedly Marxist movements such as Marxism-Leninism, Stalinism, and **Maoism** (page 163).

(Opposite) Karl Marx embraced the philosophy of "dialectical materialism," seeing humanity's evolution as a series of changing political and economic relations.

M

MERITOCRACY

In a *meritocracy*, positions within a government, business, or other organization are filled primarily on the basis of merit. The latter is sometimes determined through examinations aimed at gauging a candidate's credentials, intelligence, education, or other qualifications.

The ancient Greek thinkers Plato and Aristotle both incorporated elements of meritocracy into their respective blueprints for an ideal political system. Aristotle argued that in order to hold public office, administer **justice** (page 140), and be counted as a citizen, a person must possess sufficient reason, the ability to discuss and debate political issues, and a modicum of wealth to free up time for political participation. Aristotle deemed certain groups of people (women and slaves, for example) to be largely bereft of such capacities; he therefore excluded them from the running of the polis, or **city-state** (page 52). In his *Republic*, Plato insisted that the role of "philosopher king" should be awarded to the wisest members of society, arguing that they alone are qualified to enlighten the unenlightened about the Good—the ultimate reality. Some have argued that, in the **election** (page 92) campaigns of modern representative **democracies** (page 78), the question of merit is often overshadowed by largely symbolic considerations such as the candidate's personality or family background.

MILITARY

Along with the police, the military is an arm of the state that has the legal authority to utilize weaponry and brute force—including deadly force—to defend the state's interests and assure the security of its citizens. Unlike the police, which is primarily responsible for the control of criminal activity within the nation's borders, the military is meant to engage in **warfare** (page 256) with hostile foreign powers. In addition to national defense, it may be vested with other official or unofficial powers: among other things, it may be deployed to protect the interests of the state's corporate elites, assist with domestic population control, provide emergency services, and serve symbolic functions at state ceremonies. Modern militaries are typically composed of air, ground, and naval forces.

Regimes in which one or more members of the military assume control of the state and institute authoritarian rule are sometimes referred to as military juntas or military **dictatorships** (page 84). In most contemporary **parliamentary democracies** (page 189), the national military organization remains under civilian control; it is headed by the government's elected chief executive or a member of its Cabinet.

MILITARY-INDUSTRIAL COMPLEX

The term *military-industrial complex* was introduced by US President Dwight D. Eisenhower in his 1961 Farewell Address to the Nation; it has since become part of our everyday political vocabulary. Eisenhower picked up on a complex web of relationships between US legislators, the arms industry, and the national armed forces. These three entities, he noted, are woven together in a kind of lopsided "iron triangle." On the one hand, lawmakers are charged with setting the military budget and overseeing the arms industry. On the other hand, defense contractors and the military are well positioned to influence the legislative process through lobbying and political contributions. Historically, members of Congress have been quick to bow to such pressure, particularly those from districts whose local economies are dependent on the ongoing presence of the military, and on private arms manufacturers such as Boeing, Lockheed Martin, Raytheon, and Northrop Grumman.

Eisenhower characterized the excessive influence that arms makers and the military establishment exert over the legislative process as "unwarranted." He warned that **liberty** (page 155) and **democracy** (page 78) would be threatened if steps were not taken to guard against the growth of such interference. While others had already made similar claims, Eisenhower's "military-industrial complex" captured the gist of the problem.

The term has gained wide currency among critics of the US political system. These critics contend that, far from heeding Eisenhower's admonitions, lawmakers have continued to defer to the demands of the military establishment, thus significantly expanding its power and scope. They note that military spending in the US now far exceeds that of other nations: in 2011, America's share of global military expenditures was 41 percent—well above the amount needed, they claim, to provide for the legitimate security requirements of the nation. Meanwhile, defenders of the military-industrial complex argue that its continued growth is justified by the need to protect American citizens from the threat of global **terrorism** (page 238) in the post-9/11 world.

The term "military-industrial complex" was initially used in reference to the US only, but it is now commonly applied to other countries where similar dynamics arise. Its meaning has also been expanded to encompass the broader network of relationships that exist between private arms manufacturers, the Defense Department, Congress, and the executive branch.

N

NATIONALISM

Those who subscribe to *nationalism* pledge their abiding loyalty to the principles and institutions of the nation-state. As a modern ideal, nationalism emerged with the constitutional **republics** (page 206) established in Western Europe and North America in the eighteenth century. It has since become a feature of nation-states the world over: variants of nationalism have been observed in representative **democracies** (page 78) as well as in **fascist** (page 101) and avowedly **communist** (page 64) societies.

Nationalism was originally tied to the doctrine of popular **sovereignty** (page 226), whereby the **state**'s (page 229) authority to rule was no longer grounded in the infallible will of God or the traditions of the feudal **aristocracy** (page 30), but rather in the free will of the "people." The people, however, did not simply constitute "humanity" in the abstract: they were members of a society with clearly demarcated linguistic and cultural frontiers. Nationalism in France, for instance, makes

(Opposite) The creation of a shared national identity is central to the modern nation-state, including that of France, as seen in this depiction of the 1830 July Revolution.

sense only insofar as the French Republic was established with reference to the particular will of the French people.

From its inception, nationalism has not only been characterized by patriotic allegiance to the ideals and institutions of the nation; it has also been defined in relation to those thought to stand outside the nation and its interests. In the late nineteenth century, for example, German leader Otto von Bismarck attempted to whip up nationalist sentiment by enacting legislation under which **socialist** (page 224) workers were effectively deemed enemies of the nation. Some decades later, German nationalism was pushed to an extreme with **Adolf Hitler**'s (page 124) doctrine of racial exclusivism: during his Nazi regime, all those of "pure" German descent were enjoined to pledge their loyalty to the ancestral soil of the German Reich, while all "non-pure races" were targeted for elimination.

Although it is often associated with right-wing political perspectives, nationalism has also been espoused by social movements striving for political and cultural self-determination. For instance, under the leadership of **Mahatma Gandhi** (page 114), the campaign for Indian national independence attempted to reclaim the country's **colonized** (page 61) traditions while reasserting its people's control over their own political destiny.

N

NAPOLEON BONAPARTE

Napoleon Bonaparte was at the forefront of the dramatic political, social, and economic changes that overtook Europe as its ancient feudal monarchies began to collapse in the late eighteenth and early nineteenth centuries. He remains one of the most celebrated military and political leaders of the early modern period.

1769 *Born in Corsica*

1795 *Leads offensive against Royalists*

1799 *Overthrows Directory, establishes Consulate*

1804 *Becomes French Emperor, issues Napoleonic Code*

1815 *Defeat at Battle of Waterloo*

1821 *Dies on Saint Helena at age 51*

Born in Corsica in 1769, Napoleon championed the ideals of the **French Revolution** (page 109), which established the first modern liberal **republic** (page 206) in Europe under the slogan, "Liberty, Equality, Fraternity." His efforts to bring these principles to Corsica were rebuffed, leading to his expulsion from the island in 1793. In 1795, he led French Revolutionary troops through the streets of Paris and successfully squelched an uprising by anti-republican Royalist forces.

N

Credited with having saved the French Republic from collapse, the twenty-six-year-old Napoleon was appointed General of the Army of Italy. A year later, following his marriage to Josephine de Beauharnais, the general was deployed to Italy and undertook a series of successful campaigns that enhanced his reputation as a savvy military strategist and leader. One such operation was his 1798 excursion to Egypt, where he achieved a decisive victory in the Battle of the Pyramids and ultimately captured that Ottoman province.

In 1799, Napoleon returned to France and orchestrated a successful military coup against the ruling Directory, replacing it with a new government known as the Consulate. As First Consul, he quickly added to his already long list of military achievements with a victory over the Austrians in the Battle of Marengo.

In 1804, he was declared Emperor of the French by the Consulate's Senate. His military triumphs proceeded apace. From 1803 to 1806, he mounted a successful campaign against a coalition of nations including Austria and Russia (the alliance was severely weakened after the Ulm Campaign, and defeated in the Battle of Austerlitz). In 1806, he overwhelmed the Prussians in the battles of Jena and Auerstedt.

(Opposite) Napoleon was both an aggressive military emperor and a liberal politician who advanced legal and religious freedoms within France.

N

He went on to subject the Russians to similar defeat, crushing them a year later in the Battle of Friedland and forcing them to sign the Treaties of Tilsit, which served to increase his control of Central Europe.

Later in the decade, Napoleon sought to compel Portugal to participate in his Continental Blockade, a comprehensive embargo on British trade. He appointed his brother Joseph as the King of Spain and sent troops into Iberia. His actions precipitated the Peninsular War of 1807 to 1814, which pitted the Napoleonic Empire against the allied powers of Spain, Britain, and Portugal in a battle for control of the Iberian Peninsula. In 1809, Napoleon redirected his attention to the Austrian Empire. His victory in the Battle of Wagram dissolved an alliance against France known as the Fifth Coalition, which had been formed between the Austrians and the United Kingdom.

By 1812, the Napoleonic Empire extended across Continental Europe, bringing some seventy million people under its orbit. Buoyed by his numerous military conquests, Napoleon undertook the invasion of Russia. This time, however, he proved that he was not invincible. In October 1813, the Sixth Coalition—which included Russia, Austria, the United Kingdom, and several other nations—trounced Napoleon in the Battle of Leipzig. The following year, the coalition forces invaded France and captured Paris. The Allies restored power to the old Bourbon dynasty, stripping Napoleon of most of the territories he had conquered since the Revolution.

The former emperor was forced into exile in April 1814, but returned to France the following year in an attempt to resume his leadership. No sooner had he set foot on his native soil than he was pulled into a war with the members of a Seventh Coalition, which roundly defeated him in the Battle of Waterloo. His attempt to flee to the United States was foiled by the British, to whom he was forced to surrender. For the next six years, Napoleon was confined to the remote island of Saint Helena, where he died in 1821, at the age of fifty-one.

In addition to his military successes, Napoleon is credited with diplomatic achievements like the Concordat of 1801, which reconciled republican revolutionaries and the Catholic Church. He is also renowned for the Napoleonic Code, a framework for legal equality and religious tolerance that has been adopted by many of the world's nations.

NAZISM

Nazism arose in Germany in the 1920s and 1930s. It is associated with the doctrines of the German leader **Adolf Hitler** (page 124) and the practices of his Third Reich. Nazism shared many of **fascism**'s (page 101) views, but developed them in its own peculiar direction. Most notably, it employed **anti-Semitism** (page 23) to promote a campaign of violence against the Jewish people. To justify its anti-Semitic practices, Nazism made use of various pseudo-scientific theories and techniques. It espoused a perspective known as social Darwinism, for example, to defend the existence of a natural racial hierarchy in which people of Germanic descent were situated at the top. As the purest members of the "Aryan race," such "Nordic" peoples were declared the "master race." At the bottom of the ladder were the Jews, Gypsies, homosexuals, Jehovah's Witnesses, and a variety of other racial and ethnic groups classified as **Untermenschen** (or "sub-humans").

The Nazi Party was born in 1919 as the avowedly anti-Semitic and nationalist German Workers' Party. It was rechristened the National Socialist German Workers' Party

The swastika was the emblem of the Nazi regime under Hitler, whose ideology proclaimed the construction of a Greater Germany without "undesirables."

N

in the 1920s, when Hitler took control of the organization. With the term "National Socialism," the Nazis hoped to draw in workers opposed to **free-market** (page 108) **capitalism** (page 44), while also rejecting the **Marxist** (page 166) principle of internationalist **socialism** (page 224). Indeed, Nazism expressly repudiated Marxist notions of class struggle, social equality, and international solidarity; the "Socialism" portion of its name notwithstanding, it upheld the idea of private **property** (page 199) and free enterprise.

The Nazi program was committed to a united Greater Germany that would bar Jews, those of Jewish ancestry, foreigners, and other "undesirables" from citizenship. It sought to establish a homogeneous society of national comrades, and to preserve the traditions and practices of the country's authentic "people's community." The Nazi Party laid claim to the "historically German" territories of neighboring states and called for the expansion of Germany through the appropriation of foreign lands.

After Hitler became Chancellor of Germany in 1933, the Nazis ruled the nation as a one-party state; they subjected their political enemies, Jews, and other "racially impure" groups to systematic persecution. The Holocaust—Nazism's mass extermination program—was responsible for the deaths of approximately eleven million people.

N

NEOLIBERALISM

Neoliberalism is an economic doctrine that promotes **free markets** (page 108), the deregulation of industry, the **privatization** (page 198) of state-controlled assets and services, tariff reductions, and other pro-market policies. When the term "neoliberalism" was first coined in the 1930s, it was largely devoid of the negative connotations it carries today. At the time, figures such as Ludwig von Mises, Friedrich August von Hayek, and Wilhelm Röpke called for a revival of **liberalism**'s (page 152) core values. These values, which protect both the individual and the private market from undue governmental interference, were felt to be under attack by the rise of **communist** (page 64) societies like the **Soviet Union** (page 226), in which property was collectivized and brought under the control of the **state** (page 229). Hayek's 1944 book *The Road to Serfdom*, a critique of statism and planned economies, inspired the creation of an international liberal think tank called the Mont Pelerin Society. In his book, Hayek departed from the classical liberal portrait of markets as nature-like mechanisms directed by what Adam Smith called an "invisible hand." He argued that the state should not simply "get out of the way," but rather take an active role in promoting the growth of the free-market economy and preventing the development of state monopolies.

In the decades following **World War II** (page 266), neoliberalism was overshadowed by the theories of John Maynard Keynes, which supported the organizing principles of the **welfare state** (page 259) economies that had been established in the West. By the early 1970s, however, the political winds had begun to shift: among other developments, an economic crisis marked by high inflation rates and slow economic growth ("stagflation") led many to rethink the Keynesian model, which gave the state a significant role in the management of social and economic life.

This created an opportunity for neoliberalism to re-emerge and take center stage. A group of economists at the University of Chicago brought their neoliberal experiments to Chile.[12] In the late 1970s and early 1980s, the services of neoliberal economic advisors were also solicited by the administrations of American President Ronald Reagan and British Prime Minister Margaret Thatcher. With the support of supranational financial institutions such as the World Bank, the International Monetary Fund, and the World Trade Organization, neoliberal governments demanded that the **decolonized** (page 77) nations of the Third World winnow down their state-led development paradigms. Recipients of international loans were bound to strict repayment schedules and "structural adjustment" policies, which obliged them to undertake fiscal austerity measures, privatize state functions, liberalize trade, and deregulate markets. However, beginning in the late 1990s, the neoliberal policy consensus began to encounter staunch opposition from various social movements around the globe—notably in Latin America, where a number of governments were elected on the basis of their vocal opposition to neoliberal austerity.

Critics of neoliberal policies have underscored their untoward social consequences, including the promotion of **inequality** (page 133) and the reduction of **democratic** (page 78) accountability. The theorist Karl Polanyi argued that the project of economic liberalism ultimately turns society at large into a mere "adjunct to the market." According to the sociologist Pierre Bourdieu, in destroying forms of social solidarity fostered by the welfare state, neoliberalism promotes an ongoing state of "existential insecurity." For **Marxist** (page 166) thinker David Harvey, neoliberal privatization policies increase the power of economic **elites** (page 94), while rendering more and more spheres of life subservient to the logic of capital accumulation. Writers inspired by the work of the French philosopher Michel Foucault have likewise noted that neoliberal projects do more than relieve the market from state interference: they establish new indirect forms of power and domination.

NEPOTISM

In the city-states of medieval Italy, chastity-sworn popes and bishops had no legitimate sons to which to pass on their positions; their nephews were thus given preferential consideration for appointment to high offices within the Catholic Church. The term *nepotismo* (derived from the Latin *nepos*, for nephew) was employed to refer to this custom. In some cases, the cycle of handing over the papacy to the nephews or other relatives of existing popes was repeated over the course of many generations, resulting in the creation of papal dynasties. In contemporary times, the term nepotism refers to a situation in which a position is acquired based on one's personal or familial relationship to a current officeholder or company employee, rather than on one's relevant qualifications. Notable examples of modern-day political nepotism include Arthur Balfour's attaining the position of Chief Secretary for Ireland thanks to the efforts of his uncle, Lord Robert Cecil (resulting in the British expression, "Bob's your uncle"), and US President John F. Kennedy's appointment of his brother, Robert F. Kennedy, to the position of Attorney General. In later years, other members of the Kennedy family would likewise capitalize on their relationship to the popular president in order to advance their own political careers.

N

NONINTERVENTIONISM

When a state adopts a policy of *noninterventionism*, it declares its resolve not to interfere with the affairs of other nations. Instead, it pledges to engage with them diplomatically, leaving them free to manage their own domestic concerns and assisting them in their external affairs only with their consent. The policy of noninterventionism thus upholds the principles of state **sovereignty** (page 226) and self-determination. One must be careful to distinguish noninterventionism from isolationism, which advocates for restrictive immigration and international trade policies.

The strategy of noninterventionism was adopted in the early years of the **United States** (page 248) Republic. Presidents **George Washington** (page 257) and Thomas Jefferson, for example, both sought to maintain diplomatic and economic relations with European nations while abstaining from involvement in European wars. Over time, however, US leaders have become less enamored of the noninterventionist strategy—particularly since 1917, when America abandoned its neutral stand and entered **World War I** (page 262). More than two decades later, President **Franklin D. Roosevelt** (page 209) justified US involvement in **World War II** (page 266) by declaring that the principle of noninterventionism applies only to nations that respect the **rights** (page 208) of others.

NONVIOLENT RESISTANCE

The term *nonviolent resistance* is reserved for those acts of **civil disobedience** (page 53) and noncooperation that avoid the use of violence. Acting as individuals, members of civic groups, or supporters of political movements, nonviolent resisters make a premeditated decision to avoid aggression when challenging the **laws** (page 147) of a domestic government or foreign occupying power. This stance is maintained even if resistance is met with violent responses from authorities. It is sometimes referred to as "passive resistance"—a potentially misleading label insofar as the strategy is not one of passivity, but one of very active nonviolent confrontation. It may take various forms, including sit-ins at government offices or businesses, economic boycotts, **strikes** (page 231), and protest marches.

In withdrawing their consent from specific laws, nonviolent resisters seek to cast doubt on the legitimacy of certain aspects of the opposed government's rule. They do so with the conviction that its legitimacy can be sustained only with the citizens' ongoing consent, or at least acquiescence, to its laws—a view upheld both by **liberals** (page 152) like John Locke, and political realists like Niccolò Machiavelli.

Protesters in Tennessee conduct a sit-in at a whites-only lunch counter in 1960. Sit-ins were a nonviolent strategy used to resist Jim Crow laws.

Nonviolent resistance is often, but not always, espoused by those who are morally committed to **pacifism** (page 186). Rebels opposed to British rule of the American colonies, for example, waged an armed war against their colonial adversaries but also employed tax refusal and other nonviolent tactics to further their objectives.

Led by the decidedly pacifist **Mahatma Gandhi** (page 114), the movement against the **colonial** (page 61) rule of the British Raj in India was a seminal moment in the modern history of nonviolent resistance. Gandhi based his independence campaign on the principle of *satyagraha*, or "soul force," which counseled protesters to defy unjust laws and edicts while also maintaining an attitude of respect and compassion for the confronted authorities. Methods of resistance, Gandhi argued, must be morally consistent with the goals they seek to achieve. In the 1950s and 1960s, **Martin Luther King, Jr.** (page 141) incorporated elements of Gandhian nonviolent resistance into the American **civil rights** (page 54) movement. Guided by principles similar to Gandhi's *satyagraha*, civil rights activists in the **United States** (page 248) held peaceful public demonstrations and endured the often brutally violent responses of state authorities without responding in kind. As it is often employed by marginalized, non-powerful groups, nonviolent resistance has been nicknamed the "weapon of the weak."

NUCLEAR WEAPONS

Nuclear weapons are the most powerful explosive armaments ever created by humans; they have the potential to destroy virtually all life on Earth. There are two basic kinds of nuclear weapons: fission bombs and thermonuclear bombs. Each type of weapon can generate, from relatively small amounts of matter, a nuclear reaction that will release massive quantities of energy. One 2,400-pound thermonuclear weapon, for example, has the same explosive force as more than 1.2 million tons of TNT. The destructive power of these devices is almost unfathomable: a blast from a single nuclear bomb can annihilate an entire city, both from the sheer force of the explosion and from the fire and radiation that follow.

In the 1940s, when the threat of global nuclear annihilation first became a reality, many nations undertook measures to protect those located outside the immediate radius of a nuclear fireball from serious injury or death. A program launched in the US in the 1950s known as "duck and cover," for example, instructed schoolchildren to take shelter under their desks in the event of a nuclear attack.

The first nuclear weapons were created at the Los Alamos National Laboratory from 1942 to 1946, under the auspices of the Manhattan Project led by US physicist J. Robert Oppenheimer. Since then, nuclear weapons have been detonated in thousands of tests and demonstrations, but they have only been used

N

twice in warfare against human populations. In both cases, Japanese cities were the target.

Toward the end of **World War II** (page 266), a fission bomb with the codename "Little Boy" was dropped by the US on the city of Hiroshima; a second US nuclear device, codenamed "Fat Man," was released over Nagasaki. An estimated two hundred thousand people were killed in the immediate aftermath of the bombings; exposure to radiation would produce many more casualties over the months and years to come. President Harry S. Truman's decision to authorize the bombings has been the subject of much debate as to whether they were militarily necessary or morally justifiable.

According to a 2012 estimate, some seventeen thousand nuclear warheads exist worldwide; 4,300 of them are ready for immediate use. Today, a handful of the world's nations acknowledge possessing nuclear weapons: the United States, Russia, the United Kingdom, France, China, India, Pakistan, and North Korea. Israel claims to have no nuclear armaments, but it is widely believed to possess them. Over the years, some "weaponless" nations have been accused of having covert nuclear programs; this was recently the case with Iran, which accepted an April 2015 preliminary agreement to refrain from such programs.

The Iran deal is but the latest in a long series of international agreements aimed at limiting the production, use, and possession of nuclear weapons. The Partial Test Ban Treaty of 1963, for example, limited the testing of nuclear weapons to underground sites; this was meant to prevent contamination from nuclear fallout. Further restrictions on the development and use of nuclear armaments were imposed by the Nuclear Non-Proliferation Treaty of 1968. In addition to such official diplomatic efforts, numerous citizen campaigns have been launched with the more radical goal of eliminating nuclear weapons altogether.

(Right) A mushroom cloud expands over Nagasaki, Japan, in the aftermath of the United States's August 8, 1945, nuclear bomb attack.

O

OLIGARCHY

In an *oligarchy*, all of the powers of the state remain under the exclusive control of a small group of individuals. Oligarchs are typically granted such power on the basis of their rank or social standing; being a member of the royalty or a particular religious sect, ranking high in the military, and having excessive wealth are some of the advantageous social markers.

Oligarchs are sometimes elected, but, historically, most oligarchies have lacked electoral systems. It has been more common for oligarchs to pass down their political authority from generation to generation. Accordingly, many oligarchies have been political dynasties in which a few prominent families retain state control for decades or even centuries.

Moreover, because the powers of the state are theirs alone, oligarchs are free to act solely based on their own interests. According to Aristotle's portrayal of oligarchy, the few who rule are not the "best" (as is the case in an **aristocracy**, page 30) but rather the wealthy, who are principally concerned with enhancing their own fortunes while disregarding the interests of the poor. To assure that their hold on power remains exclusive, oligarchs tend to demand strict obedience, frequently resorting to political repression to enforce it. Oligarchies are thus often said to be **tyrannical** (page 244) in nature.

Historical examples of oligarchy include the short-lived Council of the Four Hundred, which toppled the democratic government of Athens in 411 BC. In contemporary times, the term "oligarchy" has been applied to the Russian Federation, governed by a small group of wealthy businessmen who amassed huge fortunes during the economic privatization that followed the 1991 collapse of the **Soviet Union** (page 226). Some critics also perceive elements of oligarchy in the contemporary United States. They argue that, while American citizens are formally guaranteed certain **freedoms** (page 107) and **civil rights** (page 54), and also have the ability to hold politicians accountable through **elections** (page 92), a small number of wealthy individuals and business organizations determines which policies are ultimately adopted by the United States government.[13]

O

(Above) Louis XVI of France inherited the throne from his father in 1774, only to be beheaded by revolutionaries in 1793.

OCTOBER REVOLUTION

The *October Revolution* was a seminal event in the history of modern-day Russia. It was led by a revolutionary political faction known as the **Bolsheviks** (page 41) and their Red Guards—paramilitary forces composed largely of industrial workers and peasants. On October 24, 1917, the Red Guards staged an armed takeover of some of the major facilities of the provisional government in Petrograd (then the capital of Russia and now known as St. Petersburg). The Winter Palace, which was the new government's seat, was captured the following day.

O

Staffed mainly by former aristocrats and nobles, the provisional government had been established to replace the autocratic regime of Russian Tsar Nicholas II, who had been overthrown earlier that year in the February Revolution. It soon became weak and fragmented due to political infighting and external opposition. Its decision to enter **World War I** (page 262) was widely denounced, and it was held responsible for the economic crisis that was hobbling the country's transport system and leading to shortages in critical goods and services. As industrial production plummeted, Russia was saddled with mass unemployment, inflation, a skyrocketing national debt, and the prospect of financial bankruptcy.

In this climate, sympathy for the Bolsheviks' cause was widespread. Mass demonstrations by revolutionary workers and soldiers had already been staged in May 1917 in Petrograd and other cities under the slogan, "All power to the soviets" ("soviets" being local workers' councils). In September and October of 1917, workers mounted strikes in Petrograd, Moscow, and other Russian cities, in some cases seizing control of the factories in which they were employed. Thousands of peasant revolts broke out against Russian landowners, and various sectors of the Russian armed forces declared their opposition to the provisional regime in Petrograd.

In the face of the escalating threat to its existence, the government resorted to brute force. In July 1917, it authorized an armed attack on some half a million workers and soldiers who had gathered in the streets of Petrograd to demonstrate against the regime. Hundreds were killed in the assault. Provisional government forces also raided the editorial offices of the Communist Party newspaper *Pravda,* arrested and disarmed workers, broke up revolutionary units in Petrograd, and ordered the arrest of Bolshevik leader Vladimir Lenin, who was forced to go into hiding. This wave of political repression served only to heighten disdain for the government and increase sympathy for the Bolsheviks' revolutionary campaign.

In this atmosphere, the stage was set for a full-scale attack on Petrograd; on October 10, 1917, the Bolsheviks' Central Committee

declared as much. Two weeks later, the Red Guards descended upon the Petrograd government. At the forefront of the revolt was Bolshevik leader Leon Trotsky, who would later become the first head of the Soviet Red Army. Trotsky handed out arms to his Red Guards, who faced little resistance as they proceeded to seize control of key government installations. The largely bloodless Petrograd revolt culminated in the capture of the Winter Palace on October 25, 1917.

The Second Congress of Soviets, which included 300 Bolshevik delegates, authorized the transfer of political power to the Congress of Workers', Soldiers', and Peasants' Deputies. The resolution was immediately denounced as illegal by opposition factions within the Second Congress, including the Mensheviks—the Bolsheviks' chief rivals. The Bolsheviks nevertheless prevailed: on October 26, 1917, a Council of People's Commissars led by Lenin was elected by the Congress. The Council, which became the foundation of a new Soviet government, proceeded to arrest and imprison Menshevik leaders and other opponents of the October Revolution.

A major counterrevolutionary offensive, which proved to be the last gasp of the toppled regime, took place on October 29, 1917. The attack was waged by Kerensky, the ousted leader. Riding into Petrograd on a white horse, he ordered his Cossack forces to fire upon a rifle garrison that had refused to obey his order to lay down its arms. Eight men were killed in the assault, fueling contempt for Kerensky among the soldiers of Petrograd and dealing the final death blow to his government.

The October Revolution was a key event within the larger Russian Revolution of 1917, which ultimately led to the establishment of the Russian Socialist Federative Soviet Republic in 1917 and the **Soviet Union** (page 226) in 1922.

(Above) Russian soldiers gather in the Winter Palace in Petrograd to pledge allegiance to the new Bolshevik government.

P

PACIFISM

Proponents of *pacifism* advocate an end to war and **violence** (page 253). While many pacifists concede that violence may sometimes be necessary as a means of self-defense, "absolute" pacifists completely abjure it. Pacifism has been advanced from various philosophical, religious, and moral-ethical standpoints. Religious philosophies associated with it include **Daoism** (page 76), Buddhism, Hinduism, and Jainism. **Christian** (page 46) pacifists find doctrinal support for their beliefs in the Bible—for example, "Love your enemies, bless them that curse you" (Matthew 4:44). In politics, pacifism has been a key tenet of various **nonviolent resistance** (page 179) struggles, including **Mahatma Gandhi**'s (page 114) campaign against British **colonial** (page 61) rule and the American **civil rights** (page 54) movement led by **Martin Luther King, Jr.** (page 141). In his 1795 treatise *Perpetual Peace*, Immanuel Kant pleaded for the establishment of a cosmopolitan federation of nation-states tasked with permanently eradicating human warfare. His normative and institutional blueprint for world peace significantly anticipated the diplomatic missions of the **League of Nations** (page 148) and its successor, the **United Nations** (page 245).

PAPACY

The papacy is the office held by the pope, head of the worldwide Roman Catholic Church. It dates back to the first century, when, according to Church doctrine, **Jesus** (page 138) appointed Peter the Apostle as the first Bishop of Rome and gave him the keys to Heaven. The authority of all succeeding popes is said to derive from Saint Peter. In addition to serving as the Bishop of Rome, the pope presides over the Diocese of Rome, or the Holy See—the governing body of the Catholic Church. Vatican City, an independent **city-state** (page 52) located within the Italian capital of Rome, is also his jurisdiction.

As one of the world's oldest religious and political institutions, the papacy has significantly influenced the course of the last two millennia of human history. In antiquity, popes helped spread Christianity across the European continent and resolve various disputes over Church doctrine. In the Middle Ages, they often mediated conflicts between the Christian monarchs of Western Europe. The current pope, Francis, has worked to modify and expand the tenets of the Catholic faith, with particular attention to issues of social **justice** (page 140) and **human rights** (page 128).

PARLIAMENT

A *parliament* is a governmental chamber where proposed legislation is debated and ultimately passed into law. The discursive aspect of the parliamentary process is reflected in the term's linguistic origins: it derives from the French word *parlement*, which means the act of speaking or discussing. In modern **parliamentary democracies** (page 189), members of parliament are charged with formulating national laws, representing the interests of their local constituencies, and holding the executive (or law-enforcing) branch of the government accountable for its actions.

Although aspects of the modern parliament were present in earlier forms of **government** (page 118), it was not until the mid-fourteenth century that the term was applied to the deliberative political bodies of England and Ireland. In 1707, the parliaments of England and Scotland were absorbed into the Parliament of Great Britain, which in turn merged with the Parliament of Ireland to form the Parliament of the United Kingdom in 1801.

Often called the "Mother of Parliaments," the British Parliament not only became a model for most of the world's other parliamentary systems; it itself established many of these systems under the authority of various Acts of Parliament. The parliaments of the British Commonwealth and those of most European nations reproduce the British Parliament's basic three-tier structure, which features a large elected lower chamber, a smaller upper chamber, and a ceremonial head of **state** (page 229) who opens and closes each parliamentary cycle.

In the United Kingdom these three parliamentary components are known, respectively, as the House of Commons, the House of Lords, and the royal monarch. The lower House of Commons consists of 650 elected Members of Parliament, each representing a single constituency. The smaller upper chamber, the House of Lords, is composed of two types of unelected officials—the Lords Temporal and the Lords Spiritual—some of whom retain their positions for life. Either chamber can propose legislation. Once introduced, a bill must move through a complicated series of stages, or readings, during which it is debated and amended several times over. If it passes the final amendment stage, Royal Assent is granted and the bill passes into law. Despite the convoluted nature of this process, British prime ministers have a relatively easy time passing their legislative agendas, as their parliaments are populated by a majority of members from their own party. This, in stark difference to US presidential **democracy** (page 78), where a president's **Congress** (page 69) is often dominated by a rival political faction.

The Palace of Westminster in London is home to both the House of Commons and the House of Lords.

PARLIAMENTARY DEMOCRACY

Parliamentary democracies arose in the late eighteenth century as replacements for the feudal monarchies and **aristocracies** (page 30) that had preceded them. Great Britain was the first major parliamentary democracy, but the system eventually spread throughout Western Europe. Consistent with the **separation of powers** (page 216) doctrine, parliamentary democracies divide the authority of the state into a law-enforcing executive, a law-interpreting judiciary, and a law-making **legislature** (page 149). The legislative branch or **parliament** (page 187), which is responsible for translating the will of the citizenry into law, is the foundation of the state's democratic legitimacy—the executive branch remains accountable to it. By contrast, in a **democracy** (page 78) with a presidential system such as the **United States** (page 248), the authority of the executive is not rooted in the legislature; rather, the different branches of the government remain accountable to one another. The separation of powers is thus stricter in a presidential system than in a parliamentary system, where the executive is appointed by, and in fact constitutes part of, the legislative body.

In parliamentary democracies, new governments are created by the party (or coalition of parties) that wins the greatest number of seats in parliamentary **elections** (page 92). The leader of the majority party becomes the chancellor or prime minister and selects members of the parliament to serve in his cabinet. Cabinet members have executive authority, advising the prime minister on matters of relevance to the agencies or departments they administer. Parties that fail to win a majority of seats in the legislature serve as the minority opposition, and are obliged to regularly contest the policies of the party in power. Should the prime minister lose the confidence of the parliament or her party, a call may be raised for her dismissal and an early dissolution of her government. In a presidential system the legislature has no such authority, which is another notable difference between presidential and parliamentary democracies.

Parliamentary systems are sometimes preferred over their presidential counterparts owing to the greater ease with which they are able to pass laws. Indeed, with the backing of her party or a majority coalition, a prime minister has generally little difficulty bringing her legislative agenda into effect. For a president, the going is not so easy: his legislature may not only be independently elected, but it may also be dominated by members of a different political party who can stall or block his legislative proposals.

PATERNALISM

The term *paternalism* derives from the Latin *pater*, or "father." In the nineteenth century, it began to be used in reference to the social hierarchies of patriarchal societies, where fathers (or father figures) were assumed to have authority over their family members and responsibility for their welfare. It also seemed an apt description of governments that positioned kings or other heads of state in a protective, fatherly relationship to their subjects. Later, similar bonds between the main dominant and subordinate groups of the industrial age—factory owners and laborers, the privileged wealthy and underprivileged poor—would sometimes be portrayed as paternalistic.

The idea of paternalism was roundly criticized by the great liberal philosophers of the European Enlightenment—notably, Immanuel Kant and John Stuart Mill. Such thinkers viewed paternalism as an affront to the **liberty** (page 155) and **autonomy** (page 33) of the individual; in a paternalistic society, they argued, one's decisions remain under the control of an authority that is not one's own. Whether or not paternal rule is seen as benevolent (that is, as acting in favor of the subordinate), claimed Kant, it keeps one in a state of "immaturity."

PERESTROIKA

In the mid-1980s, a climate of political change began to take hold in the **Soviet Union** (page 226). At the forefront of this new atmosphere was the state's leader, Mikhail Gorbachev. Gorbachev, who became General Secretary of the Communist Party in 1986, initiated a series of reforms aimed at decentralizing the command structure of the Soviet economy, under which all decisions regarding the production of goods and services remained under tight state control. Gorbachev's program was referred to as *perestroika*, or "economic restructuring."

Perestroika introduced some elements of the **free market** (page 108) into the Soviet system in order to make it more efficient and better able to meet consumers' needs. However, despite this nod toward market liberalization, the foundations of the Soviet Union's command economy remained basically intact. *Perestroika* was blamed for producing logjams in production, and was not especially well received in Russia and in the Soviet republics of Eastern Europe, such as Poland and Czechoslovakia. Here nationalist sentiments and a general distaste for the Soviet government and its leadership were already on the rise. Ironically, in attempting to liberalize the Soviet economy, Gorbachev's *perestroika* helped fuel a wave of resistance that ultimately led to the demise of the Soviet Union in 1991.

POSTCOLONIALISM

Postcolonialism is a catch-all term for the historical events, political and social upheavals, and theoretical redefinitions that have accompanied European **decolonization** (page 77) over the last century. During the 1960s and 1970s, an academic field known as Postcolonial Studies began to consider how conceptions of race, ethnicity, gender, and class were once shaped by colonial relationships of power and domination, and how vestiges of those relationships have persisted since the withdrawal of the colonizing powers in the early to mid-twentieth century.

According to postcolonialism, the "grand narratives" of Western art, literature, and philosophy leave little place for the self-understanding and lived experiences of colonized people: they depict colonized subjects as less than fully human, and as utterly dependent on the **paternalistic** (page 190) assistance of the conquering colonial powers. Postcolonial critique—which has been elaborated in disciplines such as philosophy, literary studies, and sociology—endeavors to disarticulate the universal categories of knowledge and power set forth by colonialism, and to open up spaces for the colonial subject to "speak." Frantz Fanon, Edward Said, Homi Bhabha, and Gayatri Spivak are some of the major thinkers associated with the postcolonial tradition.

POSTMODERNISM

Postmodernism is an umbrella term meant to encompass a broad range of philosophical, cultural, literary, and aesthetic movements that have developed over the last fifty years. Curiously enough, the term has been rejected by many of the major figures with whom it has been popularly associated, including Jacques Derrida, Michel Foucault, and Judith Butler. As its name suggests, postmodernism breaks with the discourses of Modernism and the Enlightenment. One of its principal objectives is to shatter the universal ideals of modernity such as **freedom** (page 107), equality, nature, humanity, morality, truth, falsity, subject, object, and so forth, and thereby expose the existence of a multiplicity of cognitive and cultural paradigms. In "decentering" the categories through which the Enlightenment has sought to understand the world, it urges a radical reconceptualization of the terms under which knowledge is acquired, retained, and disseminated.

Nineteenth-century thinker Friedrich Nietzsche is often credited with inaugurating the postmodernist shift, insofar as he tried to release philosophy from its absolute ideals and move it toward a perspectival understanding of morality, culture, and knowledge. His philosophical upheaval was based on "an incredulity toward metanarratives," as French author Jean-François Lyotard put it. "Meta" or "grand" narratives, claimed Lyotard, attempt to establish a single, all-encompassing vantage

P

point through which the world can be understood and a fixed goal or endpoint realized. The Enlightenment narrative of scientific and civilizational progress, for example, aims to reach an ultimate resting place where all uncertainties will be resolved and the absolute truth will be known. In signaling the "death" of this grand narrative, postmodernism has sought to disabuse us of the hope of understanding the world in its totality; instead, it posits a multiplicity of incommensurable worlds with no common center. Unburdened by the Enlightenment's investment in the totalizing concept of consensus, oppressed and marginalized groups can now make claims upon the notion of **justice** (page 140) and other **liberal** (page 152) ideals without divesting themselves of their "otherness" in the process.

By the 1980s, the postmodern movement was well underway in the academy. In the social sciences, many authors had begun to question the legitimacy of conceptual systems; they had also taken note of the limitations of research agendas anchored in the insular authority of "grand theories." No longer seeking to establish infallible universal truths from "on high," their new investigative approach invited multiple interpretations; it left room for irony, contradiction, paradox, uncertainty, and an appreciation of the "otherness of the other."

For those eager to contest the homogenizing effects of European colonialism and imperialism, postmodernism provided critical conceptual resources. From its standpoint, these political projects did little more than expunge the irreducible differences of non-Western cultures, absorbing their "otherness" into the dominant metanarratives of a singular European modernity. The literary critic Edward Said made some of the most significant contributions to the postmodern critique of colonialism and imperialism, notably in his books *Orientalism* and *Imperialism and Culture*.

POVERTY

For much of human history, *poverty* was upheld as the ideal state of both individuals and human communities; it was only in the eighteenth century that this sanguine view dissolved, and poverty came to be viewed as a deplorable condition in need of correction.

Some of the earliest champions of poverty can be found among the Stoics of ancient Greece and the ascetics of early **Christianity** (page 46). Both linked poverty to human **virtues** (page 255) such as simplicity, austerity, and temperance. They took poverty to be a self-imposed or voluntary condition that endowed its adopter with a sense of control over his body and its actions. Although the ancient Greek thinker Aristotle did not defend the ideal of poverty per se, he did distinguish between those who are capable of exercising discipline over the passions through reason and conscious choice, and those who lack such capacities and therefore succumb to the excessive desire for bodily pleasures. Later, in the thirteenth century, Saint Thomas Aquinas expressly promoted the establishment of Christian institutions based on the ideal of voluntary poverty.

With the dawn of the modern era, the shift in these attitudes was palpable. The eighteenth-century British economist Adam Smith, for instance, argued that the lot of the poor should be improved; he portrayed the **wealth**-generating (page 259) mechanisms of the **capitalist** (page 44) market as the ideal means of bringing about that end. A century later, important studies such as Friedrich Engels's *The Condition of the Working Class in England* began to cast doubt on Smith's thesis. Informed by this research, Karl Marx maintained that the increasing pauperization of the **working class** (page 261) could not be relieved by the operations of the capitalist market. Indeed, he claimed, poverty was symptomatic of structural problems within capitalism itself, which could only be corrected by the establishment of a new **communist** (page 64) society. In *The Poverty of Philosophy*, he upbraided the French writer Pierre-Joseph Proudhon for entertaining the moral ideal of poverty as a response to the destructive effects of capitalist competition. For Marx, the "problem of the poor" resided not in the poor themselves but in the economic system responsible for their impoverishment.

P

PRESIDENCY

In the **United States** (page 248), the president is the head of the executive branch of the federal government. As the nation's chief executive, he must implement the law of the land. This power, granted to him under Article Two of the US **Constitution** (page 72), is distinct from those given to the other two branches of the national government: the lawmaking **Congress** (page 69) and the law-interpreting **federal courts** (page 103). In addition to making him the nation's top law enforcement official, Article Two assigns the president a number of other roles: he serves as the commander-in-chief of the US Armed Forces, appoints Supreme Court justices and other federal officials, settles treaties with foreign nations with the counsel and consent of the Senate, and issues federal pardons. Under exceptional circumstances, he is authorized to call into session or adjourn one or both chambers of Congress. Although the position of president is largely ceremonial in most **parliamentary democracies** (page 189), many view the presidency of the US as the most powerful elected office in the world today.

A head of state vested with such formidable powers is perhaps unexpected in a nation whose founders were leery of excessive executive authority—after all, the US Republic was established as a counterpoint to British colonial rule. The American revolutionaries saw the power wielded by King George III and his governors over the colonies as **tyrannical** (page 244) and inconsistent with the ideals of **liberty** (page 155), equality, and **republicanism** (page 206) later to be championed in the *Declaration of Independence* of 1776. Accordingly, the Articles of Confederation—which served as the Republic's first constitutional document from 1781 to 1789—narrowly restricted the powers of the national government; in fact, they contained no provisions for the creation of an executive branch.

The political climate would soon change, however. In May 1787, the Constitutional Convention was assembled to draft a replacement for the Articles of Confederation. The difficulties of managing the various political and economic problems created by the American Revolutionary War and its aftermath made the idea of a stronger national government appealing to many of the Convention's delegates. While a political faction known as the anti-Federalists remained opposed to such a move, a Constitution that endowed the presidency with a considerable degree of authority was ultimately adopted. The latter, however, was limited: the Constitution called for (among other things) a **separation of the powers** (page 216) of the presidency from

(Opposite) Columbia, the female embodiment of the United States, surrounded by portraits of the country's first 16 presidents.

P

those of the legislative and judicial branches, creating a system of "checks and balances" against potential power abuse.

These "checks and balances," however, have proven to be relatively weak: over the years, the power of the executive has grown precipitously. This shift became especially evident in the early twentieth century, when President Theodore Roosevelt added the executive order to the president's strategic toolkit. An executive order enables the president to implement national policies expeditiously, without the need to consult Congress or even the Constitution. Although the Supreme Court has ruled that the authority of the legislature and the Constitution cannot be circumvented in this way, the executive order has been wildly popular among occupants of the White House: by the early twenty-first century, US presidents had issued more than

P

The modern US presidency's enhanced authority allows it to establish most of the nation's foreign and domestic policies.

fifty thousand such directives. The rise of the executive order has been accompanied by the codification of other presidential prerogatives. The president's role in managing foreign affairs, for instance, has been interpreted as giving him the authority to decide when it may be appropriate to set aside the laws of individual states.[14] Although the US Constitution grants the president no formal legislative powers other than that of approving or vetoing bills passed by Congress, the modern US presidency's enhanced authority allows it to establish most of the nation's foreign and domestic policies.

Congress, for its part, has been increasingly disinclined to challenge the chief executive's role as the nation's key lawmaker. More often than not, it has been prepared to endorse—or at least acquiesce to—the president's proposed general legislation, especially with regard to military and foreign policy. It may at times object to these proposals, but it is rarely an independent initiator; nor is it common for it to exercise its authority to prevent the president from overstepping his constitutionally prescribed powers. **Marxist** (page 166) critics have argued that such heightened powers have equipped the chief executive to protect and promote the general interests of powerful business elites, while leaving the formulation of legislation addressed to the narrower concerns of particular constituencies in the hands of Congress.

(Opposite) Teddy Roosevelt, the 26th US president, summarized the country's foreign diplomacy with the phrase, "Speak softly, and carry a big stick."

PRIVATIZATION

The term *privatization* generally refers to the **government**'s (page 118) transfer of control over public operations to the private sector. The doctrine came into force in the 1980s and 1990s, as the foundational principles of the **welfare state** (page 259) fell into disfavor in many advanced industrial nations. In such countries, **state** (page 229) monopolies were dismantled and control of resources such as electricity, gas, water, steel, and railroads were turned over to private businesses. Eventually, other variants of privatization emerged: for example, governments began to experiment with "outsourcing," that is, the hiring of private contractors to perform various public services and functions.

As one of the main tenets of the economic doctrine known as **neoliberalism** (page 176), privatization was taken up by Chilean President Augusto Pinochet's authoritarian **military** (page 168) regime in the early 1970s, and by the **conservative** (page 71) governments of British Prime Minister Margaret Thatcher and American President Ronald Reagan in the early 1980s. Soon, privatization schemes were adopted by many other Western nations and developing countries in Asia, Africa, and Latin America. The collapse of the **Soviet Union** (page 226) and its satellite states was accompanied by the institution of a neoliberal program known as "shock therapy," which mandated the extensive privatization of publicly owned resources and assets.

The warm reception that privatization has received over the last twenty-five years reflects a general neoliberal consensus against centralized, state-controlled economies and governmental **bureaucracies** (page 43). According to neoliberals, privatization is a superior approach because of its demonstrated ability to foster economic growth and stability. With its emphasis on **entrepreneurialism** (page 95) and the **free market** (page 108), it efficiently distributes goods and services while promoting individual initiative, scientific and technological innovation, prosperity, and a wide range of economic opportunities.

As the twentieth century drew to a close, however, the social costs of privatization began to generate significant opposition. Some economists now argue that the mere fact that public resources and assets are owned by the state is less important than what the state actually does when it retains control over the economy. They claim that, if its policies are properly executed, the state can play an important role in redressing market failures and promoting long-term equitable development. Many have also noted that with privatization, jobs remain vulnerable to the prospect of outsourcing to "external labor markets," while consumers face the threat of increased prices for goods and services.

PROPERTY

Like many other concepts in the political vocabulary, *property* has taken on different meanings over time and across human **cultures** (page 74). Many authors have nevertheless attempted to identify some of its universal features. The English philosopher Jeremy Bentham, for one, noted that "property" refers not simply to the mere physical possession of something, but to a legal or moral relation between a person and the object that he or she owns. In this sense, it can be characterized as a "metaphysical" (rather than a material) relationship. Property may be claimed by the public, the government, or private individuals and corporations.

Our understanding of private property has evolved over the last 500 years. The most significant early modern theorist of private property was the seventeenth-century political philosopher John Locke. Locke argued that private ownership of property is a natural **right** (page 208), and that it cannot be usurped arbitrarily by the **state** (page 229). In fact, he insisted that the right to acquire and accumulate property is, like human **liberty** (page 155), both conceptually and historically prior to the state. When an individual mixes her **labor** (page 143) with some portion of the natural world in the pre-political "state of nature," she expresses a fundamental aspect of her own selfhood. She thus transforms that formerly shared portion of the world into something over which she possesses an exclusive right. She may now use it as she sees fit—sell it, transfer it, or turn it into an asset designed to generate income, for instance. Other people are barred from taking over her property without her consent. In fact, for Locke, the basic purpose of the state is to assure that the property rights of the individual are not infringed upon by others.

Since the conclusion of **World War II** (page 266), commodities—that is, saleable, privately held objects—have become the paradigmatic manifestation of private property. Moreover, upon the dissolution of the ideological divide between the **communist** (page 64) East and the **capitalist** (page 44) West in the early 1990s, the legitimacy of the private ownership of the means of production has gained near-universal acceptance. Even the People's Republic of China, which once stood alongside the **Soviet Union** (page 226) as one the world's great champions of collectivized property, had by the early 2000s established constitutional protections for private property rights.

R

RACISM

The term *racism* refers to belief systems that assume the human species can be divided into socially and biologically distinct "races," and that such races can be ranked on a superior-to-inferior continuum. There is a direct causal association, these ideologies maintain, between inherited racial traits (e.g., skin color) and an individual's personality, intellect, physical capacities, and moral attitudes.

Throughout human history, certain groups have used race as a basis for asserting their prerogative over others, and racial stereotypes are still embedded in the symbols, beliefs, and assumptions of many cultures. In some cases, racism is explicitly incorporated into the practices of the political order. Such institutionalized racism often involves distributing **rights** (page 208), **freedoms** (page 107), social privileges, or **wealth** (page 259) unequally on the basis of race.

Racism has been a prominent feature in North America since the arrival of European settlers more than five hundred years ago, when it was used to justify violence against Native American tribes. It was also the principal ideological prop for the institution of **slavery** (page 217), which resulted in the subjection of African slaves to separation from their families, mental and physical torment, violence, and death—for no fewer than 425 years.

The rationale underlying the slave system faced a formidable conceptual challenge in the late eighteenth century, with the establishment of the **United States** (page 248) Republic: in its *Declaration of Independence* and **Constitution** (page 72), the new nation proclaimed equality of opportunity and individual **liberty** (page 155) as two of its highest ideals, directly contradicting racist ideology.

Be that as it may, slavery was not dismantled in the US until the end of the **Civil War** (page 58) in 1865—almost a century after the **American Revolution** (page 18). Over the ensuing century and a half, institutionalized and symbolic forms of racism against African Americans and others have persisted. Racism in America has been the target of

Although slavery was abolished in 1865, the South's Jim Crow laws codified racial segregation for another century, as seen at this 1938 North Carolina water fountain.

R

various resistance movements, including the **civil rights** (page 54) struggle led by **Martin Luther King, Jr.** (page 141), and liberation campaigns mounted by groups such as the **Black Panther Party** (page 38).

Racism was a key ideological component of empire-building projects during the period of European **colonial** (page 61) expansion (1820–1939). The great Western empires subjected conquered populations to exploitative labor practices and systematic discrimination; they also denied them **sovereignty** (page 226) over their own political affairs. They legitimated these practices by portraying their colonial subjects as racially inferior members of the human species. In many cases, this mindset was turned against groups residing within the borders of the colonizing nations themselves. The racism that accompanied European colonialism fueled enormous resentment among the colonized peoples of the Third World. In the mid-twentieth century, independence movements such as **Mahatma Gandhi**'s (page 114) campaign against British rule in India gained momentum, eventually bringing colonialism to an end.

One of history's most notorious examples of racism occurred under the **Nazi** (page 175) regime led by **Adolf Hitler** (page 124) during the 1930s and 1940s. For more than a decade, Nazism waged a campaign of prejudice, hatred, violence, and genocide against European Jews and members of other ethnic and religious groups. It attempted to defend its **anti-Semitic** (page 23) practices by propounding the idea of a natural racial hierarchy that placed people of Germanic descent at the top, and Jews and other racial subgroups at the bottom—a proposition for which it claimed to have discovered scientific proof.

Throughout the twentieth century, racism was at the core of many other political campaigns and practices—notably those of **apartheid** (page 24) South Africa. The apartheid regime legally restricted the civil rights, liberties, and movements of blacks and other ethnic groups, which comprised the majority of the nation's population. The state of Israel has also been accused of adopting racist practices toward indigenous Palestinians and Arabs. Although roundly refuted by Israel and its allies, this charge was upheld in a 1975 **United Nations** (UN) (page 245) resolution (which has since been repealed) equating **Zionism** (page 270) with racism. For almost seventy years, the UN's 1948 *Universal Declaration of Human Rights* has been the basis of calls to end institutionalized racism and the dissemination of racist beliefs and practices the world over.

RADICALISM

The term *radicalism* was coined in the late eighteenth century by the British statesman Charles James Fox. Derived from the Latin *radix*, or root, it was initially associated with Fox's campaign to fundamentally reform the British parliamentary system by extending the right of suffrage to all adult males. The radicals of Fox's era cheered the demise of Europe's old feudal orders and championed the **liberal** (page 152) ideals of modern Enlightenment: they upheld **republicanism** (page 206), freedom of the press, the abolition of titles based on social status, the principle of private **property** (page 199), and secularism. In Britain and continental Europe, their cause was eventually absorbed into the tradition of liberal progressivism. By the late nineteenth century, radicalism was radical only with respect to its opposition to a social order that had long since ceased to exist.

In the **United States** (page 248) and other countries, the term "radicalism" has generally had different connotations. Historically, it has been used in reference to **Marxist** (page 166) organizations and other groups on the far left side of the political spectrum, although it is now also applied to **terrorist** (page 238) groups and elements of the far right.

REDISTRIBUTION

Redistribution refers to the process of transferring income or **wealth** (page 259) from some groups to others; it generally flows downward, from the wealthier to the poorer. In today's global political climate, where the principles of market **liberalism** (page 152) are widely embraced, it is a controversial idea.

In any case, redistribution has been a feature of most Western constitutional **democracies** (page 78) since the conclusion of **World War II** (page 266), and governments have adopted a number of institutional mechanisms to ensure it. Some, for instance, have instituted progressive **taxation** (page 236), which obliges those with higher incomes to incur higher rates of tax. Schemes that provide government subsidies to individuals with low incomes (e.g., the Supplemental Nutrition Assistance Program) are another popular tactic.

Redistribution is supported by many currents within the Western philosophical tradition. Aristotle's ideal of distributive justice, for instance, points to a more equitable allocation of commonly held goods. This argument was developed by the philosopher John Rawls, who portrayed a fair society as one in which inequalities are tolerated only insofar as they redound to the benefit of the least well-off.

REFORMATION

The Protestant Reformation, or simply the *Reformation*, was a theological and political movement that began in sixteenth-century Europe. It was initiated by a group of theologians, clergy, and statesmen who challenged the reigning doctrines of the Catholic Church, helping to fuel widespread disenchantment with the **Papacy** (page 187) and the Holy See.

Such critical sentiments and calls for reform had already surfaced in the fourteenth century, during the early Renaissance. However, the official start of the Reformation is generally attributed to Martin Luther's famous *Ninety-Five Theses*, published in 1517 and widely disseminated thanks to the introduction of the printing press. Luther questioned some of the powers granted to the Pope, along with many of the Catholic Church's doctrines and devotional practices. The Counter-Reformation, an attempt on the part of the Catholic Church to quell the movement, did not prevail. The Reformation spread the Lutheran and Calvinist versions of Protestantism throughout Europe, ending the dominance of Catholicism in the continent. In his book *The Protestant Ethic and the Spirit of Capitalism*, Max Weber argued that Protestantism, with its emphasis on hard work and worldly achievements, created a cultural environment conducive to the rise of modern **capitalism** (page 44).

REGICIDE

Regicide is the intentional killing or judicial execution of a king, emperor, or other member of the reigning royalty. In most contemporary nations, the role of such figures has become largely symbolic, divested of all real political power. However, this has not always been the case: in the **aristocratic** (page 30) societies of medieval Europe, monarchs enjoyed the power of **absolute** rule (page 15). As God's mortal representative on earth, the king wielded his all-encompassing authority in accord with the divine will. Regicide was thus viewed as a particularly grave offense, an affront to both God and the doctrine of the king's **divine right** (page 87).

This meant that regicides were often subjected to harsh punishments. In France prior to the Revolution of 1789, those convicted of the crime had to endure barbaric forms of torture—for example, burning and dismemberment—carried out both before and during the implementation of their death sentences. Notable historical cases of regicide include the execution of Mary, Queen of Scots, who was found guilty of conspiring to assassinate Queen Elizabeth I of England; the execution of Charles I of England by Parliament supporters during the English Civil War; and the murder of Henry III of France at the hands of a knife-wielding assassin.

REPUBLIC

Taking its name from the Roman *res publica* (Latin for "the public thing"), a *republic* is a **state** (page 229) in which citizens elect a body of representatives to public office, conferring upon them the authority to govern in accordance with the rule of law. In a republic, then, the **sovereignty** (page 226) of the state resides with the citizenry—the definition of which has varied over time and from nation to nation. Because the people themselves do not participate in the running of the government, a republic is not considered to be a direct **democracy** (page 78), but rather a representative democracy.

This modern description of a republic was not always the prevalent one. Before the seventeenth century, all regimes aimed at upholding the common good—including **aristocracies** (page 30), monarchies, and **oligarchies** (page 182)—were referred to as republics; only **tyrannies** (page 244) were not classed as such, since their objective was to further the interests of a single private individual. In the late eighteenth century, as the old **hereditary** (page 123) monarchies and aristocracies of feudal Europe collapsed in the aftermath of the **French Revolution** (page 109) and the **American Revolution** (page 18), the term took on its modern sense: it was applied only to states that are governed by a written constitution and whose leaders are periodically elected or appointed.

While some thinkers of the European Enlightenment advocated constitutional monarchies, others weighed in on the side of republics. Baron de Montesquieu and Jean-Jacques Rousseau, for example, doubted that republics could be viable in large nation-states such as France; they believed, however, that a republic modeled along the lines of the ancient Geek *polis* could work very well in small city-states like Corsica. Rousseau in particular argued that such city-states offered the best prospects for a democratic-republican **social contract** (page 221), in which citizens would obey their own self-prescribed laws and implement the "general will" out of a sense of moral and civic obligation. Constituted by a system of small self-governing assemblies, such a republic would be an ideal political arrangement.

On the other side of the Atlantic, the case for a republic was advanced by opponents of British rule over the American colonies. The anticolonial rebels insisted that the British monarchy had abrogated its colonial subjects' **rights** (page 208) to representative government, which rendered it little more than a tyranny. A federal republic was eventually established upon the ratification of the **Constitution** (page 72) of the **United States** (page 248) in 1789.

REPUBLICANISM

In *republicanism,* as opposed to other forms of political organization, **sovereignty** (page 226) over the **state** (page 229) resides not with its rulers but with its citizens; the latter endow the government with the authority to formulate and enact legislation on their behalf and in accord with their will. In other words, state officials represent not themselves but the people. While citizens do not participate directly in the running of the state—as would be the case in a "pure" **democracy** (page 78)—republicanism is hospitable to the idea of representative democracy, in which citizens are afforded certain institutional mechanisms (e.g., **elections,** page 92) and **rights** (page 208) (e.g., the freedom of speech and public assembly) to contest the actions of the government and guard against abuses of state power.

Historically, republicanism emerged as a significant political doctrine upon the advent of the Roman Republic in 509 BC. It was resuscitated during the Florentine Renaissance of the early sixteenth century. In the late eighteenth century, the **French Revolution** (page 109) and the **American Revolution** (page 18) both opposed **hereditary** (page 123) monarchy and other non-republican governmental arrangements that abjured popular sovereignty.

REPUBLICAN PARTY

Along with the **Democratic Party** (page 82), the *Republican Party*—also referred to as the Grand Old Party, or GOP—is one of the two major political parties in the United States today. The Republican Party grew out of the movement against slavery in the northern US in the nineteenth century. Officially established in 1854, the party gained the White House for the first time in 1861 with the election of President Abraham Lincoln.

Despite its origins in the progressive anti-slavery cause, the Republican Party's platform is now largely based on **conservative** (page 71) ideological principles. These include the belief that government should have a limited role in regulating the **free market** (page 108) and providing for the social **welfare** (page 259) of disadvantaged individuals and groups. The party also supports strengthening the American armed forces in the name of national defense, and is generally opposed to labor unions, abortion rights, and illegal immigration (although there is some disagreement within the party about how to handle the latter problem). While Republicans tend to favor fewer controls on market activities than do Democrats, there is broad agreement between the two parties about the need to promote an economic climate that is hospitable to the interests of American corporations.

REVOLUTION

In the premodern era, the word *revolution* usually referred to the replacement of one form of **government** (page 118) by another—an **aristocracy** (page 30) substituted for a **republican** (page 206) **city-state** (page 52), for example. However, beginning in the late eighteenth century, the term was used to describe a social and political upheaval whereby one type of society is replaced by a radically different one. This new usage reflected recent developments in Western Europe, where the old systems of aristocratic feudalism had been supplanted by new constitutional republics.

The first great upheaval of this sort was the **French Revolution** (page 109) of 1789. Inspired by the philosophy of the Enlightenment, the French revolutionaries tore down established traditions and systems of political

Nineteenth-century painting depicting French insurgents burning royal chariots at the palace of Château d'Eu.

R

authority; they proclaimed the dawn of a new era in which social institutions and governments would be based on reason and citizens' free will. Such ideals were also taken up and instituted across the Atlantic in 1776, although the **American Revolution** (page 18) was principally a campaign for independence from **colonial** (page 61) rule, rather than an overthrow of an ancient order of peasant vassals and their aristocratic landlords.

In the nineteenth century, the German thinker Karl Marx contributed significantly to the theorization of revolution. Drawing on the philosophy of Georg Wilhelm Friedrich Hegel, he claimed that the seeds of a new political order are present in each historical epoch. History, he argued, does not progress in a linear fashion (one event after another); rather, it unfolds according to the logic of the "dialectic." As encapsulated in Hegel's concept of *Aufhebung*, the three basic moments of the dialectic can be translated roughly as negation, preservation, and transcendence. Marx, however, maintained that the dialectic is grounded not in the realm of ideas—as Hegel would have it—but rather in the material conditions of production: the present **capitalist** (page 44) mode of production has given rise to a historical agent (the **working class**, page 261) that is positioned to negate the rule of the **bourgeoisie** (page 41). Following the logic of the dialectic, this negation will also entail a preservation of some elements of the order for which the bourgeoisie is itself responsible—notably, its ideals of **liberty** (page 155), equality, and fraternity, and its revolutionized means of production. Thus, proceeding in this dialectical fashion, the revolution will transcend the present conditions of "unfreedom" and create the material bases for a truly liberated society.

RIGHTS

See *civil rights, human rights*.

R

FRANKLIN D. ROOSEVELT

1882	*Born in Hyde Park, New York*
1910	*Launches political career as senator*
1933	*Begins first presidential term*
1933	*Initiates New Deal reforms*
1935	*Signs National Labor Relations Act*
1941	*US enters World War II after Pearl Harbor attack*
1945	*Dies while still in office*

Franklin D. Roosevelt was the longest-serving president in United States history. A **Democrat** (page 82), Roosevelt was first elected to the presidency in March 1933. He went on to serve a record four consecutive terms, relinquishing the office only upon his death in April 1945. The period in which Roosevelt led the nation was arguably the most momentous in twentieth-century US history. Roosevelt oversaw America's involvement in **World War II** (page 266), and confronted the global economic crisis known as the Great Depression. He also inaugurated the New Deal, a program that significantly augmented the government's role in regulating the **free market** (page 108) and providing for the social welfare of American citizens. Roosevelt's reform initiatives were dogged by controversy from the outset; efforts to roll back the **welfare state** (page 259) that he helped bring to life have become an enduring feature of US politics, finding champions among both Republicans and Democrats.

Roosevelt began his political career in 1910, upon his election to the New York State Senate at the age of twenty-eight. He went on to serve as President Woodrow Wilson's Assistant Secretary of the Navy. Running alongside presidential contender James M. Cox, Roosevelt lost a bid for the vice presidency in 1920. Having lost the use of his legs due to polio, he then took a hiatus from politics. But he reentered the fray some years later, serving as Governor of New York from 1929 to 1932. As governor, Roosevelt promoted a number of economic relief programs that anticipated the New Deal initiatives he would later champion as president.

Roosevelt won the presidency for the first time in 1932, having defeated Republican candidate and previous White House occupant Herbert Hoover. Within the first hundred days of his term, he began to lay the foundations of the New Deal through a series of major legislative proposals and executive orders. Initially, the New Deal's chief aim was to provide relief from massive unemployment and other economic ills created by the Great Depression, as well as to stimulate the recovery of the economy. In order to achieve the former, Roosevelt provided millions of unemployed Americans with government jobs—specifically, jobs in

R

various public works programs designed to build up the nation's public infrastructure: its highways, its **energy** (page 95) grid, and so on. To stimulate economic growth and stabilize the volatile financial market, Roosevelt imposed tighter regulations on American corporations and the finance industry.

Some years later, in 1935, Roosevelt would sign the National Labor Relations Act, a key piece of New Deal legislation. Under the act, workers were guaranteed a number of federal rights, including the right to form unions, to bargain collectively with management, and to participate in strikes. (The Taft-Hartley Act, authorized by President Harry Truman in 1947, would significantly weaken these entitlements.) 1935 also saw the establishment of the Social Security Act, a New Deal "safety net" program offering economic assistance to those who would otherwise suffer hardship due to old age, illness, or poverty.

Roosevelt's New Deal programs, along with his repeal of the Prohibition laws against

(Above) Though many of his programs were later repealed by anti-welfare politicians, Franklin D. Roosevelt is known for his New Deal, which pulled the US out of the Great Depression.

the sale of alcohol, were well received; this led to a landslide reelection in 1936. From 1937 to 1938, Roosevelt had to contend with the effects of an economy that had relapsed into a deep recession, as well as stiff opposition from a newly formed Conservative Coalition. The Coalition blocked his nominations of liberal justices to the Supreme Court, while also obstructing most of his newly proposed liberal legislation (his minimum wage bill was the only exception). As the economy emerged from recession and unemployment dropped to two percent, Roosevelt's New Deal relief programs were repealed. Starting in the mid-1970s, many of the regulations he had imposed on American business were also discarded.

Initially, Roosevelt kept America out of World War II—which broke out in 1939—although he did provide diplomatic and financial aid to China and the United Kingdom. However, after the Japanese attack on Pearl Harbor on December 7, 1941, Roosevelt could no longer remain neutral. Partnering with British Prime Minister **Winston Churchill** (page 50) and **Soviet** (page 226) leader Joseph Stalin, he incorporated the United States to the coalition of Allied forces arrayed against the Axis Powers (Germany, Italy, and Japan). He also launched the Manhattan Project, which led to the development of the **nuclear weapons** (page 180) that were eventually dropped on the Japanese cities of Hiroshima and Nagasaki.

In addition, he sent some one hundred thousand Japanese American civilians, who were said to be threats to US security, to internment camps during the war.

Although his domestic and foreign policies have been criticized by both the left and the right, Roosevelt's presidency remains one of the most significant in US history—one that has had lasting effects on the scope and direction of American politics and society.

(Above) The Works Progress Administration generated mass employment by funding the construction of large public works like dams and bridges.

S

SENATE (US)

Along with the **House of Representatives** (page 126), the *Senate* is one of the two chambers that comprise the **Congress** (page 69), the federal law-making body of the United States. The Senate was established in 1789 under Article One of the US Constitution. The Article requires that each US state, regardless of its geographic size and number of residents, be represented by two Senators, each elected to a six-year term in office. The Senate is subject to a staggered election cycle: every two years, one-third of the one-hundred-member chamber stands for re-election. An individual can run for the office of Senator only if he or she is at least thirty years old, has been a citizen of the United States for a minimum of nine years, and is a resident of the state in which he or she is running at election time. The Senate and the House deliberate on proposed legislation separately, but the approval of both chambers is required in order for a bill to be passed into law.

The Senate was incorporated into the US Congress on the conviction that it would serve as an important internal check on the activities of the House. According to the framers of the US Constitution, such a check was needed in order to protect the rights and interests of the individual states and, in particular, the rights and interests of the wealthy property owners residing therein. Such protections would be absent, they argued, if the Congress were simply a one-chambered body representing the citizenry at large—a so-called "People's House." As James Madison, one of the Constitution's main authors, noted, "Landholders ought to have a share in the government, to support these invaluable interests, and to balance and check the other. They ought to be so constituted as to protect the minority of the opulent against the majority. The senate, therefore, ought to be this body."[15] Senators were thus given certain exclusive powers denied to their counterparts in the House—for example, their consent must be given if a treaty is to be ratified, and they have the power to confirm the appointments of certain federal officials, including Cabinet secretaries, federal judges, and ambassadors. In general, the office of Senator carries more prestige than the office of Congressperson. Senators are fewer in number and serve for lengthier terms; they are also assigned more staffers and participate in more congressional committees.

The Senate, pictured here circa 1873, was conceived of by James Madison as the chamber that would represent the interests of the landed elite.

S

SCIENCE AND POLITICS

In the West, the principles of the modern scientific method were developed during the European Renaissance of the fourteenth to seventeenth centuries. Modern science radically transformed the way that humans understood not only the physical universe, but also the world of politics. The groundbreaking scientific discoveries of Galileo, Nicolaus Copernicus, Johannes Kepler, and other Renaissance thinkers had immediate political ramifications. The medieval church-state was now forced to grapple with a new conception of the universe that threatened to shatter the doctrinal foundations of its rule. The seminal development in this regard was the astronomical model developed by Copernicus, which placed the sun, rather than the Earth, at the center of the solar system. Copernicus's heliocentric theory would later be championed and empirically substantiated by Galileo. The response from the Catholic Church was swift: its Roman Inquisition declared Galileo's findings "foolish" and "heretical," while Pope Paul V ordered him to "abandon completely" the perspective of heliocentrism.

In attacking the discoveries of modern science, the Church was not simply engaged in a scholastic dispute about the correct interpretation of the Bible; it was also responding to what it perceived to be a *political* threat. Indeed, if the scientific method was correct, then the Church's divine cosmology and derived authority could no longer be accepted *prima facie*. Modern science prescribed an epistemology based not on avowedly infallible canonical texts, but rather on processes of verification and falsification. The laws of the entire universe, including those of the political institutions on Earth, were now fair game for scientific inquiry. If prevailing assumptions about the way the world worked were shown to be false, then a rational mind would have little choice but to abandon them.

The emergence of the scientific method had a profound impact on the political philosophers of the early modern era. Although few were prepared to disavow the existence of God, the great political minds of the period (Niccolò Machiavelli, Thomas Hobbes, and John Locke, for example) were eager to discard divine authority as a foundation of the nation-state. In accordance with the epistemological convictions of modern science, they considered men to be rational, self-directed, and capable of charting their own destinies. Men, they added, could also utilize modern science to predict the behavior of nature and control it in the service of their ends. This anthropocentric perspective wrested control over both nature and politics from God and his earthly representatives, and placed it in the hands of mere mortal men.

By the late eighteenth century, the demise of the old feudal **aristocracy** (page 30) was

complete. The **French Revolution** (page 109) and ensuing political upheavals led to the establishment of constitutional **republic**s (page 206), whose founding legal documents offered citizens formal guarantees of **liberty** (page 155) and equality. With the Church divested of its authority to direct the political life of the nation, modern science and technology were free to develop apace. Many have noted, however, that decisions about what science should study and how it should be utilized are now often made to suit private industry objectives. This raises the question of whether a political element has been introduced into the scientific process. Is the development of modern science and technology driven by the quest for truth, or is it fueled, in large measure, by a **capitalist** (page 44) market?

Modern science has faced this basic conundrum from the outset. On the one hand, it is committed to the principle of value neutrality: it strives to be impartial in the face of truth. On the other hand, it has often been forced to operate in environments where economic and political considerations take precedence over the imperative to simply discover what is. One notable historical example of the politicization of science is Lysenkoism, which took hold in the **Soviet Union** (page 226) in the late 1920s. The biologist and agronomist Trofim Lysenko was the director of the Lenin All-Union Academy of Agricultural Sciences. Backed by Communist Party leader Joseph Stalin, he used his position to manipulate the scientific process, constructing scientific models on the basis of predetermined political objectives. During this same period, scientists in **Nazi** (page 175) Germany distorted Charles Darwin's evolutionary theory in an effort to substantiate the regime's belief in the existence of a natural racial hierarchy that placed those of "pure" Germanic descent at the top, and members of "subhuman" races at the bottom.

(Above) Fifteenth-century astronomer Copernicus's discovery that the sun (rather than Earth) lay at the center of the solar system presented a grave threat to the Catholic Church.

SEPARATION OF POWERS

The *separation of powers* doctrine is an argument for dividing the state into branches, each with its own distinct powers and responsibilities. The origin of the idea can be found in Aristotle's *Politics*, in which he defends the institution of a "mixed government": one combining features of **oligarchy** (page 182) and **democracy** (page 78). However, credit for our modern understanding of the separation of powers must go largely to the French Enlightenment thinker Baron de Montesquieu. In his 1748 treatise *The Spirit of the Laws*, Montesquieu made the case for splitting the powers of the government in three: a separate legislature, executive, and judiciary would prevent the king or other head of state from monopolizing political power, and thereby guard against the prospect of **tyranny** (page 244). While this argument had already been anticipated by John Locke, who advocated dividing the powers of the king and the parliament in his *Two Treatises of Government* of 1689, most modern presidential **democracies** (page 78) were ultimately drawn to Montesquieu's tripartite division.

The model proved especially attractive due to its accompanying system of "checks and balances." With their powers duly separated, argued Montesquieu, the three branches are positioned to surveil and control one another, assuring that each adheres to its respective mandates and does not emerge as a supreme power unto itself. In other words, it does not just fall on the electorate to keep the government on its toes; the checks and balances system provides the state with its own internal means of guarding against political power abuse.

James Madison argued precisely this in *Federalist No. 51*. He noted that since the government, like the citizenry, is not comprised of "angels," the state must possess some internal mechanism that will "oblige it to control itself." Madison went on to incorporate the separation of powers doctrine into the **Constitution** (page 72), the founding legal document of the **United States** (page 248). As a result of his intervention, the Constitution does not just parcel out the authority of the government among three branches; it also splits **Congress** (page 69), the legislative body, into the **House of Representatives** (page 126) and the **Senate** (page 212). In proposing this additional division, Madison was not simply looking for a further check against the emergence of tyrannical state power; his hope was that the Senate would "balance and check" the lower "People's House," protecting the interests of the "opulent minority" against the schemes of the propertyless majority.

S

SEPARATISM

In adopting the doctrine of *separatism*, religious, cultural, ethnic, tribal, or other kinds of groups seek to sever ties with a larger community to which they belong. Separatism is sometimes associated with segregation—as implemented under **apartheid** (page 24) South Africa, for example—but is different from it in that it is generally undertaken voluntarily.

Groups may be drawn to separatism for a variety of reasons. They may, for instance, have a longstanding rivalry with the community from which they wish to separate, or they may be seeking relief from religious, ethnic, or cultural repression; they may also wish to remove themselves from a situation in which political power and economic privileges are held disproportionately by others.

Some have characterized separatist groups as practicing a form of "identity politics," meaning that their desire for separation stems from a belief that continued integration with the dominant group will compromise their identity and capacity for self-determination. However, in many cases, economic and political factors may be the primary motivation for separatist action.

SLAVERY

Slavery is a condition under which some human beings are owned by others. A slave is legally recognized as the **property** (page 199), or chattel, of his or her owner. Some slave systems consider slaves as transportable property, while others take them to be immovable assets similar to land or real estate. As property, slaves are denied most of the **freedoms** (page 107) and **rights** (page 208) enjoyed by other members of society, including the right to vote and hold public office. They become objects of the **law** (page 147) rather than its subjects. Accordingly, in most slaveholding societies, they are neither held legally responsible for their actions nor granted the same legal protections as non-slaves. Moreover, as mere objects of the law, they have no legally recognized kin or progeny, no legal claim on the products of their own labor, and often no right to make decisions regarding their biological reproduction and prospective sexual partners. It must be said, however, that many slave societies throughout time established conventions limiting the extent to which slaves could be abused.

Slavery has existed since the origins of recorded history. In China, for example, it was practiced from the eighteenth century to the twelfth century BC during the Shang dynasty, and from 206 BC to AD 25 during the Han dynasty. It persisted in certain regions through the twentieth century. Yet China is hardly an isolated case: over the ages, slavery

S

was instituted in Asian countries such as Korea, India, Thailand, Burma, the Philippines, Nepal, Malaya, Indonesia, and Japan; it was also implemented in European nations such as France, Germany, Poland, Lithuania, and Russia.

Since their inception, slave systems have fallen into two basic types: household slavery and productive slavery. Under household slavery, slaves are obliged to work primarily within the domestic sphere, with only occasional duties (harvesting, for example) outside of it. Household slaves often serve as status symbols for their owners—evidence of their high levels of surplus **wealth** (page 259). By contrast, the principal purpose of productive slavery is to extract **labor** (page 143) from slaves in order to produce marketable goods such as coal, timber, and sugar. This was the aim behind the slave systems that were established in, among other places, Classical Athenian Greece and Rome, ninth-century

Slavery in the United States lasted from 1619 to 1865, serving as the violent foundation of the South's plantation economy.

S

Iraq, nineteenth-century sub-Saharan Africa, and the Caribbean and Americas following Columbus's arrival in 1492.

In the Southern **United States** (page 248), slavery was introduced in 1619, when slaves were first transported involuntarily from Africa and deposited in Virginia. A productive slave system utilizing captured Africans was soon established throughout the South, replacing an earlier system in which white landowners enlisted indentured laborers from England. At first, slaves were forced to work primarily on Southern tobacco plantations. However, with the arrival of Eli Whitney's cotton gin in 1793 and the incorporation of Alabama, Mississippi, Louisiana, and Texas into the Southern fold, the demand for slave labor changed: almost two-thirds of Southern plantation slaves were engaged in cotton production by 1850. The slave system would meet its demise only upon the conclusion of the American **Civil War** (page 58) in 1865. It may be argued that despite the abolition of slavery, the extension of legal **civil rights** (page 54) to African Americans in the 1960s, and the 2008 and 2012 electoral victories of Barack Obama (America's first black president), US society has yet to rid itself completely of its cultural and ideological legacy of **racism** (page 200) and discrimination.

SOCIAL ACTIVISM

Social activism is a broad term that refers to the efforts of individuals or groups to bring about social, economic, political, or ideological change. It typically involves either support for or opposition to a controversial matter, such as same-sex marriage or national foreign policy; it may focus on issues of concern to a local community or the society at large. Social activists' campaigns may take a variety of forms, including **nonviolent resistance** (page 179), **direct action** (page 86), and **civil disobedience** (page 53). Specific tactics include **strikes** (page 231), demonstrations, sit-ins, riots, economic boycotts, and political **lobbying** (page 158). Today, many activist groups have taken advantage of the growing availability of the Internet to bring their causes to national or international attention: social media activism has been credited with mobilizing support for the various campaigns of the **Arab Spring** (page 28), for instance.

The degree of social activism within a society has been understood by many as an important barometer of its **democratic** (page 78) legitimacy. Low levels of social activism are indicative of a situation in which citizens have "immunity from service," as the seventeenth-century **social contract** (page 221) theorist Thomas Hobbes put it. In such societies, the running of the **state** (page 229) is left to public officials; citizens are divested of oversight and control over its affairs. Many observers have underlined

S

DEMAND
ILLINOIS
CHICAGO UNIT
RANK & FILE
NOW
BONUS
UNIT
WHEN TO COME
WHEN TO GO
VETERANS
UNITE
BONUS

the authoritarian implications of such a scenario, noting that changes in the direction of national policy—particularly with respect to the interests of disadvantaged groups—have generally come about as a result of pressure exerted on the **government** (page 118) by social activists. Few would deny that the Civil Rights Act of 1964 and the Voting Rights Act of 1965, for example, were a direct response to the massive **civil rights** (page 54) campaign led by **Martin Luther King, Jr.** (page 141)

In the **United States** (page 248), the **freedom** (page 107) to engage in social activism is upheld by the First Amendment to the **Constitution** (page 72), which guarantees citizens the right to assemble and "petition the government for a redress of grievances." However, in recent years, the US government has often exercised the authority granted to it by anti-**terrorism** (page 238) laws such as the 2001 USA Patriot Act to limit the constitutional rights of citizen activists.

(Opposite) Veterans march in front of the US Capitol building in Washington, DC, in the 1930s.

SOCIAL CONTRACT

The idea of the *social contract* emerged in the seventeenth and eighteenth centuries, and quickly established itself as one of the tenets of modern political theory. It proposes that a legitimate government, or commonwealth, will take the form of an agreement specifying the rights and obligations between citizens and their rulers. In order to illustrate why such a pact is necessary, social contract theory imagines what life might be like without it. It refers to such a situation as the "state of nature." Here, social contract theorists argue, individuals are free to exercise their natural liberties and rights; in so doing, they may be happy or unhappy (depending on the version of social contract theory consulted). At some point, however, natural reason shows them that morality and justice can be achieved only by leaving the **anarchic** (page 22) conditions of this state of nature, and entering into a civil contract with a sovereign government. A principal aim of social contract theory is to demonstrate why people would freely agree to be bound by the obligations that such a government imposes.

The modern social contract tradition is principally associated with the work of Thomas Hobbes, John Locke, and Jean-Jacques Rousseau. In his famous 1651 text, *Leviathan*, Hobbes portrays men in a state of nature as absolutely free and absolutely equal, but not accountable to a law that would have them behave peaceably; free to pursue

S

their self-interests without constraints, they become embroiled in a perpetual battle over scarce resources—a "war of each against all." Reason, however, eventually leads them to surrender some of their natural rights and freedoms to an all-powerful sovereign, who will in turn assure peace and security through the coercive force of the civil **law** (page 147).

Locke will later make important revisions to Hobbes' account. In particular, he will reject the defense of monarchical **absolutism** (page 15) and posit the safeguarding of **property** (page 199) rights as the social contract's principal objective. Meanwhile, Rousseau's political theory is notable for its postulation of rather peaceful individuals in their state of nature, and its claim that the moral ends of the social contract are not best realized through laws imposed by an authority external to the citizenry; rather, he argues, citizens should exercise their "general will," i.e., implement their own self-prescribed laws out of a collective sense of moral responsibility and civic obligation.

SOCIAL DEMOCRACY

As a political movement, *social democracy* shared classical **Marxism**'s (page 166) goal to replace **capitalism** (page 44) with a **socialist** (page 224) alternative; it rejected, however, Marxism's revolutionary means of achieving such a goal. Instead, it sought to peacefully attain socialism through the **liberal** (page 152) political processes that had emerged alongside capitalism. Because of this, many Marxist critics derided social democracy as a form of revisionism.

The contemporary social democratic movement took hold in 1875, when two previously existing workers' organizations merged to form the Social Democratic Party of Germany. Theoreticians such as Eduard Bernstein helped promulgate social democracy's belief that socialism should be instituted incrementally and lawfully rather than through revolutionary force. The Social Democrats were elected to the Reichstag (the German parliament) in 1871. By 1912, they had become the largest single party in that chamber, fueling the spread of social democracy throughout the continent. They were also behind the rise of the robust **welfare states** (page 259) established in post-**World War II** (page 266) Europe. Contemporary Marxists continue to criticize social democracy; they insist that, in adopting an increasingly accommodationist stance toward capitalism, it has betrayed its original socialist goal.

S

SOCIAL GROUPS

Social groups are collections of individuals who are at least partially dependent on one another and share at least some elements of a common identity. Members of a group generally interact with each other on a face-to-face basis, although this is not always so (as is evident, for example, in the case of today's increasingly popular Internet groups or "online communities").

In modern sociology, one of the first major efforts to distinguish between different types of groups was made by the German theorist Ferdinand Tönnies. Tönnies used the terms *Gesellschaft* and *Gemeinschaft* to describe two types of groups on the basis of their economic and social structures. The members of groups of the *Gesellschaft* type are oriented toward the achievement of instrumental objectives; they are bound by formal social relations, rather than interpersonal or communal ties. In contrast, members of *Gemeinschaft* groups belong to small communities that share cultural traditions and beliefs, as well as mutual bonds of kinship. Another classical sociologist, Émile Durkheim, emphasized the importance of religious rituals in assuring control and cohesion among the members of a social group.

SOCIAL INSURANCE

Social insurance programs provide citizens with government-sponsored safeguards that the **free-market** (page 108) economy is unable to offer, such as protections against the loss of employment due to illness, disability, or old age. Participation in, and contributions to, government social insurance programs are usually compulsory. Credit for the first modern nationwide social insurance scheme goes to German Chancellor Otto von Bismarck, who in the 1880s offered workers old-age and invalidity pensions. By the early twentieth century, many European countries had followed his example.

The **United States** (page 248) was a much slower adopter: it waited until 1935 to pass the Social Security Act, which provides some protections against risks associated with old age, poverty, and unemployment. The Act would eventually be followed by social insurance programs like Medicare, which offers **health care** (page 121) assistance to individuals over the age of sixty-five. Departing significantly from the Medicare model, the 2010 Patient Protection and Affordable Care Act requires citizens without health care coverage to subscribe to a modestly subsidized, means-tested private health insurance plan. Some argue that this scheme, in which each state can opt to run its own health insurance "marketplace," is less a government social insurance program than an essentially **neoliberal** (page 176), market-based solution to a pressing social problem.

SOCIALISM

Socialism is a political program that opposes the private ownership of **property** (page 199), and advocates for its control by the society at large. In contrast with classical **liberalism** (page 152)—which portrays people as inherently self-interested and inclined to pursue their affairs in isolation—socialism espouses a sanguine view of human nature: it affirms people's capacity to live and work cooperatively, and sees production as a fundamentally social process whose outcomes can and should be shared by everyone involved.

Socialism is thus at odds with capitalism, which calls for an economy based on private ownership of the means of production. Under capitalism, decisions regarding the creation and distribution of goods and services are not made cooperatively: they are left to the unplanned motions of the **free market** (page 108). Socialists view capitalism as an inherently exploitative system that enables an elite class—the capitalist class—to accumulate enormous amounts of **wealth** (page 259) and power by controlling the production process. Having failed to triumph in free-market competition, the majority working class must seek employment in capitalist enterprises, which then appropriate the surplus[16] of their labor in the form of profits.

Socialists further argue that, as the dominant economic class, capitalists exert disproportionate leverage over the political process: they make large contributions to **election** (page 92) campaigns and often hold high positions within the government itself. Assisted by the latter, capitalists in representative **democracies** (page 78) appropriate **liberal** (page 152) principles such as **freedom** (page 107) and equality to legitimate the very power structures over which they preside. Democratic socialists do not reject these ideals per se, but argue that they cannot be objectively realized under capitalist conditions. They maintain that true human emancipation, equality, and prosperity are dependent upon the establishment of social control of the material means by which society is reproduced.

Despite these basic points of agreement, socialists differ in their opinions of how their social order is to be organized and achieved. Some among them argue that existing liberal institutions—such as elections and the legislative process—should be utilized to develop socialism incrementally and lawfully out of the capitalist order. This "reformist" course was originally advocated by European **social democracy** (page 222). Radical socialists, in contrast, contend that true socialism can only be brought about through revolutionary force.

Socialists also disagree about which types of property should be socially controlled. In his 1516 book *Utopia*, Thomas More imagined a world in which almost all property, with the exception of personal effects such as clothing, is publicly owned. Other socialists depart from this vision and are receptive to the idea of some small or medium-sized farms and businesses remaining in private hands. Some argue that property and natural resources should be brought under a single central authority such as the state. Others agree, but would like to see such ownership backed by the authority of a political party, in line with the model of socialism established in the former **Soviet Union** (page 226). Proponents of decentralized socialism insist that decisions about the production, use, and distribution of public property should be made at the local level by those who stand to be most directly affected. This is basically the view of **syndicalist** (page 235) socialism, which argues for the creation of multiple cooperative political units that will manage the production process internally, democratically, and locally.

Karl Marx and Friedrich Engels are widely recognized as the most important modern theorists of socialism. They argued that it could not be established by building idyllic communities amidst the existing capitalist order, as writers such as Henri de Saint-Simon, Charles Fourier, and Robert Owen had imagined—such experiments were "utopian," they claimed, and insisted that the true, "scientific" road to socialism must involve the resolution of capitalist class antagonisms through revolutionary change. They saw the working class of advanced industrial society as the historical agent destined to carry forth socialism's emancipatory project.

In the twentieth century, various socialist movements modified Marx and Engels' revolutionary prescriptions, adapting them to new social and historical circumstances. The campaigns of the **Bolsheviks** (page 41) in Russia and **Mao Zedong** (page 163) in China led to the advent of ostensibly socialist orders in regions of the world where industrial capitalism had yet to take hold. Although these and other contemporary versions of socialism veered significantly from the ideals upheld by Marx and Engels, they left indelible marks on the world's political landscape.

(Above) Male and female railroad workers labor together in 1922 Petrograd after the socialist Bolshevik Revolution.

SOVEREIGNTY

Sovereignty refers to the supreme source of authority within a **state** (page 229) or other form of political association. Within its own geographical boundaries, the sovereign state retains the final power to determine how government should proceed. Moreover, it claims the right to exercise this power without interference from external authorities. The theory of sovereignty is at least as old as Plato, who entrusted the rule of the state to an **elite** (page 94) class of wise men known as philosopher-kings. The sixteenth-century authors Niccolò Machiavelli and Jean Bodin each argued, in his own way, for endowing the ruler with the power to determine the **laws** (page 147) of the state and the conditions under which they are implemented. Their views of sovereignty would later be challenged by **social contract** (page 221) theorists such as Thomas Hobbes and John Locke, who maintained that in a properly constituted political order, citizens transfer some of their own personal sovereignty to an external agent, the state, thereby authorizing it to implement the law on their behalf and to rule the commonwealth at large. This idea of sovereignty would eventually be incorporated into the founding political doctrines of the modern nation-state.

SOVIET UNION

Throughout its seven decades of existence, the *Soviet Union* fundamentally altered the world's political landscape. Founded in 1922, it was officially known as the Union of Soviet Socialist Republics (USSR). Before collapsing in 1991, its satellite states encompassed much of the Eurasian continent; its total territory amounted to nearly seventeen percent of the Earth's landmass. From its earliest days, the USSR's highly centralized government and economy remained under tight control of the Communist Party. The party's directives were issued from the Kremlin, a fortified complex in the heart of Moscow, the capital of the regime.

The rise of the Soviet Union began in the aftermath of the Russian Revolution of 1917. Vladimir Lenin—the leader of a political faction known as the **Bolsheviks** (page 41)—had just succeeded in ousting a provisional government led by Alexander Kerensky and creating a new regime, the Russian Socialist Federative Soviet Republic. But he was now confronted with a burgeoning civil war, which pitted the pro-revolutionary forces of the Reds against those of the counterrevolutionary Whites. In a bid to crush the Whites and defend the Revolution, Lenin marched his Red Army into Poland and several other territories of the old Russian Empire. With the assistance of local communist forces, he seized power and established soviets (councils representing the interests of workers and peasants) throughout these regions. Lenin ultimately triumphed over the White backlash in 1922, unifying the republics of Russia, Transcaucasia, Ukraine, and Byelorussia under the banner of the Soviet Union.

Lenin died only two years after the creation of the new regime, at which point Communist Party leader Joseph Stalin took over all the powers of the state. Stalin ruled autocratically and ruthlessly. He suppressed his political opponents and established his own rigid version of **Marxism**–Leninism (page 166) as the official state doctrine. He abandoned Lenin's more liberal "New Economic Policy" in favor of a planned economy in which all decisions regarding the production and distribution of goods were made under the centralized authority of the state. This resulted in a period of rapid collectivization and industrial development, positioning the Soviet Union as a major industrial power and a dominant player in **World War II**

The Kremlin in Moscow housed the highly centralized government of the Soviet Union from 1922 to 1991.

(page 266). According to his critics, these achievements hardly compensated for the massive wave of political repression unleashed by his regime: military officials, Communist Party members, and ordinary citizens were arrested arbitrarily and sent to forced labor camps known as *gulags*; during the Great Purge of 1936 to 1938, tens of thousands of these inmates were executed for engaging in alleged counterrevolutionary activities.

At the start of World War II, Stalin invited the United Kingdom and France to join forces against **Nazi** (page 175) Germany. When his proposal was rejected, he signed a non-aggression treaty with the Nazis. In 1941, however, the Germans invaded the USSR, launching one of the war's largest and deadliest battles—especially for the Soviet side. Stalin's fortunes improved, however, in 1945, when he succeeded in taking control of Berlin. He went on to capture additional territories from the Axis in Central and Eastern Europe; these were eventually incorporated into the sphere of Soviet influence as satellite republics.

After his death in 1953, Stalin was succeeded by Nikita Khrushchev as the Communist Party's leader. In an attempt to liberalize the USSR's social and economic structures, Khrushchev passed a series of modest reforms. His initiative is often referred to as "de-Stalinization" or the "Khrushchev Thaw." During this time, the Soviet Union made significant strides on the technological front: its Sputnik 1, for example, became the world's first artificial satellite orbiting the Earth, and its Vostok 1 was the first spacecraft to carry humans to outer space. Cold War tensions between the Soviets and the Americans were at their height during the Cuban Missile Crisis of 1962, a conflict that drew the two superpowers to the brink of nuclear annihilation. Relations eased somewhat during the early 1970s but re-escalated toward the end of that decade, when the Soviet Union sent troops into Afghanistan in support of the socialist Afghan government's campaign against Mujahideen insurgent groups.

Under the leadership of Mikhail Gorbachev, a group of policies known as *glasnost* and ***perestroika*** (page 190) was introduced in the late 1980s; their aim was to further liberalize the USSR's economy and democratize its rigid political **bureaucracy** (page 43). However, Gorbachev's reforms were not well received by the USSR's satellite republics, where a push to separate from the Soviet government was already under way. In August 1991, a group of hardliners opposed to Gorbachev's policies attempted to seize control of the government. Although the coup did not succeed, Gorbachev ultimately relinquished power in December. He also dissolved the twelve remaining constituent republics of the Soviet Union, which were then reconstituted as independent nation-states.

STATE

One of the earliest and most influential accounts of the *state* can be found in Aristotle's *Politics*. Aristotle referred to the *polis*, or **city-state** (page 52), as the highest form of political association. He argued that a properly constituted *polis* would satisfy all communal needs, enabling man to develop morally and carry forth his true nature as a "political animal." Aristotle's view of the *polis* as a self-sufficient community of people sharing linguistic and cultural traditions anticipates our contemporary understanding of the nation. The modern concept of the state, however, is more closely related to the Roman *res publica*, which binds all citizens to the same system of laws, specifies their civic obligations, and guarantees their **rights** (page 208).

In the sixteenth century, Italian thinker Niccolò Machiavelli contributed significantly to the theorization of the modern state. In his book *The Prince*, he argued that the state's true ends are the acquisition, maintenance, and expansion of power. The ruling prince may achieve these objectives via two key tools of **statecraft** (page 230): brute force and ideological manipulation. For Machiavelli, the latter is especially important. The prince must set aside all moral considerations and deceive his subjects about his ultimate goals; in so doing, he will elicit their consent to his rule, and thereby confer legitimacy upon it. In unlinking the ends of the state from morality and associating them with power instead, Machiavelli broke with the tradition of Plato and Aristotle.

His argument was challenged by the seventeenth-century **social contract** (page 221) theorist Thomas Hobbes. Although Hobbes endorsed Machiavelli's claim that man is self-interested and competitive by nature, he rejected his assertion that power is the state's proper end. For Hobbes, the state is justified in employing the coercive force of the law to constrain the private will, but only in cases where the free exercise of such a will threatens to undermine the commonwealth's peace and security. The latter are the proper, and decidedly moral, ends of the state. While they disagreed with Hobbes in many important respects, later social contact theorists such as John Locke and Jean-Jacques Rousseau endorsed his basic contention that the state, anchored in the will of the people, exists to serve moral objectives. Many of the social contract theorists' proposals were incorporated into the political doctrines of the **republican** (page 206) states established after the **French Revolution** (page 109).

STATECRAFT

Statecraft is a broad term meant to encompass the strategies that states adopt to advance their political, military, economic, and ideological interests, particularly through the use of power. The first great theorist of modern statecraft was Italian Renaissance thinker Niccolò Machiavelli, whose 1532 book *The Prince* has served as a playbook of sorts for practitioners of the art over the ages. Machiavelli theorized that power is an indispensable tool for governing the population and advancing the interests of the state. Power, he claimed, does not simply involve the use of blunt force through **military** (page 168) action or economic pressure, for example; it also entails the dissemination of ideas. Indeed, no less than muskets, cannons, and truncheons, ideas enable the statesman to keep his subjects under control. Such control is critical, thought Machiavelli, because left to their own devices the people might rise up against the statesman and depose him. Thus, if the latter is to succeed in politics, he must persuade the citizenry that his interests and objectives are coextensive with theirs. Once convinced, the citizenry will consent to his rule and leave him free to pursue his power objectives without fear of a legitimation crisis from below.

For Machiavelli, then, ideology is one of the critical tools of modern statecraft. When political discourse is ideologically manipulated, the state's underlying power objectives and relations of domination are concealed from the masses. From this perspective, which is sometimes associated with the doctrine of political realism, the most successful practitioners of statecraft are precisely those who are able to set aside all substantive moral or normative commitments to the ideals they champion—"**freedom**" (page 107) and "**democracy**" (page 78), for example—and use them solely as an ideological cloak to be thrown over the actual conditions of their rule. The frequent use of hard power is a sign of a weak prince, one who must resort to blunt force to stave off a legitimation crisis that could have been more effectively prevented by using ideology (or "soft power") to manufacture the consent of the governed.

S

STRIKES

A *strike* is a collective stoppage of work organized by the employees of a private company, organization, or government agency. Strikes are generally undertaken in hopes of compelling management to address specific worker grievances. Less frequently, they are part of a broader social movement aimed at destabilizing or overthrowing a particular government or political party. The word "strike" entered the English language in 1768, when a group of British sailors made certain demands known by striking the sails of docked merchant ships.

The first documented strike dates back to ancient Egypt, when the artisans of the Royal Necropolis stopped work in 1152 BC because they had not received their wages. Similar events took place over the ages, but it was not until the rise of the Industrial Revolution in the early nineteenth century that strikes became a tool of political action.

(Below) Workers pictured during a 1938 labor strike at King Farm in Morrisville, Pennsylvania, demanding better wages and working conditions.

At that time, the ranks of the working class swelled as private industry grew like never before. Factory conditions were notoriously horrific: long hours, unsafe work environments, pitiful wages—all of which spurred the development of numerous working-class movements. The first modern general strike took place in England in 1842, with workers in many different industries asking for higher wages and better working conditions. These workers understood the power of a strike as a means of extracting concessions from industry owners—after all, the withdrawal of labor has the potential to cripple an industry and deprive it of profits.

S

As the nineteenth century wore on, the working class returned time and again to the strike. In 1937, in the midst of the Great Depression, some 4,740 strikes were staged in the United States alone—the largest such groundswell in American history. These actions were often countered with brute force: owners would threaten to close or move their plants; scabs (strikebreakers willing to cross picket lines) were brought in; and company "goons," sometimes assisted by the police, would be summoned to forcibly crush strikes so that plant operations could resume. After the end of **World War II** (page 266), the massively high unemployment rates of the Depression dropped, the economy began to recover, and the big industrial unions started cozying up to factory owners from whom they had managed to extract various concessions. The unions abandoned their more radical demands and pledged their commitment to the legitimacy of the **capitalist** (page 44) system. Strikes were mostly replaced with peaceful collective bargaining over wages, benefits, and working conditions; their heyday was over.

In the US, moreover, strikes became increasingly difficult to mount as a consequence of the legal restrictions imposed by the Taft-Hartley Act of 1947; it didn't help that collective bargaining agreements between employers and unions often contained "no-strike" provisions. In the late 1960s and early 1970s, groups like the Dodge Revolutionary Union Movement in Detroit opposed the new ideal of comfortable labor-management relations, attempting to reclaim the strike as a tool of revolutionary working-class mobilization. When these radical movements declined in the mid-1970s, however, the strike receded with them.

SUFFRAGE

Suffrage refers to the **right** (page 208) to vote in **elections** (page 92) for **government** (page 118) representatives and public initiatives or referenda. Voting rights combined with the right to run for public office are sometimes known as full suffrage rights. Dating back to the ancient Roman Republic, suffrage in its various guises has been a feature of many political orders. However, it was the first constitutional **republics** (page 206) of late eighteenth-century Western Europe and North America that brought the modern ideal of suffrage into existence. By voting, citizens were provided with a mechanism through which they could express their public policy preferences and participate in the selection of candidates for public office. A conduit was thus established between the will of the citizenry and the will of the government, institutionally shoring up a fundamental tenet of Enlightenment political philosophy: the idea that the legitimacy of the state's authority is grounded in popular **sovereignty** (page 226).

(Below) Suffragist leader Inez Milholland at the National American Woman Suffrage Association's 1913 parade in Washington, DC.

S

The modern system of suffrage was nevertheless a highly politicized institution from its inception. In the United Kingdom, suffrage rights were initially extended only to male owners of land and property. Having come to the conclusion that the "great, outrageous and excessive numbers of people" were "of small substance and of no value," King Henry VI of England enacted a series of statutes in 1432 aimed at restricting the franchise to male owners of land worth at least forty shillings a year—a voting pool of perhaps no more than a half-million people. These limitations became a key issue during the English Civil War two centuries later. The Radical movement's demands for an extension of enfranchisement were met with staunch resistance from Oliver Cromwell, Lord Proctor of the Commonwealth of England. Cromwell expressed his dismay about where such demands would ultimately end. Would the vote, he complained, eventually be extended to men "who have no interest but the interest of breathing"? The British Crown's opposition to the lifting of suffrage rights restrictions proved to be quite tenacious: King Henry VI's statutes remained in effect for another two centuries, until they were finally relaxed by the Reform Act of 1832. However, universal adult male suffrage was not fully implemented in the United Kingdom until the passage of the Representation of the People Act in 1918.

In the pre–**Civil War** (page 58) **United States** (page 248), individual states were at liberty to deny people the right to vote on the basis of gender, religion, race, wealth, tax status, mental competence, literacy, and other arbitrary considerations. The states were eventually stripped of such authority with the passage of the Fifteenth Amendment to the **Constitution** (page 72) in 1870. Various battles were subsequently waged in an effort to widen the field of eligible voters beyond adult males. Launched in the mid-nineteenth century, the **women's suffrage movement** (page 106) campaigned for an end to gender-based voting rights restrictions, a right that was ultimately secured with the passage of the Nineteenth Amendment in 1920. In the 1950s and 1960s, African Americans began to press for the elimination of race as a limiting factor. Although black men and women had been extended full suffrage rights by then, many states were deploying institutional roadblocks (poll taxes and literacy tests, for example) to prevent them from exercising these rights on a par with whites. Under the massive pressure of the **civil rights** (page 54) movement led by **Martin Luther King, Jr.** (page 141), these institutional tactics were outlawed by the Voting Rights Act of 1965. Despite these victories, voter participation rates in the US continue to be notoriously low, comparing poorly with those of other representative **democracies** (page 78).

SYNDICALISM

Along with market socialism and planned-economy socialism, **syndicalism** is one of the three principal models of socialist economics. In some countries, the term is simply a synonym for "trade unionism" or "militant trade unionism." However, socialist syndicalism breaks with the more reform-oriented objectives of the trade union movement. Under syndicalist socialism, private ownership of the means of production gives way to a system in which industries are controlled by multiple cooperative political units known as syndicates. In each syndicate, or confederation, the production process is owned and managed internally and democratically by workers specializing in a particular trade or field; some are selected to serve as representatives of the syndicates to which they belong. Syndicates operate independently of the state and are not subject to the authority of central planning.

The most familiar variety of syndicalism is a revolutionary, anti-state strain known as anarcho-syndicalism. Anarcho-syndicalism arose in Western Europe and North America in the early twentieth century, and was especially prominent in Spain during the 1936–1939 Spanish Civil War. Its advocates campaigned not only for the abolition of capitalism and its wage labor system, but also for the eradication of the state—an aim that distinguished them from other syndicalists. They argued that, in a capitalist society, the state is a top-down structure whose basic purpose is to protect and promote the interests of the capitalist class while depriving workers of control over their labor and basic life conditions.

Under anarcho-syndicalism, the workplace, the economy, and society at large are democratized, decentralized, and cooperatively controlled, rendering the very idea of a state superfluous. This sets anarcho-syndicalism apart from traditional versions of **Marxism** (page 166) and Leninism, which hold that in the aftermath of the communist revolution the state will play a role in empowering the workers. Anarcho-syndicalists are skeptical of the state's capacity to do this, arguing that it will ultimately accumulate power for itself or its elites, and turn against the interests of the workers. Such a belief underscores the **anarchist** (page 22) standpoint of anarcho-syndicalism. According to this view, safeguarding the conditions of a liberated society is not up to politicians, bureaucrats, or other third parties; it depends on workers' direct participation in, and democratic self-management of, economic and political life.

T

TAXATION

Taxation is a scheme or policy employed by **governments** (page 118) to extract money or other items of value from their citizens. Backed by **law** (page 147), taxes are imposed on individuals, corporations, and other entities. Their main objective is to generate revenue for government expenditures; they may also be implemented to redistribute income, maintain high employment rates through the financing of public works, or stabilize prices.

Almost all contemporary nations levy taxes, and money is the prevailing medium for their calculation and collection. Throughout history, however, taxes were often leveled "in kind"—that is, in terms of goods or services. In countries such as China, for instance, taxes on peasant grain farmers were often assessed according to the number of units of grain produced, and payment was made with the grain itself. In the eighteenth and nineteenth centuries, the local governments of American frontier settlements extracted value from adult males by asking them to contribute a certain amount of their time toward the construction of roads, schools, and other community facilities.

Taxation presupposes that at least some of the society's **wealth** (page 259) remains in private hands. Even in societies like the former **Soviet Union** (page 226), where property is collectivized and brought under state control, there is usually a modicum of personal wealth available for taxation (e.g., in the form of individual savings accounts). However, governments that control large amounts of the society's wealth are less dependent on taxes to cover their expenditures than governments that control little of it.

The strategy of tax resistance has long been employed by individuals and groups opposed to certain governmental policies and laws, and by those opposed to the very idea of taxation itself. In refusing to pay legally mandated taxes, resisters engage in a form of **civil disobedience** (page 53): they attempt to undermine the legitimacy of governmental practices by withdrawing their consent from the tax policies that sustain them. Notable historical examples of tax resistance include the Salt March tax boycott led by **Mahatma Gandhi** (page 114) in opposition to British **colonial** (page 61) rule in India; the Women's Tax Resistance League's campaign for American women's suffrage **rights** (page 208); and the National War Tax Resistance movement, which seeks to deprive the **United States** (page 248) government of revenue for its military operations and weapons development programs.

TEA PARTY MOVEMENT

A key launching point of the *Tea Party movement* in the United States was a 2009 speech delivered on the floor of the Chicago Mercantile Exchange by CNBC financial analyst Rick Santelli. Santelli lambasted US President Obama's plan to provide 75 billion dollars in aid to homeowners whose mortgages were jeopardized by the financial crisis of 2008. He characterized the would-be recipients of such assistance as "losers" who "drink the water" and contrasted them with the "silent majority" of Americans who "carry the water." Santelli's outburst and subsequent call for the establishment of a "Chicago Tea Party" were picked up by media outlets such as the *Drudge Report*, the *Rush Limbaugh Show*, and Fox News, and were met with widespread approval from their **conservative** (page 71) audiences.

Taking its name from the Boston Tea Party—a famous 1773 protest by American colonists against the unfair **taxation** (page 236) policies of the British Crown—the Tea Party soon emerged as a major force in US electoral politics, throwing its support behind various **Republican Party** (page 206) candidates and running numerous contenders of its own. In the tradition of George Wallace and other right-wing populists, the Tea Party has built a mass base of followers by championing the **libertarian** (page 154) virtues of personal responsibility, limited government, and the **free market** (page 108). At the same time, it condemns "socialistic charity programs" (such as Obama's Affordable Care Act) and their "undeserving" recipients, as well as Wall Street "fat cats" and bankers who have done little to earn their bloated paychecks.

With its predominantly white demographic base, the Tea Party has long faced charges of racism. According to a 2010 survey, 73 percent of strong Tea Party backers believed that "if blacks would only try harder they could be just as well off as whites."[17] Meanwhile, caricatures of President Barack Obama as a "foreign-born Muslim" have featured prominently in the party's rhetoric. Its credentials as a genuine populist movement have also been questioned. It has been deemed a "fake" or "Astroturf" movement in view of the massive financial and logistical support it receives from wealthy sponsors like industrialist David Koch and the right-wing advocacy group FreedomWorks, led by Dick Armey and other prominent conservative politicians. Some observers note that such financial backing is only partially responsible for the Tea Party's success and that it remains, despite a decline in its initial level of support, a genuinely populist political movement.

T

TERRORISM

Although **violence** (page 253) has been a perennial feature of human society, the classification of specific forms of violence as *terrorism* is a relatively recent development. The term entered the political lexicon in the aftermath of the **French Revolution** (page 109), with the unleashing of a "Reign of Terror" characterized by the use of excessive, and often brutal, force on the part of the new **bourgeois** (page 41) **republic** (page 206). In the late nineteenth century, the term "terrorist" was applied mainly to groups that perpetrated antigovernment violence. Since the twentieth century, the question of which groups and actions should be classified as terrorist has not been as clear-cut.

According to some defenders of the institution of **government** (page 118), almost all acts of violence that are not carried out under the legal authority of the **state** (page 229) can be categorized as terrorism. Political scientists tend to adopt a somewhat more nuanced definition, reserving the term for forms of violence perpetrated by non-state actors against civilian populations. Other scholars—including sociologists, historians, and **international law** (page 133) experts—are prepared to bring the state into the fold

(Opposite) Aside from the World Trade Center in New York City, the September 11, 2001, attacks also targeted the Pentagon in Washington, DC, among other stuctures.

of potential terrorists if it employs violence against noncombatants. Under this more expansive definition, German Nazi Party leader **Adolf Hitler** (page 124) and Chilean **military** (page 168) chief General Augusto Pinochet, for example, both qualify as heads of terrorist states: each made methodical and systematic use of violence against civilian populations. Those opposed to the very existence of government—**anarchists** (page 22), for instance—take it a step further and maintain that the state *as such* must be seen as an exemplar of terrorism, as it is predicated on the repression and control of its own population. There are, in fact, so many competing definitions of terrorism that it is difficult to home in on its universally accepted characteristics. Its single undeniable trait is that it employs (or at least threatens to employ) violence.

Many observers agree that another distinguishing feature of terrorism is that it is often carried out by politically motivated organizations. The motivations themselves can vary widely. Some may be drawn to terrorist tactics simply out of frustration with a government or institution standing in the way of

T

their political goals. Others may have a highly developed ideology, and an associated analysis of the political relationships they would like to disrupt or overturn.

The September 11, 2001 attacks on New York City and Washington, DC, elevated the problem of terrorism to the top of the foreign policy agendas of many nations—particularly the **United States** (page 248). Since President George W. Bush's post-9/11 proclamation of a "War on Terror," the US has devoted unprecedented military, legal, and political resources to fighting militant Islamist organizations such **al-Qaeda** (page 16).

In 2013, President Barack Obama winnowed down the scope of the US counterterrorism campaign to "a series of persistent, targeted efforts to dismantle specific networks of violent extremists that threaten America."[18] Despite Obama's official proclamation of an end to the War on Terror, critics have noted that it has continued apace. As of June 6, 2015, 368 drone attacks had been carried out in Pakistan alone under Obama's tenure, killing an estimated 423 to 965 civilians. Some have argued that a more effective and morally appropriate means of reducing terrorism would be to eliminate the conditions of **poverty** (page 193), despair, and political repression that make it an attractive option for people with little hope of leading better lives.

TOTALITARIANISM

Social scientists generally use the term *totalitarianism* to describe a specific type of political order that emerged in the early twentieth century. Similar to **tyrannies** (page 244) and **dictatorships** (page 84), totalitarian societies lack mechanisms of **democratic** (page 78) accountability. However, what sets the totalitarian **state** (page 229) apart from other nondemocratic regimes is its effort to administer almost every facet of private and public life.

Although there is some debate among social scientists about how to flesh out this basic description, some essential features of totalitarianism are widely recognized. Most scholars agree that the ideology behind a totalitarian regime is all-encompassing and oriented toward the realization of a perfect end-stage of society. To achieve this goal, the regime declares an ongoing state of emergency and a "perpetual revolution"; by suspending the rule of **law** (page 147), it acquires the authority to act arbitrarily.

Headed by a single mass party with a charismatic leader, the totalitarian state has the power to annihilate many legal, political, and social traditions; it seeks to transform society into a seamless, homogenous system. It pursues these goals with the aid of the police, who are authorized to employ terror tactics against the population. All individuals and groups (whether situated in private or public spaces) are potential targets of terror—a fact that produces generalized uncertainty and social anxiety. To disseminate its ideology, the state also assumes control of all forms of mass communication. It establishes various social and political organizations which citizens are made to join. These groups often single out certain segments of the population as enemies of the state and target them for elimination.

Most observers maintain that these general features of totalitarianism were evident in **Adolf Hitler**'s (page 124) **Nazi** (page 175) Germany, especially from 1939 to 1945, and Joseph Stalin's **Soviet Union** (page 226) from 1927 to 1953. There is ongoing debate, however, about whether other societies—Benito Mussolini's Italy, **Mao Zedong**'s (page 163) People's Republic of China, and the Khmer Rouge's Cambodia, for instance—should be classified as totalitarian.

Social scientists also differ with regard to the question of why totalitarian regimes arise in the first place. For many, a key factor behind the rise of totalitarianism in Germany was the economic depression that the nation experienced in the wake of **World War I** (page 262), which contributed to the widespread resentment against the Weimar Republic. Hitler's Nazi Party exploited this politically unstable atmosphere in order to mobilize support for the **fascist** (page 101) cause. He suppressed political dissension and labor unrest, rallying the masses around a program of militant **nationalism** (page 170) that eventually led to the Nazis' seizure of state power.

One of the most well-known fictional portrayals of a totalitarian state is George Orwell's *Nineteen Eighty-Four*. The novel devotes particular attention to how a totalitarian regime can employ modern science and technology to surveil and control its population. According to philosopher Herbert Marcuse, modern science and technology are themselves partially responsible for totalitarianism. Marcuse writes that "science, by virtue of its own method and concepts, has projected and promoted a universe in which the domination of nature has remained linked to the domination of man—a link which tends to be fatal to this universe as a whole."[19] For Marcuse, then, there are aspects of totalitarianism inherent in all modern scientific-technical civilizations.

TRADE

As one of the main processes linking members of different communities together, *trade* is often regarded as a basic aspect of human existence. While exchange encompasses the general movement of all goods among individuals or groups, trade has a narrower meaning: it assumes that such a movement will be reciprocal and serve some practical purpose. Early anthropological investigations examined how social relations are shaped by the expectation that trade will take place on reciprocal terms. In his classic study of the inhabitants of the Trobriand Islands, for instance, Bronislaw Malinowski considered how social status was created and sustained by a complex system of mutual trade.

T

In the early 1970s, Marshall Sahlins built on earlier anthropological studies of trade as reciprocity. He emphasized that the latter is not always evenhanded: some forms of trade are unequal and contain an element of exploitation. A decade later, this thesis was developed by the anthropologist Eric Wolf. Wolf identified three basic "modes of production": kin-based (where trade reciprocation is balanced and generalized); tributary (where trade is managed by a centralized authority through the collection of tribute or taxes); and **capitalist** (page 44) (where trade is characterized by "negative reciprocity"). In line with the perspective of **Marxism** (page 166), Wolf saw trade under capitalism as inherently exploitative: workers must be paid less than the actual worth of their **labor** (page 143) if capitalists are to turn a profit and perpetuate the system. Moreover, capitalists are free to roam the globe in search of ever cheaper labor and raw materials, exploiting the underdeveloped world to advance their own economic interests. To explain the geographical hierarchy of trade under capitalism, the sociologist Immanuel Wallerstein developed a "world systems" theory. From the **colonial** (page 61) era to the present, he claimed, equity in trade relationships has been entirely absent as capitalists from the "core" Western nations have plundered the resources of the non-Western "periphery" to create new products and markets.

Capitalist modes of trade introduce not only Western goods, but also many aspects of Western culture, into non-Western societies. Many observers contend that modern trade relations impose doctrines such as individualism, modernization, and **free-market** (page 108) **liberalism** (page 152) on these cultures, displacing their indigenous traditions and systems of belief. In drawing the cultures of the world together into a single, global economy, international trade has been a major driving force behind this Westernization process—a process that many regard as one of the key elements of **globalization** (page 117).

TRADE UNIONS

Trade unions are organizations set up to represent the collective interests of their employee-members. Today, they typically bargain and negotiate with employers in order to secure worker benefits such as higher wages, decreased working hours, improved working conditions, pensions, job security provisions, and health and disability insurance.

In Great Britain, which is often depicted as the "cradle" of the Industrial Revolution, workers began to form trade unions to protect and advance their interests during the late eighteenth century. From their standpoint, such efforts were necessary because the newly established **capitalist** (page 44) system left them both dependent upon, and highly vulnerable to, the practices of the factory owners who employed them: the latter had no incentive to pay them anything beyond a subsistence wage, or to invest in the improvement of the conditions under which they labored. Organized on the model of the craft guilds of feudal Europe, the British trade unions of the late eighteenth century were initially prosecuted under English common law for restraining **trade** (page 242); they were eventually granted legal recognition with the passage of the Trade Union Act of 1871. Over time, they emerged as a prominent feature of British politics: by 1979, some 13.5 million laborers could be counted among their ranks. The **election** (page 92) of Conservative Prime Minister Margaret Thatcher that same year, however, led to a decrease in their strength and membership. Thatcher championed the passage of the Employment Acts of 1980 and 1982, under which union agreements with "no-**strike**" (page 231) clauses became more common, while plant bargaining began to be favored over national negotiations.

In the *United States*, trade unions faced similar setbacks from the beginning of **Republican** (page 206) Ronald Reagan's first term as **president** (page 194) in 1981. Not long after assuming office, Reagan declared that a strike initiated by the Professional Air Traffic Controllers Organization (PATCO) was "a peril to national safety"; he then proceeded to fire 11,435 PATCO workers for refusing to obey his order to return to work. Some have argued that the anti-union policies carried forth by Reagan and his White House successors were ultimately little more than an extension of powers already granted to the **government** (page 118) under the Taft-Hartley Act of 1947, a law that abridged the right of trade unions to engage in strikes and other "unfair labor practices."

T

TYRANNY

In a tyranny, the powers of the ruler are **absolute** (page 15), that is, unchecked by any legal restrictions or by the principles of a written constitution. Criticisms of tyranny date back to the ancient period of Western philosophy: Plato and Aristotle, for example, both saw tyranny as an affront to the proper tasks of government. For Plato, a legitimate king is reluctant to rule and is concerned only with guiding the unenlightened away from ignorance, and towards an understanding of the ultimate reality: the ideal of the Good. This lofty objective, he adds, is of little interest to tyrants, who are principally concerned with advancing their own political agendas and retaining power. Aristotle portrayed tyranny as a corrupt form of kingship. A properly constituted *polis* or **city-state** (page 52), he argued, is one that enables its citizens to freely discuss questions of the good life. By accumulating power for the sole purpose of furthering their own personal and political ambitions, tyrants rule against the appropriate goals of political life.

T

Guarding against the emergence of tyranny was one of the objectives of the modern constitutional **democracies** (page 78) that were set up in the aftermath of the **French Revolution** (page 109). Various institutions were established to assure that the actions of the government would reflect the wills of the citizenry and that the citizenry, for its part, had the ability to hold its representatives accountable. These arrangements included free and fair **elections** (page 92), a system of just and equitable **laws** (page 147), and **lobbying** (page 158) on the part of competing interest groups.

Such formal political processes have been said to indicate the decidedly non-tyrannical character of constitutional democracies. Some critics have questioned the accuracy of this view, arguing that the existence of democratic institutions has often served to conceal and legitimize the highly disproportionate political influence exercised by powerful economic elites and corporations. Be that as it may, the anti-tyrannical potential of constitutional democracies should not be dismissed: they have provided fertile ground for numerous campaigns on behalf of **civil rights** (page 54) and social **justice** (page 140). Rather than characterizing them as tyrannical, some observers have described them as **oligarchic** (page 182), insofar as they grant a small group of powerful economic actors massively unequal leverage over the political process.

U

UNITED NATIONS

The *United Nations* (UN) is an international governmental body that arose from the ashes of **World War II** (page 266) as a replacement for the **League of Nations** (page 148). Established in October 1945, it was meant to accomplish the various unfulfilled objectives of its predecessor—in particular, the prevention of future wars. The UN was initially composed of 51 member states, a figure that has now risen to 193. While it is headquartered in New York City, it remains exempt from the jurisdiction of American law (a status known as extraterritoriality). Sustained by voluntary donations from its member states, it is charged with preserving peace and mutual security between nation-states; furthering human rights and social and economic development; safeguarding the environment; and assuring that victims of famines, natural disasters, and armed conflicts are provided with humanitarian relief.

In 1945, at the instigation of US President **Franklin D. Roosevelt** (page 209), a conference was held in San Francisco with the aim of drafting a United Nations Charter. After some months of deliberation, a final document was ratified in October of that year. After the mass carnage of World War II—in which an estimated fifty million to eighty million people had lost their lives—the UN's mandate to preserve world peace seemed both urgent and daunting. The organization faced formidable obstacles early on, as the world's nations were anything but united: the state of Israel was established in 1948, giving rise to the Israeli-Palestinian conflict; the Korean War broke out in 1950; independence movements throughout the Third World were dismantling the old colonial order; and the Cold War between the **capitalist** (page 44) West and the **communist** (page 64) East was beginning to take hold. Moreover, the UN's paltry budget for peacekeeping left it ill-equipped to carry forth the formidable task of containing so many armed conflicts around the globe (it had far more funding for economic and social development programs). It was not until the end of the Cold War that the UN could point

to some limited successes in the area of international peacekeeping.

The Cold War proved to be a particularly thorny problem for the UN in its early decades. For the most part, it was forced to limit its peacekeeping efforts to neutral territories (one notable exception being the war between North Korea and South Korea). Some of the UN's major initiatives during this time were its approval of a resolution to partition Palestine, which led to the establishment of the state of Israel; its use of military force to stabilize civil conflict in the Democratic Republic of the Congo; and its deployment of peacekeepers to Cyprus.

With the spread of **decolonization** (page 77) during the 1960s, a host of newly independent nation-states began to apply for UN membership. In 1964, an Algeria-led coalition of Third World nations known as the Group of 77 emerged for a brief time as a major power within the UN. Over the strong objections of the US, the People's Republic of China was awarded a seat on the Security Council in 1971, and a resolution (which has since been repealed) was passed in 1975 equating **Zionism** (page 270) with **racism** (page 200). For some, these developments were signs of the declining influence of the US within the organization.

In the late 1980s, as the Cold War began to fizzle, the UN redoubled its peacekeeping budget and embarked on more peacekeeping missions in one decade than it had during the preceding four. The period between 1988 and 2000 also saw a doubling of the number of UN Security Council resolutions. The organization also helped to bring about a diplomatic end to the Salvadoran Civil War; undertook a successful peacekeeping campaign in Namibia; and supervised the democratic elections that were held in South Africa after the collapse of **apartheid** (page 24), and in Cambodia after the fall of the Khmer Rouge. More recently, the UN has sent peacekeepers to mediate a variety of international conflicts, including wars in Sudan and the Democratic Republic of Congo.

In 2001, the UN won the Nobel Peace Prize in acknowledgment of its peacekeeping, human development, and humanitarian relief efforts. While some observers have concurred with the Nobel Committee's judgement, others remain critical of the UN, portraying it as ineffective and corrupt. Some have even suggested that it has basically functioned as a tool to sustain and promote the agendas of its powerful member states, particularly the US, whose control of the Security Council enables it to dominate decision-making within the organization.[20]

(Opposite) The UN was founded in the aftermath of World War II with the mission of maintaining world peace, something that proved a challenge during the ensuing Cold War.

UNITED STATES

Some 240 years after emerging from under the thumb of the British Empire, the *United States of America* is one of the chief economic, military, and political powers in the world today. It is a federal **republic** (page 206) consisting of fifty states and the District of Columbia, in Washington, DC. With 3.8 million square miles of territory and 320 million inhabitants, the United States is the world's fourth-largest and third most populous country. Over its history, it has received waves of immigrants from around the world, making it one of the most ethnically and culturally diverse nations on the planet. Its mainland, which consists of forty-eight contiguous states, was first settled approximately 15,000 years ago by Paleo-Indians migrating from Eurasia. In the sixteenth century, these lands were claimed and ultimately colonized by various European nations. For Native Americans, European colonization was accompanied by bloodshed, displacement from tribal homelands, and the decimation of traditional ways of life.

1600s	*British settlers arrive on land occupied by indigenous people*
1776	*Declaration of Independence*
1840s	*First use of term "Manifest Destiny"*
1861–1865	*Civil War, slavery abolished*
1917–1918	*US involvement in World War I*
1930s	*Great Depression, New Deal*
1941–1945	*US involvement in World War II*
1945–1990s	*US wages Cold War against communist forces worldwide*
2001	*US declares War on Terror*

The government of the United States was established in the aftermath of the **American Revolution** (page 18), an upheaval sparked by a conflict between the British Empire and the original thirteen American colonies. The colonists objected to British rule, arguing that it saddled them with obligations to a monarchical government in which they had no representation. Their resistance ultimately led to the American Revolutionary War in 1775, and to the *Declaration of Independence* in 1776. The eight-year war—the first successful campaign against European colonial rule—was settled in 1783, with the United States emerging as an independent nation freed from the authority of the British Crown. The US **Constitution** (page 72), the nation's governing document, was ratified by all of the republic's newly formed states in 1788. In 1791, ten amendments to the text were accepted. Known collectively as the **Bill of Rights** (page 37), their aim was to guarantee American citizens certain fundamental **rights** (page 208) and **freedoms** (page 107).

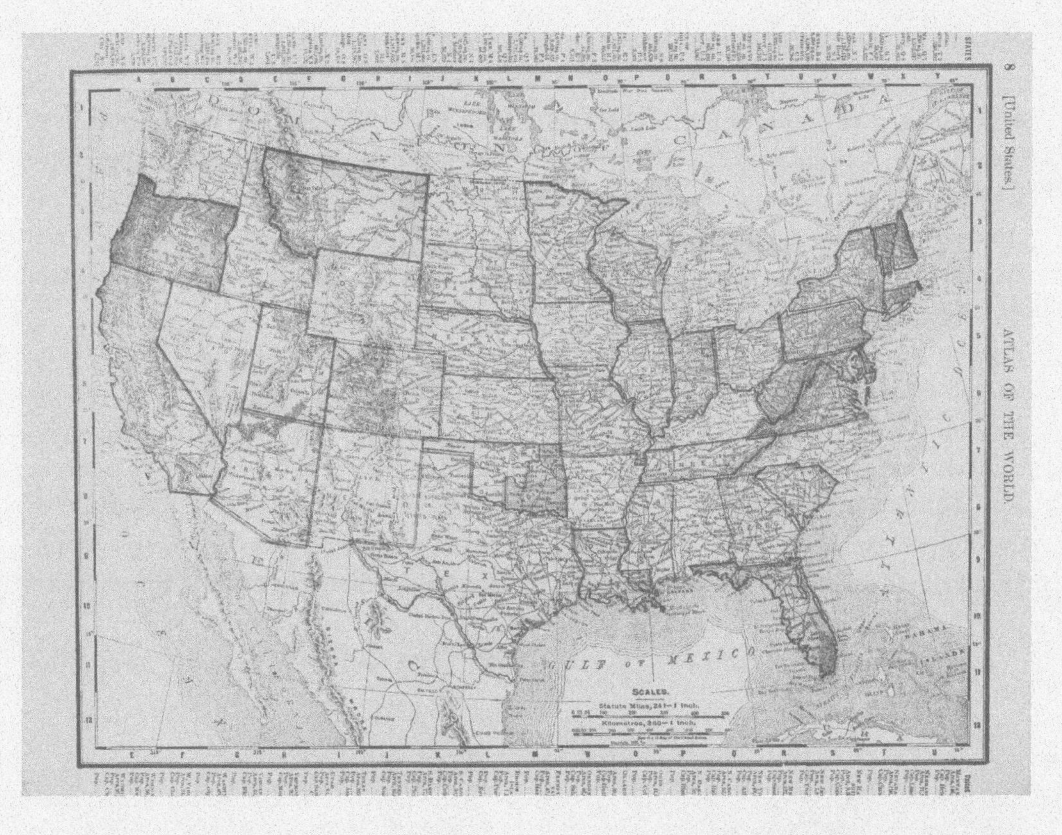

(Above) The 48 states that now form the mainland United States were acquired through territorial expansion guided by the ideology of "Manifest Destiny."

After independence, the United States resolved to extend its territory beyond the boundaries of the original thirteen colonies. The drive to settle the western frontier was justified under a doctrine known as Manifest Destiny, which held that the expansion and settlement of the North American continent was the special responsibility of the American people. The campaign, carried out throughout the nineteenth century, displaced Native American tribes and brought new territories into the American fold; these were eventually incorporated into the union as states. (In 1912, Arizona became the last contiguous state to be admitted, followed by Alaska and Hawaii in 1959.) The American **Civil War** (page 58) threatened the young republic with the prospect of secession on the part of its Southern slaveholding states. Upon the victory of Union forces in 1865, legalized **slavery** (page 217) was abolished under the Thirteenth Amendment of the US Constitution.

The twentieth century dawned with America showing its resolve to defend an increasingly wide swath of territory across the western hemisphere; extending from Greenland to its north and the tip of South America to its south, its pre–**World War II** (page 266) "zone of security" is estimated to have encompassed some 40 percent of the Earth's landmass. As the Industrial Revolution catapulted its economy forward, the United States became a key player in armed conflicts such as the Spanish–American War and **World War I** (page 262). This helped establish its reputation as one of the world's economic and military superpowers. In World War II, America became the first nation to develop and use **nuclear weapons** (page 180). Since becoming a permanent member of the **United Nations** (page 245) Security Council in 1946, the US has played a dominant role in international affairs.

The country emerged as the world's top global superpower upon the collapse of the *Soviet Union* in 1991. Buoyed by a long period of economic expansion that lasted from the early 1990s until 2001, America continued to flex its military muscles overseas: the administration of George H.W. Bush launched a

U

number of campaigns in the Middle East, including the US-backed expulsion of Iraqi troops from Kuwait in the Persian Gulf War of the early 1990s. With the election of Bill Clinton in 1992, the **Democratic Party** (page 82) recaptured the **presidency** (page 194)—an office that no Democrat other than Jimmy Carter had occupied since 1969. Though the parties had switched, many of Clinton's initiatives were consistent with those of his **Republican** (page 206) predecessor. In fact, with Clinton, a **conservative** (page 71) shift in American Democratic Party politics was initiated, elements of which are evident in many of the foreign and domestic policies of President Barack Obama.

Over the course of American history, numerous protest movements have arisen in defense of ideals such as social **justice** (page 140), equality, **civil rights** (page 54), and **freedom** (page 107). While these principles are upheld in the Constitution, many argue that they have often been absent from the practices and institutions of American life.

(Above) The seal of the United States bares the motto *E pluribus unum*, or "Out of many, one."
(Opposite) The current US flag was adopted in 1960, with 50 stars to represent the 50 states, and 13 stripes to represent the original colonies.

UTILITARIANISM

The modern philosophical tradition of *utilitarianism* was inaugurated by English thinkers Jeremy Bentham and John Stuart Mill, who wrote in the late eighteenth and mid-nineteenth century, respectively. Bentham and Mill saw the promotion of the greatest amount of happiness for the greatest number of people as the proper moral end of society. According to this principle—known as the principle of net utility—actions are morally correct if they promote the happiness of those who perform them and those who are affected by them, whereas those that diminish such happiness are not. Thus, for utilitarians, morality is not based on furthering one's immediate self-interests in disregard for the harm it may cause others; nor is morality based on independent, abstract principles—"Thou shalt not kill," for example. Rather, to determine the moral worth of an action, one must examine its consequences: does it promote or decrease net utility? If consequences are all that really matter when assessing the rightness or the wrongness of an action, then the agent's motivations are morally negligible: one can do the right thing for essentially bad reasons (though one may not necessarily deserve praise for doing so).

UTOPIANISM

The term *utopia* was introduced by Sir Thomas More in his 1516 homonymous book. More portrayed an orderly and dignified society, a pagan-**communist** (page 64) **city-state** (page 52) based entirely on rational principles. He conceived his utopia as the ideal flip side of medieval Europe's corrupt Church-states. Over the centuries, More's account of a near-perfect world promising to liberate humanity from its present miseries inspired many other utopian schemes in fiction, social theory, and practice. At least one blueprint for utopia predates More's: although it did not feature the term, Plato's *Republic* set forth a decidedly idealistic vision of a class-based social order ruled by philosopher kings.

In the nineteenth century, utopian **socialism** (page 224) took hold in response to the various social ills that accompanied the rise of industrial **capitalism** (page 44). It was associated with fictional works such as Edward Bellamy's *Looking Backward* and William Morris's *News from Nowhere*. Utopian socialism was also defended by theorists such as Henri de Saint-Simon, Charles Fourier, and Robert Owen. While Karl Marx and Friedrich Engels were critical of utopian socialists, they, too, pined for an ideal society that would create the material conditions for true human emancipation.

V

VIOLENCE

In very basic terms, *violence* can be described as the use of physical force with the intention of causing bodily harm. On a political level, both **state** (page 229) and non-state actors may inflict or be subjected to violence.

Today, most of the world's nations possess well-developed **militaries** (page 168) and state **bureaucracies** (page 43), designed to manage the material and human resources needed to carry out violence against the state's enemies under conditions of **warfare** (page 256); within national limits, police forces or militia are empowered to use violence against citizens who break the law. Both types of violence are recognized as legal and legitimate because they are anchored in the state's **sovereign** (page 226) authority. As the German sociologist Max Weber famously remarked, the "monopoly of the legitimate use of physical force" is one of the distinguishing features of the modern state.

In the 1960s, French philosopher Michel Foucault noted that the state does not only engage in "brute" force to control its citizenry, but also employs more subtle forms of violence, inscribed in small crevices of the social order, so that individuals ultimately coerce *themselves* into behaving as prescribed.

He also emphasized the fact that people often turn state violence against the state itself, using its disciplinary discourses and technologies to resist its coercive efforts.

Foucault's analyses helped reframe contemporary debates about the nature of political violence, shifting the focus away from concepts such as interstate war and physical force. While contemporary states still have recourse to these traditional tools of **statecraft** (page 230), Foucault highlighted the subtler, more highly regulated forms of violence that they employ to govern the activities of individuals and maintain social control.

American B-29 airplanes drop bombs on Chinese Communist military targets in North Korea at the height of the Korean War in 1951.

VIRTUE

In philosophy, the term *virtue* may refer to a valued human trait (such as excellence) or a combination of esteemed human characteristics. Virtue is therefore a normative concept, meaning that its purpose is to distinguish between better and worse kinds of qualities. Derived from the Latin *virtus* (which in turn originates in the Greek *arête*), it has been a key notion in Western political thought since antiquity.

The ancient Greeks initially used the term in reference to the superlative, masculine, and ruggedly individualistic prowess exhibited by the heroic warrior. (Interestingly, the terms "virtue" and "virility" share *vir,* or "man," as a common linguistic root.) With the rise of the ancient Greek *polis* or **city-state** (page 52), the connection between virtue and manly warfare began to unravel. The term was now employed to refer to the qualities of the citizen, who was understood to be bound by the **laws** (page 147) and customs of the community. Thinkers such as Plato, Aristotle, and Pythagoras saw the citizen's moral character as a reflection of the character of the *polis* at large. The ancient Greeks recognized many human qualities as worthy and estimable, but spoke of four "cardinal virtues": wisdom, courage, justice, and temperance.

The Greeks' efforts to associate private virtue with public virtue were taken up by the ancient Romans. The latter distanced themselves from philosophical doctrines such as Stoicism and Epicureanism, which prioritized the individual's personal well-being and happiness over the public good. Instead, they linked virtue to the sacrifices made by government officials and citizens in pursuit of civic objectives. Medieval Christians likewise held political leaders accountable to standards of virtue—notably, the principles of hope, faith, and charity.

Some have argued that during the European Renaissance, a politically oriented doctrine known as "civic humanism" helped resuscitate the link between virtue and politics. However, by the early sixteenth century, the Italian thinker Niccolò Machiavelli had already begun to sever the connection. He argued that, should the circumstances warrant it, the ruler of the **state** (page 229) must be prepared to act in terms that are inconsistent with his personal virtue. With the dawn of the modern era, virtue became increasingly less relevant to the organization of political life. It was replaced with the ideals of classical **liberalism** (page 152)—i.e., rationalism, equality, self-determination, free will, and individual **autonomy** (page 33)—as the basis of political citizenship.

W

WAR

Simply put, a *war* is an armed conflict between one or more political groups. Today, wars are generally conducted by **sovereign states** (page 229), who may wage them against one another (interstate wars), against political factions within their own borders (civil wars), or against non-state actors (the post-9/11 "War on Terror," for example). To be classified as a war, an armed conflict must rise to a sufficient level of intensity and duration (a small-scale riot summarily suppressed is not a war); it will also typically sprout from escalating tensions between hostile parties. For example, an exchange of threats may lead to military preparations, troop mobilizations, border hostilities, and ultimately outright warfare. Wars can be initiated by a formal declaration, a time-limited ultimatum, or an action aimed at advertising the intention to commence an attack. They are normally ended by peace treaties or armistices designed to bring about a permanent cessation of hostilities.

Under conditions of war, **violence** (page 253) and other types of behavior that would be illegal or inappropriate in a state of peace become permissible. Unlike "neutrals" (who neither participate nor take sides in the conflict), belligerents engaged in warfare have license to subject one another to armed force and are accorded legal equality. The legal **rights** (page 208) of combatants in the state of war were recognized throughout much of modern history and were even codified, to some degree, in the Hague Conventions of 1899 and 1907. However, these entitlements were significantly curtailed by the **League of Nations** (page 148) Covenant of 1920. The agreement obligated member states to present their disputes before the League for arbitration and to refrain, for a period of at least nine months, from violating the political **sovereignty** (page 226) and territorial integrity of other states. League members that failed to adhere to these terms were liable to economic sanctions. The League's successor organization, the **United Nations** (page 245), placed similar provisions into its 1945 Charter.

Such efforts notwithstanding, warfare among nation-states persisted throughout the twentieth century and continues to be a prominent feature of today's political landscape. While rapid advances in science, industry, and technology have dramatically enhanced the ability of human beings to annihilate one another, the political conditions that would forestall such destruction and assure the advent of perpetual peace seem more remote than ever.

GEORGE WASHINGTON

As the first President of the United States, George Washington sits atop the pantheon of America's founding fathers. The story of his life and times is required reading for American schoolchildren, although it has often been surrounded by much hero worship and mythmaking.

In 1732, Washington was born into a family of wealthy tobacco growers. The family put slaves to work on its Virginia plantations and passed them down to Washington, who owned hundreds of slaves during his lifetime. Washington was also the Commander-in-Chief of the Continental Army during the **American Revolution** (page 18), which aimed to overturn British colonial rule. Under Washington's command, the army drove the British out of Boston in 1776. During the winter of that same year, Washington crossed the Delaware River—an event immortalized in an iconic painting by Emanuel Leutze—and retook New Jersey. His attempt to capture New York City a year later, however, did not succeed. In fact, throughout the war, Washington's forces were frequently outmaneuvered by the larger armies of the British Crown. The Continental Army nevertheless prevailed; its victory over the British was finalized in 1783. Reluctant to simply replace one **tyranny** (page 244) with another, Washington stepped down from his position as Commander-in-Chief and declined to assume political power by *fiat*.

In 1789, Washington was elected as the first president of the United States by the Electoral College, garnering 100 percent of its votes (a tally no successor has been able to match). As president, Washington quickly established himself as an advocate of Alexander Hamilton's program for a strong, well-funded federal government. To help defray the mounting debt that the new **republic** (page 206) had accumulated, he imposed a tax on distilled spirits. The tax was contested by war veterans and other citizens in the swiftly crushed "Whiskey Rebellion." Washington also helped bring the United States Constitution into existence, chairing the convention at which the document was ratified to replace the Articles of Confederation. Many of the other defining institutional features of the American government, including the cabinet system and the inaugural address, were established by him. After two terms in office, he retired from the presidency and was succeeded by his vice president, John Adams, in 1797.

Born into a slaveholding Virginia family, George Washington led the Continental Army in the fight for independence, and was elected the first US president in 1789. Pictured below with one of his grandchildren, George Washington Park Custis.

WEALTH

Over the ages, *wealth* has been both championed and denounced: some have associated it with **virtue** (page 255), while others have linked it to vice. In any case, the concept itself has a central place in political and economic theory. In the modern era, the claim that wealth should be shared equitably was upheld by a surprisingly wide range of thinkers. Adam Smith claimed that **free market** (page 108) competition would lead to a more equitable distribution of goods and services—an important goal, since their unequal spread would render the greater part of society "miserable" and corrupt its "moral sentiments." John Maynard Keynes noted that **capitalists** (page 44) created artificial scarcity and used it to justify wealth inequalities, which state intervention in the market economy could help correct. While Smith had defined wealth in relation to the production of goods and services, Karl Marx described wealth under capitalism as "value" (wealth calculated in monetary terms). He criticized the basis for capitalist wealth creation ("exchange value") and advocated for a society in which the production of wealth is based on the deliberate fulfillment of human needs ("use value").

WELFARE STATE

In a *welfare state*, the government assumes some responsibility for the economic and social well-being of its citizens—especially the most disadvantaged among them—under the belief that all law-abiding nationals are entitled to certain standards of living. Measures taken to ensure such standards include distributing wealth more equitably and offering certain public benefits—homeless shelters, low-cost housing, and food assistance programs, for instance—to the least well-off. Welfare states also seek to protect citizens from the unplanned social costs of free market activity, such as unemployment, hazardous workplace conditions, and environmental pollution. This is done by imposing various **taxation** (page 236) schemes and regulations on private businesses.

Economic life is not completely taken over by the state, however—some aspects of the market are left unregulated. Welfare states are thus said to comprise "mixed" economies: they lie somewhere between nonmarket, planned-economy **socialist** (page 224) systems, and more liberal governments fostering a **free-market** (page 108) economy and little intervention in individuals' private affairs.

A notable precursor of the modern welfare state was the medieval Catholic Church: it collected certain taxes for the express purpose of building orphanages, hospices, and hospitals for the elderly, and providing food for victims of famine and poverty. What sets

W

modern welfare states apart from such relief programs is their more extensive and universal character. The government-sponsored **social insurance** (page 223) schemes initiated by conservative German Chancellor Otto von Bismarck in the 1880s represented some of the first steps in this more comprehensive direction. Bismarck's government offered workers retirement pensions and benefits designed to protect them in the event of sickness, accident, or disability.

The rise of the contemporary welfare state was fueled by the Great Depression of the 1920s and 1930s. During this period of economic crisis, mass unemployment, poverty, hunger, and other hardships helped radicalize elements of the working class. The latter began to challenge the legitimacy of **capitalism** (page 44) and call for its replacement with a **communist** (page 64) alternative. For many Western governments, Bismarck's welfare state model offered an attractive solution to the conflict: it left the free market intact while at the same time addressing workers' demands for a government that could protect them from the social injuries to which the unregulated economy had given rise.

This "middle path" between a state-controlled communist economy and an unregulated free market was adopted by many European nations in the aftermath of **World War II** (page 266). These countries vastly expanded the scope of state intervention in the lives of their citizens, offering them a variety of social services and insurance programs. A rather less comprehensive version of the welfare state was implemented in the **United States** (page 248) under the New Deal initiatives of President **Franklin D. Roosevelt** (page 209).

Today, the most advanced versions of the welfare state are found in Nordic countries such as Denmark, Finland, and Sweden. Despite some significant differences, these nations' governments subscribe to a "universalist" welfare state model: in addition to providing a comprehensive array of social insurance programs, they aim to protect basic **human rights** (page 128) and foster individual **autonomy** (page 33), social mobility, and gender equality. The American welfare system is arguably among the world's weakest; many of its programs have been eroded significantly in recent decades and continue to be targeted for "reform" by representatives of both the **Republican Party** (page 206) and the **Democratic Party** (page 82).

WORKING CLASS

When addressing the topic of the *working class*, it is difficult to avoid reference to the seminal nineteenth-century analyses of Karl Marx and Friedrich Engels. Marx and Engels maintained that two principal classes dominate the landscape of the present **capitalist** (page 44) order: the capitalist class, which owns the means of production, and the working class, which does not. There is, in a sense, a symbiotic relationship between the two. On the one hand, capitalists need workers to generate **wealth** (page 259), which they can then appropriate to revolutionize the production process and ultimately generate more wealth. On the other hand, workers must sell their labor power to capitalists to assure their own economic subsistence, since they lack control over the means of production. While seemingly complementary, the relationship between the two classes is inherently contradictory: workers must invest more time in the laboring process than is necessary to guarantee their own survival. Capitalists appropriate this excess labor as "surplus value," using it to reproduce themselves as a class. The working class thus has an intrinsic interest in ending the exploitative conditions of capitalism and establishing a new **communist** (page 64) society that allows for true emancipation.

In the latter half of the twentieth century, significant shifts in the capitalist production process led some to wonder whether it was time to bid the working class *adieu*, as French philosopher André Gorz put it. The industrial manufacturing jobs that had once been the basis of working-class employment had begun to disappear, and "blue-collar" labor had been supplanted by "white-collar" labor—work carried out by clerical workers, skilled professionals, and managers, for example. This new occupational makeup, the decline of **trade unions** (page 243), and the displacement of anti-capitalist labor struggles by "identity politics" had many rejecting the classical Marxist conception of the working class. Writers such as John and Barbara Ehrenreich argued that a new "professional-managerial class" had arisen from within it. Far from promoting working-class solidarity and revolutionary action, this new class expropriates the skills and culture of laborers, often making decisions adverse to their interests. Some have countered that the anti-working class actions of professional managers are not an indication of their status as a new class, so much as a reflection of their loyalties to the objectives of their capitalist employers.

WORLD WAR I

World War I marked a turning point in the history of human warfare. Staged on the European continent between 1914 and 1918, the conflict was the first to employ modern industrial technology for the mass destruction of life and property. Its casualty toll was one of the highest ever recorded for a single war: at its conclusion, some sixteen million people, including military combatants and civilians, had lost their lives. The conflict altered the European political landscape in significant ways, laying the groundwork for **World War II** (page 266).

June 1914	*Archduke Ferdinand assassinated in Sarajevo*
July 1914	*Austria-Hungary declares war, invades Serbia*
August 1914	*Germany attacks Belgium, establishing Western Front*
November 1914	*Ottoman Empire joins Central Powers*
1917	*US joins Allied Powers*
1918	*Germany signs peace treaty, marking Allied victory*
1919	*Paris Peace Conference*
1920	*League of Nations founded to prevent future wars*

W

The war began with several European nations splitting into two opposing coalitions: the Allied Powers (the United Kingdom, France, and the Russian Empire) and the Central Powers (Germany and Austria-Hungary). As the conflict progressed, Italy, Japan, and the **United States** (page 248) entered the Allied camp; the Ottoman Empire and Bulgaria joined the Central Powers. At this point, the war had drawn in all of the world's great economic players; with more than seventy million military personnel spread across Europe, it became one of the largest wars in history.

The war was sparked by an incident involving Archduke Franz Ferdinand of Austria-Hungary. In June 1914 the Archduke—heir presumptive to the throne of his Empire—was shot dead by a Yugoslav nationalist in Sarajevo. The gunman, Gavrilo Princip, was allied with forces seeking to unite several territories with majority South Slavic populations under the Kingdom of Serbia. In response to the assassination, Austria-Hungary initiated a coercive program aimed at weakening the Kingdom's threat. The move triggered a diplomatic crisis that revived decades-old international alliances. In just a matter of weeks, these coalitions were at war with one another, spreading the conflict across Europe and drawing in reinforcements from around the world.

The war officially started on July 28, 1914. After issuing a declaration, Austria-Hungary

invaded Serbia as Russia mobilized its forces on Serbia's behalf. Germany stoked the flames by attacking neutral Belgium and Luxembourg, and then setting its sights on France. Angered by these moves, Great Britain declared war on Germany. The Allies halted the German march through France and Belgium, while both they and the Germans began digging a line of fortified trenches that would become known as the Western Front. The contours of the front would remain more or less intact for the remainder of the war. For its part, the Russian army made inroads against the Austro-Hungarians, although the Germans were able to foil its incursion into East Prussia. When the Ottoman Empire joined the Central Powers in November 1914, the scope of the war widened: its fronts now extended into the Caucasus, Mesopotamia, and the Sinai. The Central Powers gained the support of Bulgaria in 1915, while the ranks of the Allies were swelled by a succession of new coalition partners: Italy in 1915, Romania in 1916, and the United States in 1917.

In the aftermath of its successful **October Revolution** (page 184) of 1917, Russia's new Bolshevik government faced the threat of further advances by Germany and Austria.

(Above) After the 1914 assassination of Astro-Hungarian emperor Archduke Ferdinand, most of Europe became divided between the Allied and Central powers.

W

Already saddled with a civil war at home, the beleaguered Russians signed a treaty with the Central Powers at Brest-Litovsk, ending their involvement in the war. The Russian capitulation was a feather in Germany's cap, albeit a short-lived one. Buoyed by their victory, the Germans amassed along the Western Front in 1918 and mounted an assault. Their campaign, however, was beaten back by the Allies in a series of counteroffensives. Overwhelmed by the strength of the Allied defenses, the Austro-Hungarian Empire submitted to an armistice. Germany, burdened with revolutionary resistance at home, followed on its heels; it agreed to a peace treaty with the Allies on November 11, 1918, bringing the war to an end.

With the victory of the Allies, the long reigns of the German, Russian, Austro-Hungarian, and Ottoman Empires were over. Europe's political fault lines were

W

reconfigured: some nations were reestablished as independent nation-states, while others were created anew; to the victors went the spoils of Germany's colonies. At the Paris Peace Conference of 1919, Britain, France, the United States, and Italy ironed out the details in a series of treaties, whose terms were imposed on the defeated Central Powers. In a bid to prevent a replay of another war of mass death and destruction, **The League of Nations** (page 148) was founded in 1920. The League's lofty goal was not to be realized, however: in the aftermath of the war, Germany was grappling with a major economic depression and a sense of humiliation over its defeat, both conditions that German leader **Adolf Hitler** (page 124) later capitalized on to fuel the rise of **Nazism** (page 175)—a development that ultimately gave rise to World War II.

(Above) The 1915 sinking of British Royal Navy ship HMS *Irresistible* during the Dardanelles Campaign against the Ottoman Empire. (Opposite) German soldiers fight from the trenches of the Aisne River in France, circa 1914.

W

WORLD WAR II

World War II was the deadliest, most destructive, and most widespread armed conflict in human history. The six-year war, which began in 1939 and ended in 1945, drew in most of the world's nations, which organized themselves into two opposing military coalitions: the Allied Powers and the Axis Powers. Involving some one hundred million people (including military personnel and noncombatants), the war had a staggering scope: it mobilized the economic, industrial, and scientific resources of more than thirty countries. The number of people killed during the conflict is also astounding. Just the Nazi Holocaust—the mass extermination of Jews and other targeted populations—was responsible for the deaths of approximately eleven million people. An additional one million people were killed in various strategic bombings, including those involving the use of **nuclear weapons** (page 180) on the Japanese cities of Hiroshima and Nagasaki. In total, the war resulted in the deaths of an estimated fifty million to eighty-five million people.

1933 *Adolf Hitler appointed Chancellor of Germany*

1939 *Germany invades Poland; France and England declare war*

1941 *Germany invades Soviet Union; Pearl Harbor attack marks US entry into war*

1942 *Battle of Midway staves off Japanese advance*

1944 *Allied invasion of Normandy liberates France from Nazis*

1945 *Germany surrenders; US drops atomic bomb on Hiroshima and Nagasaki; United Nations replaces League of Nations*

Prior to the official start of the war, the first storm clouds were already gathering: in 1937, the Empire of Japan was in the midst of a war with the Republic of China—an initial step in its broader plans to bring all of Asia and the Pacific under its control. However, World War II did not formally begin until September 1, 1939, when France and the United Kingdom declared war on Germany following its invasion of Poland. In the first two years of the conflict, Germany proved to be a formidable foe. It brought Italy and Japan into the Axis alliance and proceeded to conquer much of continental Europe. It acquired territory from Poland, Finland, Romania, and the Baltic States under the terms of a nonaggression treaty with the **Soviet Union** (page 226), which also appropriated land from these nations. At this point, the military campaign against the Axis Powers was being waged only by the United Kingdom and the British Commonwealth. The Allied front launched the Battle of the Atlantic—the longest continuous military campaign of the war—and brought its troops into North Africa and

W

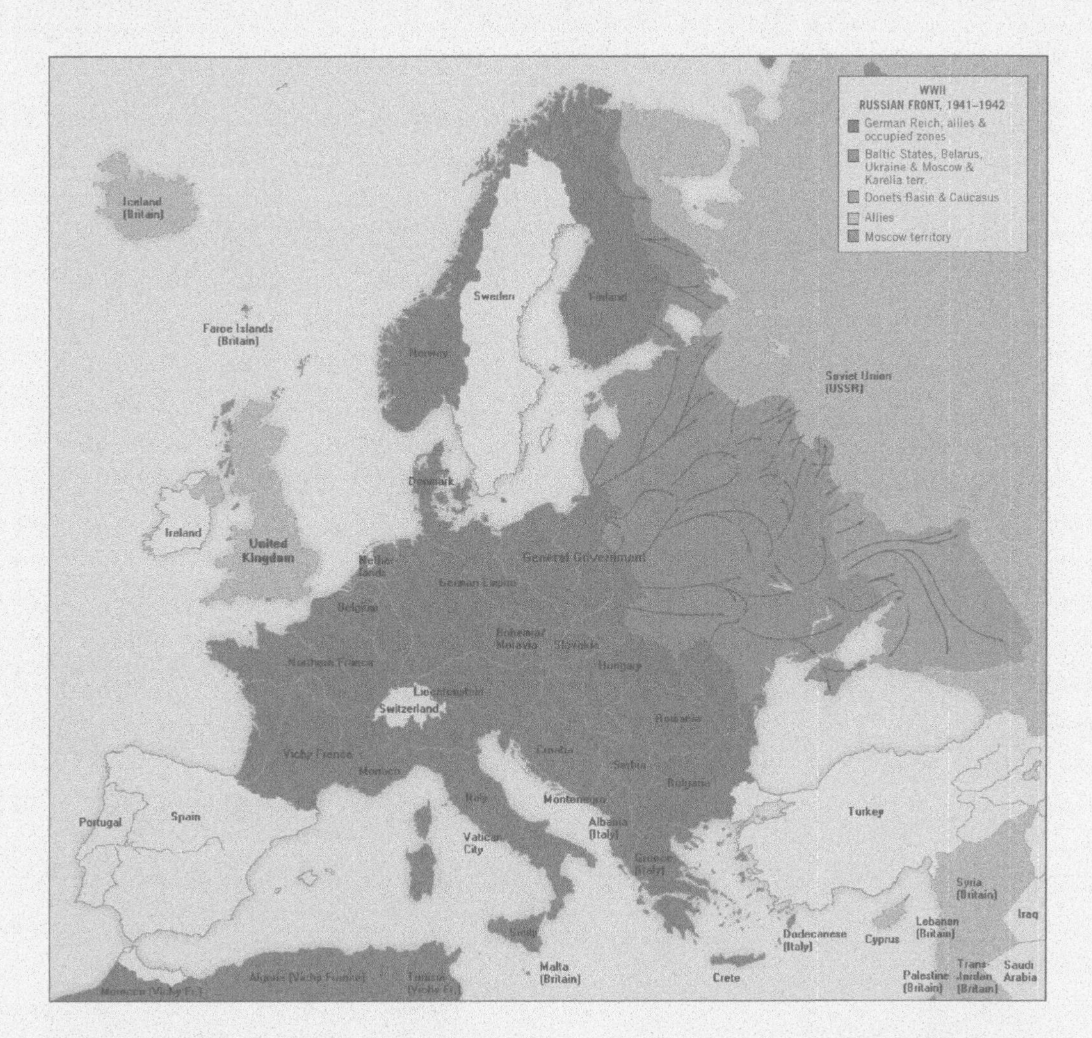

the Horn of Africa. In June 1941, Germany's short-lived armistice with the Soviets came to an end when the Axis Powers invaded the Soviet Union. The incursion opened up the largest land-based battleground in military history. As 1941 drew to a close, Japan launched assaults on various American and European territories in the Western Pacific, ultimately taking control of much of the land in this area.

The fortunes of the Axis Powers would soon sour, however. In 1942, Japan suffered a major defeat at the Battle of Midway. The Allies went on to take over a number of Western Pacific islands. The Germans were upended in North Africa and also lost the critical Battle of Stalingrad in the Soviet Union.

(Above) A map showing the Russian front and the Allies in 1941 to 1942

W

In 1943, Germany was subjected to additional setbacks on the Eastern Front. Overwhelmed by the Allied invasion of Sicily, Italy offered its outright surrender. These defeats, along with the Allied victories in the Pacific, forced the Axis Powers to view retreat on all fronts as their best strategic option. Things only got worse for them in 1944, when the Allies' massive seaborne invasion of Normandy liberated France from Nazi control. Meanwhile the Soviet Union, which had recaptured the territories lost earlier in the conflict, mounted an attack on Germany and its allies. Japan did not fare any better: with its Navy badly bruised by the Allied onslaught, it suffered major defeats in South Central China and Burma.

(Above) Austrian concentration camp prisoners in 1945. (Opposite, top to bottom) American troops landing at Normandy in 1944; London air raids in 1940.

For the Axis Powers, the Allied invasion of Germany was the final death blow of the long, bloody war. The conflict ended with the seizure of Berlin by Soviet and Polish troops, forcing Germany to agree to an unconditional surrender on May 8, 1945. On July 26, the Allies issued the Potsdam Declaration, which demanded that Japan follow suit. Although some historians have pointed to evidence of Japan's preparedness to surrender, US President Harry S. Truman—insisting that there were no such signs—ordered atomic bombs to be dropped on Hiroshima and Nagasaki in August 1945. The Soviet Union had recently declared war on Japan, launching an invasion of Manchuria. This, together with the prospect of further US nuclear attacks and a planned Allied assault on the Japanese archipelago, was more than Japan could withstand. It surrendered on August 15, 1945. The Allies had won the war in Asia and the war at large.

The political landscape of the world was significantly altered by World War II. In its aftermath, the **United Nations** (page 245) was set up in the hope of preventing future armed conflicts and promoting cooperation among nation-states—a goal that had eluded its predecessor, the **League of Nations** (page 148).

Z

ZIONISM

The term *Zionism* is derived from the Hebrew word *Zion*, a biblical name for the city of Jerusalem. In the late nineteenth century, Eastern Europe saw a flourishing of grassroots organizations seeking to resettle the Jewish people in the Land of Israel, their presumptive ancestral homeland. The campaigns of the "Lovers of Zion" also called for the rejuvenation of the decimated Jewish culture and the disused Hebrew language. Later, these groups would be collectively referred to as the Zionist movement. Most Zionist leaders embraced the objective of establishing a Jewish state in Palestine, which had been ruled by the Ottoman Empire from 1516 to 1918 and by the British since **World War I** (page 262). They envisioned this new state as one to which the Jewish people had a right to return after having been exiled and dispersed throughout the world in what was known as the Jewish diaspora. It would serve as a haven for Jews, liberating them from the **anti-Semitic** (page 23) discrimination and persecution they had endured for millennia.

In the early twentieth century, the international community made various attempts to address the demands of the Zionist movement. In 1903, the British proposed establishing a Jewish homeland in the nation of Uganda. The recently formed Zionist Congress swiftly declined the offer, while Zionist leaders such as Chaim Weizmann continued to press the British for the creation of a Jewish state in Palestine. Fearing that American Jews would encourage the US government to side with Germany—Britain's enemy during World War I—the British issued the 1917 Balfour Declaration, a document calling for the establishment of a Jewish national homeland in Palestine. Thirty years later, in the aftermath of the mass extermination of Jews during the **Nazi** (page 175) Holocaust, this demand was endorsed by the **United Nations** (UN) (page 245). Its Special Committee on Palestine recommended the partitioning of western Palestine into three territories: a Jewish state, an Arab state, and another area to be controlled by the UN. The resolution, which was later ratified by the UN General Assembly, was rejected by Palestinian Arabs and their Arab state allies.

Temporary housing for Jewish settlers arriving in the newly formed state of Israel, circa 1950.

Z

On May 14, 1948, when the British mandate to administer the territory of Palestine expired, Jewish Agency leader David Ben-Gurion proclaimed the creation of the State of Israel. That same day, seven Arab countries launched a military assault on the newly declared Israeli nation. The ensuing Arab–Israeli War resulted in the evacuation of over seven hundred thousand Palestinian Arabs. Upon the conclusion of the war in March 1949, the victorious Israelis established a number of laws aimed at reclaiming property from Palestinians and preventing their return to soil claimed by Israel, resulting in a Palestinian diaspora that exists to this day. Critics blame the Israeli government's forced exodus of Palestinians and its demolition of Palestinian villages for the subsequent Palestinian refugee crisis. Some supporters of Israel dispute this account, insisting that although the new government attempted to persuade them to remain, most Palestinians left voluntarily or were pressured into leaving by other Arabs.

Since the founding of Israel almost seventy years ago, the relationship between its Jewish inhabitants and the indigenous Palestinians has remained highly tense; it has been marked by a series of armed conflicts between the Israeli state and resistance movements such as Hamas and the Palestinian Liberation Organization. Throughout it all, Israel and the Zionist movement have been accused of subjecting Palestinians to systematic violence, hostility, and **racism** (page 200). Such charges have been repeatedly dismissed by Israeli partisans, who claim that the Zionist founders of the state, such as Ben-Gurion, advocated nondiscriminatory policies toward Palestinians and other minority ethnic groups.

Nevertheless, in 1975, the UN General Assembly passed a controversial resolution declaring that "Zionism is a form of racism and racial discrimination." Backed by the Soviet Union and various Arab and African states, it likened the ideology of Zionism to that of **apartheid** (page 24) South Africa, and deemed its alleged belief in a racially superior group of people to be scientifically and morally unjustifiable. The declaration was roundly denounced by the US, a longtime political ally and financial patron of Israel with a powerful Zionist lobby. It was revoked by the UN in 1991, when Israel agreed to participate in a Madrid conference aimed at reviving the stalled Israeli–Palestinian peace process.

ENDNOTES

1. Kant, Immanuel, "An Answer to the Question: What is Enlightenment?" in *Perpetual peace, and other essays on politics, history, and morals*. Translated by Ted Humphrey. Indianapolis: Hackett Pub. Company, 1983, p.41
2. Mill, John Stuart, "On Liberty," in Steven Scalet and John Arthur (eds.), *Morality and Moral Controversies, 9th Edition*. New York: Pearson, 2014, p. 387.
3. Greenberg, Edward S., *The Struggle for Democracy: A Radical Approach (Fifth Edition)*. Glenview: Scott Forseman, 1989, p. 263.
4. Greenberg, Edward S., *The Struggle for Democracy: A Radical Approach (Fifth Edition)*. Glenview: Scott Foresman, 1989, p. 88.
5. Riegert, Bernd, "A Philosophical Critique of EU Politics," *Deutsche Welle*, April 27, 2013, www.dw.com/en/a-philosophical-critique-of-eu-politics/a-16776364.
6. "The Nobel Peace Prize 2012." www.nobelprize.org/nobel_prizes/peace/laureates/2012/.
7. Greenberg, Edward S., *The Struggle for Democracy: A Radical Approach (Fifth Edition)*. Glenview: Scott Forseman, 1989, p. 55.
8. Held, David; McGrew, Anthony; and Goldblatt, David; *Global Transformations: Politics, Economics and Culture*. Stanford: Stanford University Press, 1999, p. 15.
9. In announcing his intention to stand in the 2016 presidential **elections** (page 92), **Republican** (page 206) Donald Trump declared that Mexican immigrants are "bringing drugs, they're bringing crime, they're rapists and some I assume are good people." "Donald Trump Announces U.S. Presidential Run with Eccentric Speech." *The Guardian*, June 16, 2015. www.theguardian.com/us-news/2015/jun/16/donald-trump-announces-run-president.
10. For Locke, the natural law prescribes only two moral limitations on the right to homestead private property: leave the commons as good as it was before, and leave enough for others. Beyond this, there are no limitations on the right to appropriate land and other natural resources as private property.

11. For Marx, estrangement is a feature of both capitalist and pre-capitalist societies, although the concept is most prominently developed in his analysis of capitalism. See Isidor Wallimann, "Is Estrangement Limited to Capitalist Societies?" in *Estrangement: Marx's Conception of Human Nature and the Division of Labor*. Westport: Greenwood Press, 1981.

12. At that time, Chile was under the authoritarian rule of General Augusto Pinochet, who came to power following a **military** (page 168) coup; sponsored by the American Central Intelligence Agency, the action ousted Marxist president Salvador Allende in 1973.

13. Winters, Jeffrey A. and Page, Benjamin I., "Oligarchy in the United States?" in *Perspectives on Politics*, Vol. 7, No. 4, December 2009, pp. 731–751.

14. This power was upheld by the Supreme Court in its 2008 ruling in *Medellin v. Texas*. See Daniel Silverberg, "The President as Lawmaker: Moderating Executive Authority in Wartime." *National Security Law Brief* 5, no. 1 (2014): 37–64.

15. Farrand, Max, ed., *The Records of the Federal Convention of 1787, Volume 1*. New Haven: Yale University Press, 1911, p. 431.

16. As used here, surplus is that portion of a laborer's work for which he or she is not compensated in the form of wages.

17. Parker, Christopher, "2010 Multi-State Survey on Race & Politics," University of Washington Institute for the Study of Ethnicity, Race & Sexuality. Accessed May 16, 2015. https://depts.washington.edu/uwiser/mssrp_table.pdf.

18. Shinkman, Paul D., "Obama: 'Global War on Terror' Is Over." *U.S. News & World Report*, May 23, 2013. www.usnews.com/news/articles/2013/05/23/obama-global-war-on-terror-is-over.

19. Marcuse, Herbert, *One-Dimensional Man: Studies in the Ideology of Advanced Industrial Society*. Boston: Beacon Press, 1964, p. 166.

20. Bennis, Phyllis, *Calling the Shots: How Washington Dominates the United Nations*. New York: Olive Branch Press, 1996.

VISUAL REFERENCES

p. 16 Osama bin Laden, https://www.fbi.gov/wanted/topten/usama-bin-laden/image

p. 16-17 September 11th terrorist attack on the World Trade Center, courtesy of the Library of Congress, http://www.loc.gov/item/2002719353/

p. 19 Siege of Yorktown, https://archive.org/stream/battlemapsandcha00carriala#page/86/mode/2up

p. 20 Declaration of Independence, courtesy of the Library of Congress, http://www.loc.gov/item/2003656533/

p. 20–21 Battle of Lexington, courtesy of the Library of Congress, http://www.loc.gov/item/2004669976/

p. 22 Kropotkin, http://archive.org/stream/memoirsofrevoluto1kropuoft#page/n5/mode/2up

p. 25 Mandella, courtesy of the Library of Congress, http://www.loc.gov/item/2015645189/ ; Africa, © Bardocz Peter/Shutterstock; Apartheid Sign, https://commons.wikimedia.org/wiki/File:ApartheidSignEnglishAfrikaans.jpg

p. 27 Chamberlain & Hitler, © Everett Collection

p. 28 Protesters in Cairo, © Hang Dinh/Shutterstock

p. 31 La veillesse d'un prince/peint par L. Rossi, grave par Ed. Girardet. courtesy of the Library of Congress, http://www.loc.gov/item/94512098/

p. 32 Adolphe Braun, Rome, Palais du Vatican, Chapelle Sixtine, Michel-Ange, ca 1869, Carbon print, © The J. Paul Getty Museum, Los Angeles

p. 35 Berlin Wall, © Everett Historical/Shutterstock

p. 37 Bill of Rights, courtesy of the National Archives, https://research.archives.gov/id/1408042?q=1408042

p. 39 Black Panther Convention, Lincoln Memorial, courtesy of the Library of Congress, http://www.loc.gov/item/2003688171/

p. 47 Stained glass, © Christy Thompson/Shutterstock

p. 48 Leonardo da Vinci, The Last Supper, late 19th century, Collotype, © The J. Paul Getty Museum, Los Angeles

p. 50 Churchill, courtesy of the Library of Congress, http://www.loc.gov/item/owi2001045696/PP/

p. 53 Gandhi Spinning at a wheel, © Mary Evans Picture Library/Everett Collection

p. 55 March on Washington, courtesy of the Library of Congress, http://www.loc.gov/item/2013648841/

p. 59 Courtesy of the Library of Congress: Antietam, http://www.loc.gov/item/cwp2003000148/PP/ ; Gettysburg, http://www.loc.gov/item/cwp2003001110/PP/ ; Fort Sumter, http://www.loc.gov/item/2011648573/ ; Emancipation Proclamation, http://www.loc.gov/item/96512448/

p. 62-63 Chart of the west indies, https://archive.org/stream/atlasmaritimusor00sell#page/n82/mode/1up

p. 65 Marx, © Everett Historical/Shutterstock; communist manifesto, © IgorGolovniov/Shutterstock

p. 66 Lenin, courtesy of the Library of Congress, http://www.loc.gov/item/ggb2006006212 ; hammer & sickle, © Misha Abesadze/Shutterstock

p. 72 Howard Chandler Christy, Painting Scene at Signing of Constitution of United States of America, September 17 1787, © ClassicStock/Alamy Stock Photo; constitution, courtesy of the National Archives, https://catalog.archives.gov/id/1667751

p. 77 Gandhi meeting with Lord & Lady Mountbatten, Delhi India, 1947, © Dinodia Photos/Alamy Stock Photo

p. 79 James Madison, portrait by Gilbert Stuart, courtesy of the Library of Congress, http://www.loc.gov/item/92520495/

p. 81 Ballot box, courtesy of the Library of Congress, http://www.loc.gov/item/hec2009011227/

p. 82 Jackson, © Everett Historical/Shutterstock, Clinton, courtesy of the Library of Congress, http://www.loc.gov/item/93505822/ ; donkey, https://archive.org/stream/scripturenaturalooreli/scripturenaturalooreli#page/36/mode/1up

p. 85 Antonio Lopez de Santa Anna, © Everett Historical/Shutterstock; Stalin, courtesy of the Library of Congress, http://www.loc.gov/item/96522736/

p. 89 "Blue Marble" courtesy of NASA, https://www.nasa.gov/content/blue-marble-image-of-the-earth-from-apollo-17 ; wind turbines, courtesy of the Library of Congress, http://www.loc.gov/item/2014631722/

p. 90 Adam Smith, courtesy of the Library of Congress, http://www.loc.gov/item/91706325/

p. 93 Campaign banner, courtesy of the Library of Congress, http://www.loc.gov/item/2003656570/

p. 98 EU flag, © issumbosi/Shutterstock

p. 102 Hitler and Mussolini, © Everett Historical/Shutterstock

p. 104 Supreme Court Building, © Brandon Bourdages/Shutterstock

p. 109 Prise de la Bastille par les Citoyens de Paris, courtesy of the Library of Congress, http://www.loc.gov/item/91480935/

p. 110 Louis XVI being led to the guillotine, courtesy of the Library of Congress, http://www.loc.gov/item/2001695230/

p. 112 C'est ainsi que l'on punit les traitres, courtesy of the Library of Congress, http://www.loc.gov/item/91480935/

p. 115 Ghandi, 1931, © Everett Collection

p. 118 US Capitol, © Alexandr Junek Imaging s.r.o./Shutterstock

p. 121 Hospital, courtesy of the Library of Congress, http://www.loc.gov/item/mpc2004000694/PP/

p. 124 Hitler, courtesy of the Library of Congress, http://www.loc.gov/item/2004672089/

p. 127 House of Representatives chamber, courtesy of the whitehouse.gov, https://commons.wikimedia.org/wiki/File:Obama_Health_Care_Speech_to_Joint_Session_of_Congress.jpg ; https://www.whitehouse.gov/photos-and-video/photogallery/remarks-president-health-care

p. 130 Ellis Island, courtesy of the Library of Congress, http://www.loc.gov/item/ggb2006005961/ ; lady liberty, courtesy of the Library of Congress, http://www.loc.gov/item/2008679689/

p. 131 Machiavelli, courtesy of the Library of Congress, http://www.loc.gov/item/90714314/

p. 135 Iranian protesters, Azadi Tower, 1978, © Everett Collection/Mondadori Portfolio/Archivio Angelo Cozzi/Angelo Cozzi

p. 138 Jesus, courtesy of the Library of Congress, http://www.loc.gov/item/mpc2004000435/PP/

p. 142 Martin Luther King, Jr., LBJ Library photo by Yoichi Okamoto, http://www.lbjlibrary.net/collections/photo-archive/photolab-detail.html?id=1468

p. 144 Tire Factory, MD, courtesy of the Library of Congress, http://www.loc.gov/pictures/item/md1498.photos.384239p/

p. 148 League of Nations, © Mary Evans Picture Library/Weimar Archive/Everett Collection

p. 151 Voter at Polls, VA, 2008, © Rob Crandall/Alamy Stock Photo

p. 153 Thomas Hobbes, © Georgios Kollidas/Shutterstock

p. 157 Lincoln, courtesy of the Library of Congress, http://www.loc.gov/item/2014650148/

p. 161 Mandela, courtesy of the Library of Congress, http://www.loc.gov/item/2011634245/

p. 164 Mao, © leungchopan/Shutterstock

p. 167 Marx, © Dariush M/Shutterstock

p. 171 Delacroix, "Liberty on the Barricades", 1830, © Oleg Golovnev/Shutterstock

p. 173 Napoleon, © Georgios Kollidas/Shutterstock

p. 175 Nazi Hierarchy: Hitler, Goering, Goebbels, Hess, courtesy of the National Archives, https://catalog.archives.gov/id/196509

p. 179 Sit-in protest, © Everett Collection

p. 181 Nagasaki atomic bomb cloud, 1945, 208-N-43888, courtesy of the National Archives, http://www.archives.gov/research/military/ww2/photos/

p. 183 Louis XVI, courtesy of the Library of Congress, http://www.loc.gov/item/89709469/

p. 185 October Revolution, Square of the Winter Palace, 1917, © Everett Historical/Shutterstock

p. 188 House of Parliament, courtesy of the Library of Congress, http://www.loc.gov/item/95509019/

p. 195 Presidents of the United States, courtesy of the Library of Congress, http://www.loc.gov/item/92506068/

p. 196 Teddy Roosevelt, courtesy of the Library of Congress, http://www.loc.gov/item/ggb2005021822/

p. 201 Segregated Drinking fountain, NC, courtesy of the Library of Congress, http://www.loc.gov/item/fsa1997003218/PP/

p. 207 French Revolution, courtesy of the Library of Congress, http://www.loc.gov/item/2001699757/

p. 210 Franklin D Roosevelt, courtesy of the Library of Congress, http://www.loc.gov/item/96522736/

p. 211 WPA poster, courtesy of the Library of Congress, http://www.loc.gov/item/98518700/

p. 213 Senate chamber, courtesy of the Library of Congress, http://loc.gov/pictures/resource/cwpbh.03299/

p. 215 Copernicus, © Everett Historical/Shutterstock

p. 218 African captives, © Everett Historical/Shutterstock

p. 220 Picketers, courtesy of the Library of Congress, http://www.loc.gov/item/hec2013006965/

p. 225 Bolsheviks, Petrograd, 1922, © Everett Historical/Shutterstock

p. 227 Kremlin, Moscow 1957, © Everett Historical/Shutterstock

p. 231 Picket line, courtesy of the Library of Congress, http://www.loc.gov/item/fsa1998021234/PP/

p. 233 Suffrage parade, Inez Milholland, 1913, courtesy of the Library of Congress, http://www.loc.gov/item/ggb2005011479/

p. 239 Pentagon, 2001, © Everett Historical/Shutterstock

p. 246 United Nations flag, © SmileStudio/Shutterstock

p. 249 US map, © Jim Pruitt/Shutterstock

p. 250 US flag, courtesy of the Library of Congress, http://www.loc.gov/item/det1994020160/PP/

p. 251 US seal, courtesy of the Library of Congress, http://www.loc.gov/item/93500738/

p. 254 Bombers in North Korea, courtesy of the National Archives, https://catalog.archives.gov/id/542229

p. 258 Washington, © Everett Historical/Shutterstock

p. 263 Map of Europe, https://commons.wikimedia.org/wiki/File:Map_Europe_alliances_1914-en.svg

p. 264 German trench, courtesy of the Library of Congress, http://www.loc.gov/item/ggb2005019750/

p. 265 Sinking of British ship, Irresistible, 1915, courtesy of the Library of Congress, http://www.loc.gov/item/94505518/

p. 267 Map of Europe, https://commons.wikimedia.org/wiki/File:WWII_Europe_1941-1942_Map_EN.png

p. 268 DDay, courtesy of the National Archives, https://catalog.archives.gov/id/195515 ; London Blitz, courtesy of the Library of Congress, http://www.loc.gov/item/98505741/

p. 269 Concentration camp, courtesy of the National Archives, https://catalog.archives.gov/id/531271

p. 271 Tents in Israel, ca. 1950, © Everett Historical/Shutterstock

INDEX

***Bolded numbers** indicate major discussions of the topic*

C

D

E

F

N

O

P

Q

R

S

T

U

V

W

X

Y

Z